Teaching with Science Writing in the Humanities Classroom

Teaching with Science Writing in the Humanities Classroom

Edited by
Allison Dushane, Lisa Ottum, and Rosalind Powell

The Modern Language Association of America
New York   2026

© 2026 by The Modern Language Association of America
85 Broad Street, New York, New York 10004
www.mla.org

To order MLA publications, visit www.mla.org/books. For wholesale and international orders, see www.mla.org/bookstore-orders. The EU-based Responsible Person for MLA products is the Mare Nostrum Group, which can be reached at gpsr@mare-nostrum.co.uk or the Mare Nostrum Group BV, Mauritskade 21D, 1091 GC Amsterdam, Netherlands. For a copy of the MLA's risk assessment document, write to scholcomm@mla.org.

Options for Teaching 68
ISSN 1079-2562

Library of Congress Cataloging-in-Publication Data

Names: Dushane, Allison Leigh editor | Ottum, Lisa editor | Powell, Rosalind
    (Lecturer in English literature) editor
Title: Teaching with science writing in the humanities classroom / edited by
    Allison Dushane, Lisa Ottum, and Rosalind Powell.
Description: New York : The Modern Language Association of America, 2026. |
    Series: Options for teaching, 1079-2562 ; 68 | Includes bibliographical references.
Identifiers: LCCN 2025037318 (print) | LCCN 2025037319 (ebook) |
    ISBN 9781603297158 hardcover | ISBN 9781603297165 paperback |
    ISBN 9781603297172 EPUB
Subjects: LCSH: Science and the humanities | Humanities—Study and teaching |
    Technical writing—Study and teaching | BISAC: LANGUAGE ARTS &
    DISCIPLINES / Study & Teaching | EDUCATION / Teaching / Subjects /
    Science & Technology | LCGFT: Essays
Classification: LCC AZ341 .T39 2026 (print) | LCC AZ341 (ebook)
LC record available at https://lccn.loc.gov/2025037318
LC ebook record available at https://lccn.loc.gov/2025037319

Contents

Allison Dushane, Lisa Ottum, and Rosalind Powell

Introduction: Science Literacy and Science Writing: A Call to Humanists

The conviction that the humanities are in peril has been a mainstay of op-ed articles and scholarly publishing since at least the 1960s, leading to a characterization of a "tradition of crisis" (Ayers 25). While it is easy to caricature, as declining job listings and precarious hiring practices, shrinking departments, and dwindling student numbers testify, there is no denying that the twenty-first-century academy is no healthy habitat. Since around 2016 these material concerns have been joined by increasingly hostile political and public rhetoric in both the United States and Britain. As institutions that are very often recipients of public funding and subject to legislation, universities should of course expect some overview of their structures and processes.[1] But the expertise of academics is now routinely questioned both within and outside government. The British politician and then justice secretary Michael Gove stated in the run-up to the Brexit referendum that the British people had "had enough of experts" (Mance), thereby voicing an increasingly popular mood. Gove's now notorious dismissal of economists' knowledge has since become a byword for a more general skepticism about knowledge produced by people working in institutions of higher education. Similar rhetoric reflecting an increasing barrier between scientific practitioners and the public is seen in the United

States: according to a Pew Research Center poll conducted in November 2023, public trust in medical scientists, and scientists in general, is lower than it was before the beginning of the COVID-19 pandemic, with just twenty-three percent of US adults expressing "a great deal" of confidence that scientific experts act in the best interests of the public and twenty-seven percent expressing "not too much or no confidence in scientists to act in the public's best interests" (Kennedy and Tyson).

Knowledge that is perceived as insufficiently accessible to the broader public has become newly vulnerable to misunderstanding, misconstrual, and even weaponization, as have the processes of creating that knowledge. This leaves both scientists and humanists with—to understate—a communication problem. In the preface to a 2002 special issue of *American Literature*, Wai Chee Dimock and Priscilla Wald call upon the public responsibility that humanists have to address developments in science and technology in their scholarship and teaching, pointing out that "scientific specializations have moved at such a pace that the untrained are virtually illiterate"; "the practical impact of this specialized knowledge," they conclude, "makes science illiteracy no longer an option" (705). Some twenty years later, as educational institutions continue to allocate the bulk of their resources to STEM disciplines, this responsibility becomes doubly pressing since humanists find themselves with knowledges and methods that are both valuable to students and the public and important to leverage for the survival of their own disciplines. Reading and writing matters. And the tools that scholars of literature and rhetoric employ and teach are, we suggest, vital in the current moment of polarization.

Science writing, broadly understood in both literary and communicative contexts, involves the negotiation of boundaries between expertise and public knowledge and the recognition that these boundaries are themselves porous. This porosity has been apparent from the beginnings of experimental natural philosophy in the seventeenth century, and a long view of the history of science helps contextualize our disciplines' role in understanding the construction of knowledge and the status of science. Martin Willis devotes the first chapter of his guide to literature and science scholarship to looking at how critics have explored the interplay between scientific institutions such as the Royal Society (established in the 1660s), the professionalized Royal Institution, and the British Association for the Advancement of Science and "a much broader culture of knowledge transmission that incorporates literature and the arts and speaks directly to social, civic and political life" (11). The gradual professionalization of the sciences and the establishment of teaching laboratories at universities coincided with the emergence of English studies as an independent discipline in the long nineteenth century. These developments necessitated the establishment of disciplinary norms, in-groups and out-groups, and processes for educating students to become practitioners and even communicators in their chosen discipline.

How might it be possible, then, for humanists to intervene with authority when researching and teaching scientific concepts and texts? Dimock and Wald argue that "the discourse of science is *literature*" and that this "broad definition suggests that science literacy is a birthright and perhaps also an obligation to those of us in literature departments" (708). To support this claim, they cite perspectives from multiple disciplines: the literary critic Raymond Williams's discussion of how the word *literature* entered the English language in the fourteenth century in *Keywords: A Vocabulary of Culture and Society*, the philosopher Michel Serres's exploration of organisms as language systems in *Hermes: Literature, Science, Philosophy*, and the sociologist of science Bruno Latour's account of how scientific knowledge advances through literature and citation in *Science in Action*. To this list we add the historian of science Thomas Kuhn, whose 1962 volume *The Structure of Scientific Revolutions* catalyzed the interdisciplinary field of science and technology studies. Kuhn describes how this book, which changed the trajectory of his own career, was conceived when he "was a graduate student of physics trying to prepare a case study on the development of mechanics for a course in science for nonscientists" ("What" 8–9). Reading Aristotle's *Physics*, he first found Aristotle "not only ignorant of mechanics, but a dreadfully bad physical scientist as well." Only after he considered that Aristotle's "words had not always meant to him and his contemporaries quite what they meant to me and mine" was he able to recognize that "statements that had previously seemed egregious mistakes, now seemed at worst near misses within a powerful and successful tradition" (9). That is, it was at the moment when he began to consider science as a form of literature, as writing, that Kuhn was able to fully trace and illuminate Aristotle's impact on the development of concepts and methods in contemporary physics.

Despite the continued fragmenting of disciplines, the act of writing remains at the foundation of the production and circulation of knowledge. As Latour claims in the short treatise "Irreductions" appended to his landmark work *The Pasteurization of France*:

> We do not think. We do not have ideas. . . . Rather there is the action of *writing*, an action which involves working with *inscriptions* that have

been extracted; an action that is practiced through *talking* to other people who likewise write, inscribe, talk, and live in similarly unusual places; an action that *convinces* or fails to convince with inscriptions which are made to speak, to write, and to be read. (218)

Though a totalizing claim that science and other forms of knowledge can be reduced to writing should be avoided, it might therefore be said that recognizing writing as a constitutive action across disciplines is the first step toward engaging in productive conversations about science with the public.

Of course, as scholars and teachers of literature, it is also important to acknowledge how the limits of our own training shape this volume. The essays and resources section cover a wide range of scientific topics that are united by common questions: What are the stakes of scientific inquiry? What role does scientific inquiry play in how humans define themselves, both in relation to other human individuals, groups, and institutions and in relation to nonhuman objects, animals, and environments? However, the emphasis on science writing necessarily excludes many other activities that contribute to the construction of scientific knowledge, such as laboratory practices, the operation of specialized instruments, and technology. That is, we don't claim to directly intervene in questions concerning specific scientific practices themselves. Rather, we see teaching with science writing as beginning with the acknowledgment that the knowledge we call "scientific" is neither static nor given but nevertheless continues to shape our lives in fundamental ways. Learning how to effectively read and communicate about scientific texts and other kinds of texts that engage with scientific topics, issues, and questions is a vital skill for students and future professionals in all disciplines.

Defining science writing is just as difficult as defining science itself, and not only because genre is what Dimock calls a "weak ontology"—a "mixed attempt at cataloging, doomed to come up short because there will always be more specimens coming its way . . . unforeseen and unrecognizable on its terms" (6). In the popular market, publishers routinely group science writing with nature writing, as in the series *The Best American Science and Nature Writing*, published by HarperCollins; *Amazon*, meanwhile, stashes science writing under "science and math," a category that currently includes everything from gardening advice to pop psychology.[2] At issue is not simply marketing: in an era of climate change and global pandemic, partitioning "science" from "nature" and "culture" is not only challenging but also dubious. In his introduction to *The Best American Science and Nature Writing 2021*, which reprints articles from the previous year, Ed Yong reflects on how COVID-19 changed his practice as a science journalist. Characterizing the pandemic as a bewildering "omnicrisis," Yong explains how it exploded the "usual mode of science writing," with its practice of breaking "big stories . . . down into small components that can be quickly turned into content" (xix). For Yong, covering the pandemic meant "interviewing sociologists, anthropologists, historians, linguists, patients, and more." "The walls between [journalistic] beats seemed to crumble," he recalls. "What, I found myself asking, even counts as science writing?" (xix). Ultimately, Yong concludes that science writing "*should* be difficult to categorize," for if there is any lesson to be taken from the pandemic, it is that science is "intricately woven into the fabric of our lives," inseparable from cultural practices, relationships, and even our very cells (xxiv). While this broad definition of science writing could seem freeing for writers, it also points to some less liberating dilemmas. For example, science writing can be both appealing to readers, as it lends a precision to the accounting of day-to-day experiences and phenomena, and potentially alienating in its introduction of objectivity, jargon, and hierarchies of expertise into new domains. This particular challenge only grows the more carefully writers strive to capture the social, cultural, economic, and other contexts surrounding new discoveries.

Still, Yong's capacious view of science and science writing resonates with trends in literary and cultural criticism, where a decades-long effort to dismantle Enlightenment dualisms such as human/animal, and the uneven operations of power that such dualisms produce, has engendered the flourishing of interdisciplinary subfields. As Melissa M. Littlefield and Martin Willis point out in their introduction to a 2017 special issue of the *Journal of Literature and Science*, "Literature and Science scholarship has had a hand in creating posthumanism, animal studies, the digital humanities, the environmental humanities, and graphic medicine, just to name a few" (2). *Teaching with Science Writing in the Humanities Classroom* offers pedagogical strategies for facilitating the interchanges between literature and science that lie at the foundation of these nascent forms of inquiry and those that might arise in the future. What roles can—and should—the humanities play in confronting anti-science discourses? How, or in what ways, can we support the development of scientific knowledge while also affirming the value of the distinct forms of knowledge produced by other disciplines? And how do we acknowledge and discuss past—and ongoing—harms against vulnerable groups, human and nonhuman, in the name of "science"?

The premise of this volume is that science writing—conceived broadly and historically—offers rich opportunities to engage with these questions using the archives and methods of humanities disciplines. *Teaching with Science Writing in the Humanities Classroom* aims to both theorize and offer practical strategies for deploying science writing in literature, writing, and interdisciplinary courses, ranging from lower-division general education courses to upper-division electives and graduate courses. Contributors demonstrate how science writing can support collaborations between the humanities and science while also providing a space for cultural debate. They model science writing as a vehicle for cultural analysis, as an object of close reading, and as the foundation for justice-oriented pedagogies. The resources section situates these pedagogical essays within long-standing scholarly conversations in science and technology studies, literature and science, rhetoric, and science communication. A key argument of this volume is that the very expansiveness of science writing as a category is an asset in classroom settings, one that humanists—and especially scholars of literature, language, and writing studies—are well positioned to utilize. By defying rigid definitional markers, science writing invites conversation about communication and about science—not as separate endeavors but as mutually constitutive practices.

Science Writing in Literary and Cultural Studies

One method represented in this volume for incorporating science writing into the classroom is to draw on the long critical tradition of literature and science, putting literary texts and cultures in conversation with (the history of) science. This strategy can accomplish several important goals. First, and most fundamentally, it can affirm the value of close reading as a tool for understanding both literary and nonliterary texts. Second, it can help students cultivate the literary analysis and research skills necessary to situate complex texts in their broader cultural and historical contexts. In addition, an approach grounded in literature and science invites students to grapple with the ethical complexities of knowledge formation, a matter of increasing interest within the field, which has evolved from a primarily (although not exclusively) historicist pursuit anchored in scientific writing into a dynamic cluster of methods with diverse relationships to science, writing, and culture.

In their respective introductions to literature and science, Steven Meyer and Michael H. Whitworth characterize the field's history as a series of waves, each striving ever more forcefully to dispute the infamous two cultures thesis.[3] Thus, while the work of the first wave in literature and science sought to explain how scientific discoveries influenced literature, as in Marjorie Hope Nicolson's *The Microscope and English Imagination* (1935), subsequent scholarship took issue with the implication that influence flows unidirectionally from science to culture. By the 1970s, scholars of Victorian culture such as George Levine and Gillian Beer highlighted the imprint of literary texts on science, focusing on Charles Darwin as the avatar of a one culture paradigm.[4] In the decades since, literature and science has taken a more pluralistic approach to contesting the traditional literature/science divide, developing along trajectories influenced by science and technology studies, the history of science, literary theory, and other disciplines—and growing to encompass a range of media. To the extent that literature and science rejects any single methodology, the science writing that appears in academic criticism today takes a variety of forms, depending upon the era, place, and readerships under consideration. This is necessarily true for early modern studies: science was not truly professionalized, nor were the disciplinary boundaries we take for granted solidified, until well into the nineteenth century. The word *scientist* did not appear in English until the geologist William Whewell introduced it in 1834, offering the term as an alternative to the label *philosopher* ("Scientist").[5] Hence, teaching with science writing in a British literature survey course, for instance, might entail working with personal letters, dialogues, poetry, and other texts that may at first appear wildly *un*scientific to students.

One way to frame science writing for students is to invoke the analogy of literary canons. Just as literary studies has strived, through efforts glossed as "recovery," to incorporate new authors, genres, and geographies into its understanding of literary historical trends, literature and science has sought to broaden its purview beyond a core canon of science writing and literature about science. The stakes of both projects go beyond improved historical understanding, however: they encompass matters of injustice that are of concern to the humanities more generally. Historicist inquiry in literature and science invites a focus on practice—that is, on the ways people pursued knowledge in various settings. This includes the practices employed by marginalized groups to resist racist, sexist, anthropocentric, or otherwise exclusionary science. As scholars of Black and Indigenous studies point out, Western science has an ugly track record of silencing nondominant voices. Besides sponsoring overtly racist projects such as colonialism and the rise of phrenology in the nineteenth century, mainstream science has often obscured the contributions of Black and Indigenous people to natural history and other fields.[6] At the same time, Black and Indigenous people have also contested racist science and the politics it supported, deploying scientific knowledge as part of antislavery, anti-colonial, and other liberation movements. Britt Rusert explains that in antebellum America, for example, "science was legitimately claimed by a surprisingly broad range of practitioners and practiced in a number of nonacademic and noninstitutional spaces, from the parlor to the workshop, the church to the park" (5). Recovering that era's "science" therefore requires an expansive, even radical, definition of empiricism that encompasses various alternative modes of observation and experimentation. It also requires an expansive definition of science writing that includes nonpublic writing, creative writing, and even oral forms.[7] Thus, Rusert attends not only to the science writing found in antebellum periodicals but also to "the dynamic fluidity and exchange between black scientific and literary production during the period" (23).

This skeptical view of knowledge production can have powerful classroom applications, for it welcomes literature students into the study of science as active participants. It can also introduce science students to worthwhile questions about method, scientific writing, and the values encoded in mainstream scientific practice. A foundational assumption of literature and science is that culture and science operate within a shared social field and should be studied together. If scholarship in literature and science demonstrates this point, so, too, does recent advocacy-oriented science. The humanities have moved toward an increasingly broad understanding of "science writing" over time, and a similar trend has been led by practitioners in Indigenous environmental studies and sciences (IESS), for whom the interlinked nature of environmental problems and environmental justice requires new modes of praxis and communication.[8] Consider, for example, the issue of plastic pollution, a multiscalar problem that confounds traditional disciplinary boundaries. Microplastics interfere with the integrity of human and nonhuman communities in myriad ways that elude ecology, biology, or chemistry alone. Their presence in the water, the atmosphere, and inside organisms of all types cannot be explained by any one theory: plastic's ubiquity is a result of colonialism, capitalism, speciesism, and other unjust systems (for more on this point, see Davis). Scholars studying plastic have turned with increasing frequency to alternative modes of knowledge presentation, incorporating arguments about scientific method into their work. This is the case with Max Liboiron's *Pollution Is Colonialism*, an interdisciplinary study anchored in feminist science, technology studies, and Indigenous environmental science. Besides advocating for an anti-colonial approach to science itself, Liboiron contends that all methodologies, "whether scientific, writerly, readerly, or otherwise," are imbricated within colonial land relations (7). In this view, "science writing" cannot be neatly decoupled from the systems that create it any more than ethics can be separated from the work of science. And yet, efforts to bridge Western and Indigenous thinking do not automatically result in self-conscious critique. As Vanessa Watts points out, Western theorists frequently practice an "abstracted engagement" with Indigenous ontologies that, at best, distorts Indigenous knowledge and, at worst, replicates other forms of colonial theft and violence (28). The anthropologist Zoe Todd (Métis) writes memorably of attending a lecture by Bruno Latour in which she "waited through the whole talk, to hear the Great Latour credit Indigenous thinkers for their millennia of engagement with sentient environments" and other concepts at the heart of posthumanism and the ontological turn (6). "Once again," she recalls, "I felt as though I was just another inconvenient Indigenous body in a room full of people excited to hear a white guy talk *around* themes shared in Indigenous thought without giving Indigenous people credit or a nod" (8). Todd's essay is a reminder that more inclusive science and science writing must include a shift in discursive practices such as citation as well as other rituals surrounding academic knowledge production.[9]

Science Writing and Science Communication

The matter of what counts as science writing naturally raises questions about audience and purpose—questions that animate the field of science communication, albeit in ways, distinct from literary studies, that reflect the field's unique history and affinity with the social sciences. A number of contributors to this volume address public-facing science writing and intra-expert writing on scientific topics, largely in the context of rhetoric and composition courses. Case studies explore how students drawn from a diverse range of disciplinary backgrounds can learn interpretative skills to assess and even replicate the values and strategies of different kinds of science writing. For humanists, including contributors to this volume, some of the most urgent questions related to science communication are those that involve matters of diversity and social justice. Analyzing science communication in a humanities classroom often entails applying the same critical eye to the field that one might apply to literary canons. Much like literary studies, science communication has inherited a legacy of Eurocentrism and its attendant biases about authority and method. Lindy A. Orthia explains that, because science communication shares close affinities with the history of science, "most current conceptualizations of science communication history are geographically, culturally and temporally narrow," focused only on "the ways establishment science was popularized, and [that] popular science 'by the people' developed, in Western Europe during the nineteenth and twentieth centuries, especially in Britain and France." The upshot of this, according to Orthia, is that "attention to science communication history is often pulled towards the well-studied cultures, making it hard to conceive of science communication beyond the recent West." The consequences of this bias redound on education: as Orthia points out, traditional conceptions of the field's purview also influence the degree to which certain students can feel "more included, validated and professionally enabled" in a university setting than others can. The education scholars Douglas L. Medin and Megan Bang corroborate Orthia's observations. As they explain, "[T]he history of science taught in U.S. schools is a history of Western science, not because the West is where science developed, but rather because those determining what story will be told are Western" (161). This pattern engenders "disidentification with science and a sense of alienation" among nondominant groups (164); Indigenous students, in particular, often do not "see their own values and orientations embraced in curricula and associated practices" (165). Medin and Bang thus call for more diversity among scientists, not only to improve scientific practice—"multiple perspectives are needed for effective science"—but also as a means of engaging Indigenous and other nondominant communities in science education (162). It follows that science communication benefits from non-Western perspectives: without attending to embedded disciplinary assumptions about what science is, who does it, and why, science communication runs the risk of excluding entire groups and traditions.

Diversifying science communication is not just about engagement with history: it is also vital for problem-solving in a diverse, globalized, and turbulent present. Confronting the challenges of climate change, species extinction, and other large-scale dilemmas will require insights from multiple knowledge systems. The struggle against misinformation also demands pluralistic approaches. For some time, science communication has wrestled with how best to overcome the so-called knowledge deficit model, a paradigm that prevailed during the mid–twentieth century. According to this model, a lack of scientific literacy amounts to a simple deficit of knowledge; if people knew more about, for instance, the science of global warming, then they would support environmentalism. The limitations of this model may seem obvious, and indeed, Adam Shapiro describes an "obligatory-seeming, almost ritualistic disparagement of the deficit model" among today's science communicators. It is patronizing to imagine science communication as a matter of translating expert knowledge for an ignorant and passive public. At the same time, alternative models—including those grounded in public engagement and relationship building between publics and scientists—have clearly not solved the problem of rampant mis- and disinformation.

Shapiro suggests that science writers might look to the past for inspiration, specifically to the eighteenth- and nineteenth-century popularizers of natural theology, who "knew that reason alone may not inspire belief, but that a sense of amazement at the natural world could reinforce such religious feeling." These writers, Shapiro continues, "used certain narrative conventions, the invocation of emotion and the sense of nature as majestic in their colorful descriptions, because they knew that this writing was both expected by their readers and created emotional attachment to the world." Most science writers would probably balk at the notion that nature itself offers moral lessons, although the notion persists that good science writing should invoke emotions of awe and wonder. It is this idea that Chanda Prescod-Weinstein disputes in her introduction to *The Disordered Cosmos*, in which she invokes Alan G. Gross's study of the "scientific sublime" in popular science writing. Prescod-Weinstein notes that most science writers have historically been white men; "as a Black agender woman," she writes, "I see science differently than my science communication ancestors" (6). She elaborates:

> When you're looking at the world from the margins, a persistent feeling of "the sublime" can feel out of reach as you struggle against mundane and pervasive forces of oppression. It may, therefore, be tempting to cast this book [*The Disordered Cosmos*] as radically outside the popular science genre because I go beyond the sublime to acknowledge the big role that social phenomena play in science. (6–7)

If the issues Prescod-Weinstein alludes to are interesting to social scientists, they are equally interesting to humanists. What *is* the purpose of science writing aimed at general readers? Must it be instrumental—and if so, in what sense or senses, and for whom? What is the relationship between genre and affect? Between thinking and feeling? Between reading and moral action?

Teaching with Science Writing: Key Considerations

The essays in *Teaching with Science Writing* engage with these issues, demonstrating how science writing, when combined with student-centered pedagogy, can be deployed toward humanistic ends. The volume's sections offer one way of navigating its contents. Part 1 may be especially useful to those who teach traditional literature courses because it presents case studies for teaching literature and science topics from the medieval and early modern periods and the nineteenth century. Part 2 may be especially useful to those who teach writing and general education courses. The contributors to this section are scholars of rhetoric, writing, and ecology; they share the conviction that science writing can aid in knowledge transfer across domains. Part 3 showcases activist approaches to teaching science writing. In part 4, readers will find detailed descriptions of specific assignments and sketches of entire courses. Finally, part 5, "Resources"—which draws on the essays in this volume as well as on scholarly traditions that inform the volume as a whole—suggests additional readings, including anthologies and secondary texts suitable for classroom use. The resources section is intended as a starting point for readers interested in learning more about the scholarly traditions that inform this volume. It begins with a list of professional associations and journals whose websites reflect ongoing developments in science and literature and related fields; many link out to a wealth of additional scholarly, professional, and pedagogical resources. The section also contains suggested print and digital pedagogical resources, drawn in part from the essays in this volume. Readers will find texts suitable for literature, general education, writing, and interdisciplinary courses. Finally, the section curates a selection of foundational works in literature and science as well as a sampling of scholarship organized by subfield, including a selection of representative works on science communication and science writing pedagogy.

Another way to approach *Teaching with Science Writing* is through key concepts. All essays deal with the nuts and bolts of teaching, such as text selection, unit design, and facilitation of classroom discussion. Many also engage, explicitly or implicitly, with one or more conceptual challenges.

We highlight these sites of struggle—including experimentation within institutional constraints, ethics, literacy skills, creativity, and the tension between subjectivity and objectivity—below, not only because they are transferable to any number of contexts but also because they are pathways into genuine inquiry and student engagement.

Experimentation within Institutional Constraints

Several essays in this volume deal head-on with specific institutional demands of teaching, such as the need to accommodate students who take a course to satisfy distribution requirements (Miller) or to design courses to meet the needs of general education courses (Newcomb). More generally, course design demands the alignment of materials and assessments with intended learning outcomes and a view to the overall trajectory of a student as they develop subject specific skills and knowledge. This institutional context also informs the activities and assumptions of students: the shift from a top-down theory of pedagogy to an emphasis on seminars as sites of discussion and exchange means that students are routinely framed as active learners, sometimes even cocreators of knowledge. At the same time, the neoliberal university context of fees and loans positions students as public consumers. This context highlights how students occupy a dual role as members of the public and members of the institution. Of course, the institution/public model is in no way clear-cut and is itself a fallacy akin to that of the two cultures model. To name just one example, many instructors find themselves forced to the edges of institutions because of precarious employment that limits their pay and influence to the classroom hours. One aim of this collection is to provide avenues for the overstretched precarious academic—who may be teaching outside their specialty, perhaps across multiple institutions and contracts, as part of survey courses—small-scale, manageable suggestions for engaging in current conversations on science writing.

Even with these concerns in view, the institution/civic binary nevertheless signals the language and assumptions underpinning both literature and science writing and the teaching of the two in conjunction. Disciplines have their own language, ways of thinking, and conventions. Stefan Collini describes the process of humanities education as follows:

> Undergraduate education involves exposing students for a while to the experience of enquiry into something in particular, but enquiry which

> has no external goal other than improving the understanding of that subject-matter. One rough and ready distinction between university education and professional training is that education relativizes and constantly calls into question the information which training simply transmits. In this sense, education encourages the student to recognize the ways in which particular bits of knowledge are not fixed or eternal or universal or self-sufficient. (56)

Collini, whose study was published in 2012, just as the marketization of UK higher education was coming to fruition in terms of fees and increasingly interventionist quality assurance procedures (and as similar trends in the defunding of state institutions continued apace in the United States), is at pains to separate universities from commercial enterprises. For our purposes, however, most interesting is the focus on students' critical acquisition of a body of knowledge that is in flux and subject to both contextual factors and debate. This is of course a key factor of science writing too: the contingency of both broad areas of knowledge and their reliance on rhetoric is an important factor of tertiary-level education. By extension, the understanding of subject matter that a student takes with them outside the institution should have this critical awareness at its heart: informed skepticism is a common outcome of the seminars and courses described here.

Ethics

As Josie Gill has documented, the academy has been urged in recent years to reckon with institutions as sites of inclusion and exclusion and particularly with a still present investment in the creation and sustaining of colonial forms of knowledge that prioritize Western norms and structures. Turning to literature and science in particular, Gill confronts her readers with two important questions:

> What would it mean for us, as literature and science scholars, to examine the institutional structures and orders of knowledge that we reproduce in our work, and to understand how this connects to the humans for whom we feel pity but might keep separate from our intellectual thought? To think of truth not only in relation to science and fiction but in terms of the political realities and contexts in which we work? (287)

Several approaches to teaching science writing represented in this volume confront these ethical questions about inclusion and exclusion: some essays encourage students to recognize unequal access to knowledge (Dauer;

Chacko); others deal with the effects of classification on human and human/nonhuman relationships (Otjen; Malcolm; Merola) as well as infrastructure and environmental justice (Barclay; Knittle, Manocha, and Rivera).

Literacy Skills

Relatedly, essays in this volume explore science literacy and literacy skills not simply as the command of basic facts but also as the competencies necessary to undertake critique and to participate in movements for justice. Bryan Shawn Wang and Sandy Feinstein note that both literature and science "involve the interplay of seeing and ideating"; meanwhile, John MacNeill Miller uses the trope of "noticing" to identify commonalities between species identification and literary analysis. These kinds of commonalities inform many of the pedagogical approaches in this volume, where one important aim is to develop students' high-level literacy skills by exposing students to different kinds of texts and approaches. Many of the essays here advocate for the inclusion of science writing in curricula with these aims of developing analytical and productive skills in mind: Aylin Malcolm and Rosalind Powell both prompt students to close-read premodern science texts in order to learn about the stylistic features of the genre and to develop their analytical skills. The recognition that science writers regularly employ tropes, persuasive rhetoric, and tone to translate concepts to nonspecialist readers appears across the volume. Our contributors also demonstrate how students develop science literacy—not simply in the sense of understanding scientific facts but also in understanding science as a social practice—as they think about the processes and effects of classifying, naming, and even creating physical phenomena. A common thread here is that science writing is not neutral. This is particularly apparent in classrooms that engage with environmental writing: in this context, Robin Wall Kimmerer's best-selling *Braiding Sweetgrass* emerges as a favorite set text (and, we might note, its recurrence is a symptom of the relative paucity of Indigenous voices within pop science writing, despite a growing emphasis on amplifying Indigenous voices within the academy). Advocacy is also emphasized in the essays that promote direct dialogue between scientists and humanists: for Davy Knittle and his undergraduate STEM students Aneesha Manocha and Arielle Rivera, for example, a humanities approach can bring an ethical dimension to questions of infrastructure through the discussion of racial justice and the deleterious effects of past projects.

Creativity

Creativity emerges as an important tool for teaching and learning. Wang and Feinstein's students engage in the creation of their own physical models that translate concepts of classification and natural hierarchies in unexpected ways. This employment of creativity also lays bare the similarities between literary analogies and scientific models, affording students the chance to think between the disciplines at the same time as they exercise their factual and procedural knowledge of the course material. Creativity has enjoyed something of a renaissance in pedagogical thinking: in 2014 the educational psychologists Lorin W. Anderson and David R. Krathwohl revised Bloom's influential taxonomy of educational objectives by replacing synthesis with creation. While the revised taxonomy does not necessarily envision building models or drawing animals, it focuses on how creative assignments can enable students to apply conceptual or factual knowledge in new ways (Anderson and Krathwohl 32–34). This kind of application can be seen in this volume in creative exercises where students construct field guide entries (Miller), write creative descriptions of illnesses (Lee), or write imitations or parodies (Malcolm). In each case, creativity requires critical processes of analysis and synthesis, and students learn how to translate their new knowledge and gain experiential knowledge of scientific methods.

Subjectivity and Objectivity

Finally, a concern braided throughout this volume is the complicated relationship between subjectivity and objectivity in the formulation, presentation, and communication of new forms of knowledge. The concept of objectivity calls to mind the sets of rules and ways of seeing that are agreed upon by a community of scientists or observers—for example, the use of commonly agreed-upon measurements; the witnessing and replication of experiments; methodologies, including the use of controls, in experimental processes; norms of recordkeeping; and the exclusion of personal biases and experiences from the field of inquiry and the reports that are published. These kinds of rules can allow the results of scientific experimentation and observation to be recognized as reliable.

The agreements determining the objectivity of scientific inquiry are also locally and temporally contingent, and each discipline has its own norms and practices.[10] As Lorraine Daston and Peter Galison's groundbreaking 2007 study showed, in spite of its frequent use as a synonym for *scientific*, the epistemic virtue of objectivity is neither automatic to scientific practice nor an automatically valued part of knowledge construction (372). Daston and Galison trace a history of science in which "there was nothing inevitable about the emergence of objectivity" (197) and in which the nineteenth-century aspiration toward "knowledge that bears no trace of the knower—knowledge unmarked by prejudice or skill, fantasy or judgement, wishing or striving" (17) is only part of a "slowly expanding repertoire" (113) of forms of knowing: "Epistemic virtues," they write, "emerge and evolve in specific historical contexts, but they do not necessarily become extinct under new conditions, as long as each continues to address some urgent challenge to acquiring and securing knowledge" (113). The essays in this volume explore how that broad repertoire, and the shifting rules of inclusion and exclusion across different periods and geographies, can be introduced to students. Several contributors to this collection also incorporate Daston and Galison's insights into their teaching by unsettling the automatic connections between science and objectivity. As a number of contributors note, an emphasis on objectivity in science writing opens itself up to critique based on what the ideal of neutrality assumes and what forms of knowledge it obscures and excludes. Finally, Daston and Galison document the reemergence of the scientist into scientific discourse in the twentieth century through the figure of "the trained expert (doctor, physicist astronomer) [who] grounds his or her knowledge in guided experience, not special access to reality" (359). They refer here to the production and interpretation of scientific images, but regarding science communication more generally, the question of visible expertise and its construction is an important theme. A literary critical approach draws students' attention to processes of mediation and interpretation in the formulation of science communication. Addressing these issues provides opportunities for students to become more informed, critical, and communicative readers of science texts who understand both their own positionality and that of the texts that they encounter.

Teaching with Science Writing is not the last word on integrating science writing into humanities courses, nor should it be: if there is anything this collection demonstrates, it is that science, humanistic inquiry, and pedagogy are all enlivened by continual reexamination. Perhaps this book is more of an experiment in the nonscientific sense of the word: any "course of action, system, method, etc., which is speculatively or provisionally adopted without being sure of the outcome" ("Experiment"). A pedagogy founded on speculation is necessarily adaptive and, we would like to think, hopeful. So let's experiment. What we try may not work—or it might succeed even beyond what we expected.

Notes

1. In England and Wales, tuition fees were introduced in 1998, and in September 2012, they increased substantially following the 2010 Browne Report, also known as the Independent Review of Higher Education Funding and Student Finance, a report commissioned by the United Kingdom's Labour government in the wake of the 2008 global financial crisis. In the United States, state spending on higher education has declined precipitously following the Great Recession, leading to what the nonpartisan Center on Budget and Policy Priorities refers to as a "lost decade in higher education funding" (Mitchell et al., "Lost Decade"). For a detailed analysis of funding trends since 2008, see Mitchell et al., "Unkept Promises."

2. For more on how *Amazon*'s classificatory systems have influenced the book industry, see McGurl. Although McGurl's argument focuses on the novel, his observations about how *Amazon* has shaped readers' behavior is relevant here: as he demonstrates, *Amazon*'s algorithms have exploded traditional literary categories, reorganizing texts according to the consumerist logic of the recommendation (i.e., "users who viewed this product also viewed . . .").

3. In the often cited *The Two Cultures and the Scientific Revolution*, C. P. Snow famously declared a "gulf of mutual incomprehension" (4) between literary critics and scientists. Although Snow later modified this stance, the notion that literature and science represent opposite poles of intellectual inquiry remains an ingrained cultural belief. Martin Willis remarks that the 1959 lecture on which *The Two Cultures* was based "has a status amounting almost to myth in the present day," owing partly to the vituperative response it provoked from F. R. Leavis. Because Leavis sought to defend the value of English as a discipline, Willis explains, "Snow's thesis and Leavis's response to it have been seen as a kind of origin story for literature and science scholarship" (7).

4. See Beer; see also Levine, *Darwin* and *One Culture*. For more on successive waves of Darwin studies scholarship, see Griffiths 66–67.

5. In an 1840 volume, Whewell reiterates, "We need very much a name to describe the cultivator of science in general" (qtd. in "Scientist").

6. For more on the roles played by Indigenous and enslaved people in British colonial science, see Parrish; see also Rusert.

7. Matters of genre, style, and labeling are a familiar topic among historians of science, for whom the definition and analytical utility of the term *popular science* has sparked lively debate. Skeptics point out that *popular science* is imprecise, since it could describe anything from science education to citizen science to science-related

entertainment. Others counter that popular science is a useful umbrella category, a pragmatic heuristic for gathering related areas of interest. For perspectives on how the discipline of history has regarded popular science and cognate categories, see Bowler; see also Bensaude-Vincent; Daum; O'Connor; Pandora; and Topham.

8. Indigenous environmental studies and sciences (IESS) is an interdisciplinary enterprise focused on "Indigenous heritages and traditions for the sake of understanding how the moral fabric of a society is related (or not) to its capacity to adjust to various ecosystems" (Whyte 139). As the Potawatomi scholar Kyle Whyte explains, spirituality—defined for many Indigenous people as the sum of intra- and interspecies moral relationships—has long anchored the capacity of Indigenous cultures to "adjust to the dynamics of ecosystems to avoid preventable harms" (140). IESS therefore assumes that environmental science must attend to the cultural practices that encode human accountability to nonhuman others. IESS is worth highlighting here as a model of scientific practice that explicitly engages with matters that come up throughout this volume, such as the definition of *science* and scientific authority, the role of settler colonialism in shaping scientific practice, and opportunities for interdisciplinary collaboration in the service of justice.

9. For resources on Indigenous science, see the section "Indigenous Science and Indigenous Knowledge: Introductory Resources" in part 5 of this volume.

10. For an early exploration of how norms were operating within twentieth-century scientific spaces, see Latour and Woolgar's sociological investigation of the "process of fact construction" in *Laboratory Life* (105).

Works Cited

Anderson, Lorin W., and David R. Krathwohl. *A Taxonomy for Learning, Teaching, and Assessing: A Revision of Bloom's Taxonomy of Educational Objectives.* Pearson, 2014.

Ayers, Edward L. "Where the Humanities Live." *Daedalus*, vol. 138, no. 1, 2009, pp. 24–34, https://doi.org/10.1162/daed.2009.138.1.24.

Beer, Gillian. *Darwin's Plots: Evolutionary Narrative in Darwin, George Eliot and Nineteenth-Century Fiction.* Routledge, 1983.

Bensaude-Vincent, Bernadette. "A Historical Perspective on Science and Its 'Others.'" *Isis*, vol. 100, no. 2, 2009, pp. 359–68, https://doi.org/10.1086/599547.

Bowler, Peter J. *Science for All: The Popularization of Science in Early Twentieth-Century Britain.* U of Chicago P, 2009.

Collini, Stefan. *What Are Universities For?* Penguin, 2012.

Daston, Lorraine, and Peter Galison. *Objectivity.* Zone Books, 2007.

Daum, Andreas W. "Varieties of Popular Science and the Transformations of Public Knowledge: Some Historical Reflections." *Isis*, vol. 100, no. 2, 2009, pp. 319–32, https://doi.org/10.1086/599550.

Davis, Heather. *Plastic Matter.* Duke UP, 2022.

Dimock, Wai Chee. *Weak Planet: Literature and Assisted Survival.* U of Chicago P, 2020.

Dimock, Wai Chee, and Priscilla Wald. "Literature and Science: Cultural Forms, Conceptual Exchanges." Preface. *Literature and Science*, special issue of *American Literature*, edited by Dimock and Wald, vol. 74, no. 4, 2002, pp. 705–14.

"Experiment, *N*." *Oxford English Dictionary*, Oxford UP, Mar. 2025, https://doi.org/10.1093/OED/2775257539.

Gill, Josie. "Decolonizing Literature and Science." *Configurations*, vol. 26, no. 3, 2018, pp. 283–88, https://doi.org/10.1353/con.2018.0023.

Griffiths, Devin. "Darwin and Literature." *The Cambridge Companion to Literature and Science*, edited by Steven Meyer, Cambridge UP, 2018, pp. 62–80.

Gross, Alan G. *The Scientific Sublime: Popular Science Unravels the Mysteries of the University*. Oxford UP, 2018.

Kennedy, Brian, and Alec Tyson. "Americans' Trust in Science, Positive Views of Science Continue to Decline." *Pew Research Center*, 14 Nov. 2023, pewresearch.org/science/2023/11/14/americans-trust-in-scientists-positive-views-of-science-continue-to-decline/.

Kuhn, Thomas S. *The Structure of Scientific Revolutions*. U of Chicago P, 1962.

———. "What Are Scientific Revolutions?" *The Probabilistic Revolution: Ideas in History*, vol. 1, edited by Lorenz Kruger et al., MIT Press, 1978, pp. 7–22.

Latour, Bruno. *The Pasteurization of France*. Harvard UP, 1993.

———. *Science in Action: How to Follow Scientists and Engineers through Society*. Harvard UP, 1987.

Latour, Bruno, and Steve Woolgar. *Laboratory Life: The Social Construction of Scientific Facts*. Sage Publications, 1979.

Levine, George. *Darwin and the Novelists: Patterns of Science in Victorian Fiction*. Harvard UP, 1988.

———, editor. *One Culture: Essays in Science and Literature*. U of Wisconsin P, 1987.

Liboiron, Max. *Pollution Is Colonialism*. Duke UP, 2021.

Littlefield, Melissa M., and Martin Willis. "The State of the Unions." Introduction. *The State of the Unions*, special issue of *Journal of Literature and Science*, edited by Littlefield and Willis, vol. 10, no. 1, 2017, pp. 1–4, https://doi.org/10.12929/jls.10.1.01.

Mance, Henry. "Britain Has Had Enough of Experts, Says Gove." *Financial Times*, 3 June 2016, ft.com/content/3be49734-29cb-11e6-83e4-abc22d5d108c.

McGurl, Mark. *Everything and Less: The Novel in the Age of Amazon*. Verso, 2021.

Medin, Douglas L., and Megan Bang. *Who's Asking? Native Science, Western Science, and Science Education*. MIT Press, 2014.

Meyer, Steven. Introduction. *The Cambridge Companion to Literature and Science*, edited by Meyer, Cambridge UP, 2018, pp. 1–21.

Mitchell, Michael, et al. "A Lost Decade in Higher Education Funding: State Cuts Have Driven Up Tuition and Reduced Quality." *Center on Budget and Policy Priorities*, 23 Aug. 2017, www.cbpp.org/research/a-lost-decade-in-higher-education-funding.

Mitchell, Michael, et al. "Unkept Promises: State Cuts to Higher Education Threaten Access and Equity." *Center on Budget and Policy Priorities*, 4 Oct.

2018, cbpp.org/research/state-budget-and-tax/unkept-promises-state-cuts
-to-higher-education-threaten-access-and.

O'Connor, Ralph. "Reflections on Popular Science in Britain: Genres, Categories, and Historians." *Isis*, vol. 100, no. 2, 2009, pp. 333–45, https://doi.org/
10.1086/599549.

Orthia, Lindy A. "Strategies for Including Communication of Non-Western
and Indigenous Knowledges in Science Communication Histories." *Journal
of Science Communication*, vol. 19, no. 2, 2020, https://doi.org/10.22323/
2.19020202.

Pandora, Katherine. "Popular Science in National and Transnational Perspective: Suggestions from the American Context." *Isis*, vol. 100, no. 2, 2009,
pp. 346–58, https://doi.org/10.1086/599548.

Parrish, Susan Scott. *American Curiosity: Cultures of Natural History in the Colonial British Atlantic World*. U of North Carolina P, 2006.

Prescod-Weinstein, Chanda. *The Disordered Cosmos: A Journey into Dark Matter,
Spacetime, and Dreams Deferred*. Bold Type Books, 2021.

Rusert, Britt. *Fugitive Science: Empiricism and Freedom in Early African American Culture*. NYU Press, 2017.

"Scientist, N." *Oxford English Dictionary*, Oxford UP, June 2022, oed.com/
view/Entry/172698.

Serres, Michel. *Hermes: Literature, Science, Philosophy*. Johns Hopkins UP, 1983.

Shapiro, Adam. "What Science Writing Owes to Its Religious Origins." *American Scientist*, 17 Nov. 2021, americanscientist.org/blog/macroscope/
what-science-writing-owes-to-its-religious-origins.

Snow, C. P. *The Two Cultures and the Scientific Revolution*. Oxford UP, 1959.

Todd, Zoe. "An Indigenous Feminist's Take on the Ontological Turn: 'Ontology' Is Just Another Word for Colonialism." *Journal of Historical Sociology*,
vol. 29, no. 1, 2016, pp. 4–22, https://doi.org/10.1111/johs.12124.

Topham, Jonathan R. Introduction. *Isis*, vol. 100, no. 2, 2009, pp. 310–18,
https://doi.org/10.1086/599551.

Watts, Vanessa. "Indigenous Place-Thought and Agency amongst Humans and
Non-humans (First Woman and Sky Woman Go on a European Tour!)."
Decolonization: Indigeneity, Education and Society, vol. 2, no. 1, 2013,
pp. 20–34.

Whitworth, Michael H. "Literature and Science." *Oxford Research Encyclopedia
of Literature*, 28 Sept. 2020, https://doi.org/10.1093/acrefore/97801902
01098.013.990.

Whyte, Kyle. "Critical Investigations of Resilience: A Brief Introduction to Indigenous Environmental Studies and Sciences." *Daedalus*, vol. 147, no. 2, spring
2018, pp. 136–47, https://doi.org/10.1162/DAED_a_00497.

Williams, Raymond. *Keywords: A Vocabulary of Culture and Society*. Croom
Helm, 1976.

Willis, Martin. *Literature and Science: A Reader's Guide to Essential Criticism*.
Palgrave Macmillan, 2015.

Yong, Ed. Introduction. *The Best American Science and Nature Writing 2021*,
edited by Yong, Mariner Books, 2021, pp. xv–xxv.

Part I

Historical Science Writing

Aylin Malcolm

Before Objectivity: Pluralizing Science with Premodern Knowledge

One of the most rewarding things about teaching premodern texts is the chance to empower students to question accounts of history as constant progress. To many people, the phrase *medieval science* may seem a contradiction in terms: the medieval period is frequently understood as a time *before* science, where "science" refers to a particular form of systematic knowledge based on observation and experience.[1] In general, students who sign up for literature and science courses do not expect to encounter the Middle Ages, and students who sign up for courses on medieval literature do not expect to encounter scientific texts. These preconceptions are inaccurate: as medievalists have long argued, the Middle Ages were a time not of obscurity and ignorance but of complex astronomical calculations, sophisticated (albeit dubious by modern standards) medical practices, and meticulous observational studies of nonhuman nature—much of which was financially supported by the very religious orders that are now accused of stifling innovation (Shank and Lindberg, Introduction 1–8). However, it is also true that premodern societies engaged in knowledge practices that differ considerably from twenty-first-century empiricism. These dissimilarities are useful to address with students because they put pressure on cultural narratives that associate legitimate expertise with Western academic institutions, thus excluding many Indigenous, traditional, and domestic knowledges. Studying and teaching medieval philosophy can therefore undermine totalizing, teleological views of both the history of knowledge and the present character of knowledge.

This essay addresses the benefits of including medieval science in general or transhistorical literature and science courses. Focusing on poetry and philosophy produced between the twelfth and fourteenth centuries, I suggest that such texts can both contextualize and destabilize received notions of "literature" and "science" by revealing these to have been variable and often overlapping categories in the past.[2] Crucially, examining historical forms of natural knowledge also helps students identify plurality in the present. I therefore explore the radical potential of teaching medieval philosophy alongside critiques of Western empiricism and objectivity in Indigenous studies and Black feminist studies.

To illustrate these points, I refer to a transhistorical literature and science seminar that I taught at the University of Pennsylvania in the spring of 2020. Broadly stated, my goal in this course was to offer expansive views of both "literature" and "science" while highlighting contributions by people of color, women, queer people, and other marginalized communities. We began the semester with foundational theoretical conversations about the degree to which science is socially constructed and the need to recognize its rhetorical aspects while acknowledging the reality of scientific findings (Haraway; Latour). We critically examined contemporary perceptions of science as mechanistic, methodical, and objective, including the third-person reporting style common in scientific writing, which obscures individual human experiences.[3] These discussions laid the groundwork for students' understanding of objectivity as a historical phenomenon rather than a natural or necessary aspect of the pursuit of knowledge.[4] We then explored these issues in relation to literary texts written during the last fifty years, including a number of speculative short stories and two novels: Amitav Ghosh's *The Hungry Tide*, which depicts encounters between Western science and place-based knowledge in a region prone to ecological crises, and Jeff VanderMeer's *Annihilation*, a narrative of first contact with extraterrestrial life that also reflects on the limits of observational knowledge.[5]

The course also featured three short historical units on early modern astronomy (weeks 2–3), medieval zoology (week 4), and nineteenth-century natural history (week 11), each of which addressed a scientific problem or controversy central to its period. This essay focuses on the medieval zoology unit, which paired scholastic philosophy in translation with narrative poetry from England. Medieval philosophers were invested in clearly defining the human/animal boundary because of its importance in Christian theology; most writers affirmed that only creatures with rationality (i.e., humans) were eligible for salvation, but in practice this boundary was challenging to establish and maintain (Salisbury; Steel). Our readings accordingly centered on animals that threatened this boundary—namely dogs, with their remarkable powers of sensation and discernment, and birds, with their capacities for song and mimicry. As this case study reveals, even brief discussions of medieval philosophy can fuel conversations about the exclusions and biases of modern science while encouraging students to pursue novel, cross-disciplinary modes of written expression.

Pedagogical Goals and Methods

The strategies I outline below were developed for a junior research seminar titled Science/Fiction that consisted of a small group of seven students. Primarily intended for English majors nearing the end of their degrees, these capstone courses combine advanced study in a period, topic, or text with training in research methods and writing skills. Students are expected to build on class discussions in a final scholarly essay (comparable to a graduate seminar paper) or an equivalent creative project. Given these broad learning outcomes, readings and assignments function best in these courses when they serve multiple purposes; I have therefore found the materials I used in this seminar easy to adapt to other courses by altering the workload or shifting the emphasis.

The medieval unit of this course consisted of two class sessions of eighty minutes each. For the first class, students read Marie de France's early-twelfth-century poem "Bisclavret" ("The Werewolf") with an accompanying scholarly essay that calls attention to the interplay between gender and species in the narrative (Langdon); for instance, the titular character regains his humanity through acts of violence against his former wife. We paired this poem with the section on animals in Adelard of Bath's *Questiones naturales* (*Natural Questions*), a philosophical dialogue that atypically argues for the immortality of dog souls (102–19), and a description of dogs found in medieval bestiaries, which contain moralized accounts of animal behavior (Clark 145–48).[6]

The second class centered on Geoffrey Chaucer's *Parliament of Fowls*, a dream vision that allegorizes human social classes as bird species and appears to consider whether women might resist subjugation within the social order.[7] To complement this text, I assigned excerpts on the ostrich and the barnacle goose from Albertus Magnus's *On Animals* (1563, 1648–49). In both entries, Albertus stresses his reliance on personal experience to verify the claims of previous writers, and the ostrich description even includes an experimental study. Students also read brief excerpts from scholarly articles on *Parliament* (Crane; Kordecki; Warren) and Ibn al-Nafis's *Theologus Autodidactus* (*The Self-Taught Theologian*), a speculative philosophical narrative in which a spontaneously generated feral child acquires information about the world through observation and reason.

I had several goals in making these selections, which amounted to between forty-five and fifty pages of reading per class. One of my objectives was to include texts representative of mainstream medieval philosophy as well as those expressing less conventional ideas. I also wanted to help students situate texts from England in the broader context of European and Middle Eastern science.[8] All these texts are available in readable English translations (although we did work through the original Middle English text of Chaucer's *Parliament*), and many have a substantial body of associated criticism.[9]

The broader learning goals for this week were both theoretical and methodological. On a conceptual level, I wanted students to note the stylistic aspects of medieval scientific writing and to consider the historical fluidity of textual genres. Medieval natural philosophers' frequent references to morality and religious doctrine, as well as their (often seemingly uncritical) citations of classical authorities, differ sharply from the impersonal, ostensibly objective tone that has characterized Western institutional science since the nineteenth century.[10] John Murdoch has described medieval science as "livresque" or "carried out in books" (3), which highlights the fact that medieval philosophers viewed reading, writing, translation, and illustration as central to the process of knowledge production rather than as mere tools for the post hoc reporting of findings. In other words, medieval science bears methodological similarities to modern humanistic disciplines, and its privileging of textuality and referentiality makes it highly amenable to literary analysis. In terms of skills, I hoped that students would gain a better sense of how modern theory can inform interpretations of historical texts while honing their ability to extract information from secondary readings, building on their previous work with etymological tools (e.g., the *Oxford English Dictionary*).

Since this was not a medieval class, I kept my lesson plans simple and included time to work through readings on a literal level before moving on to more advanced interpretation. I began both days, as I often do, with ten-minute introductory lectures on the social, generic, and philosophical contexts of our readings accompanied by visual materials (e.g., images of bestiary illustrations) and relevant quotations. I provided basic information about medieval authors and genres, the philosophical importance of human exceptionalism, and the specific social contexts from which our texts emerged. While these mini-lectures do include questions directed to the room, they are meant to ease students into the class by offering basic information and identifying key issues for later discussions. Students tend to report in course evaluations that these lectures help them feel prepared to begin analyzing historical readings.

Because this week fell at the point in the semester when students were beginning to think about their own research, I reserved time in class for students to analyze secondary readings in breakout groups, while discussions of primary readings involved the whole class. Should a lesson plan call for using medieval texts in group work, I find that a multistage approach often works well. For instance, I might begin by giving students a few minutes to freewrite about a passage or question, then have them answer related questions in small groups; usually, group work involves identifying important passages, points of uncertainty, or notable literary devices. Finally, I bring the class together for a synthetic discussion, during which I often take notes in a shared document. This tiered exercise encourages students to focus on specific features of a text while offering varied opportunities for participation and engagement.

Many of the open-ended questions that I asked the whole class might also be incorporated into individual or group work. Examples include the following:

> Is Bisclavret more human or more wolf (or dog)? Who has the best claim to truth or morality in this story, and why?
>
> How do philosophers like Adelard, Albertus, and Ibn al-Nafis respond to older authorities? What kinds of evidence do they mention in their responses? What strikes you about the styles of their writing (e.g., form, rhythm, vocabulary)? Do you notice any figurative language? If so, what purpose does it serve?
>
> How is nature organized in *Parliament*? What hierarchies are at play, and how stable are they? Do you find the ending of this narrative satisfying?
>
> Which of our readings would you consider "science"? Which would you consider "literature"? Why?

In the junior research seminar, asking questions like these led students to consider the importance of observation and sensation in medieval zoology, the rhetorical complexity of science writing, and the coconstruction of species and gender hierarchies.

Student Responses and Theoretical Implications

Initial responses to the scientific texts in this unit generally fell into the realm of incredulity and confusion. Adelard's *Natural Questions* seemed to be particularly challenging for students, likely because the philosophical dialogue is no longer a standard scholarly form; some students found it difficult to square its theatricality and abundant use of figurative language with their sense of scientific legitimacy. Despite the respective similarities of Albertus's and Ibn al-Nafis's texts to modern encyclopedias and science fiction, students also pointed out differences in their underlying ideologies; for instance, the eponymous self-taught theologian's rational process leads him to affirm the existence of God. Albertus's description of the semimythological barnacle goose (a bird that grows on trees at sea) was particularly fruitful because this legend led to a discussion of how science (still) builds on authoritative precedents: many of us accept the existence of animals that we have never seen because we trust what we have read about them, and it is impossible for a single person to verify everything they know through personal observation.[11]

On a basic level, these philosophical readings enhanced our interpretations of premodern vernacular poetry. For instance, we discussed Adelard's description of a dog carefully discerning the correct path based on scent (112–15) in relation to Marie de France's equivocal depiction of humans who fully trust a dog's judgment, to the point of valuing its testimony over that of a woman. The barnacle goose discussion also exemplifies a larger tendency that emerged in many of our explorations of premodern science: the sense that turning to the past can tell us something about our present moment, especially by denaturalizing and historicizing our understanding of modern disciplines and their boundaries.

Notably, these conversations continued to inform our work throughout the semester. In the following week, we turned to twenty-first-century discourses on climate change, including critiques of apocalypticism and the Anthropocene grounded in Indigenous and Black feminist thought (Whyte; Yusoff).[12] These critiques position the current climate crisis as one of many disasters experienced by postcolonial societies and stress the role of Western science in the ongoing oppression of marginalized peoples. Students pointed out that our readings in premodern science destabilize the notion of objectivity as a central feature of science, even in western Europe. Connecting *Parliament* to the present day, they also noted the longevity of hierarchies that position some individuals as more "human" than others, leading to a discussion of how institutional sciences have bolstered these hierarchies, both explicitly and through their privileging of Eurocentric epistemologies.[13] We also touched on the challenges of applying observational methods to large-scale, long-term ecological changes as well as the potential uses of historical texts and oral histories in these efforts.

Elements of our conversations about premodern science resurfaced again in an assignment in week 8, which encouraged students to interpret texts through creative lenses. I asked them to choose any of our syllabus readings, make a list of its key stylistic devices, and then produce a creative imitation (mimicking the original text's style but introducing new content), adaptation (transposing the text's content into a different style or genre), or exaggerated parody of the text. Assignments like this are common in junior research seminars, but the exercise took on new significance given that scientific writing made up a large proportion of our syllabus. Multiple students chose to engage with the rhetorical aspects of scientific texts, and one student produced a convincing imitation of Albertus's *On Animals.*[14] This student noted how Albertus uses similes, anthropomorphism, and classical allusions to construct his authority, capture his readers' interest, and enhance his comprehensibility.

I was also pleasantly surprised to find that medieval texts informed several of their final projects: for instance, one student produced a sonnet sequence based on their research on medieval grafting, while a second wrote an essay about personifications of nature across several periods that included Chaucer's *Parliament of Fowls.* Interestingly, several students who were originally planning to write essays ended up shifting to creative final projects accompanied by critical reflections. This may have been due in part to the unique challenges of the spring 2020 term: the university closed after our eighth week of class, and libraries were still adjusting to supporting remote work. However, a student who submitted a science fiction short story (which developed into their honors thesis) also pointed out that the class had inspired them to think more expansively about ways of communicating knowledge, noting the potential for even explicitly fictional texts to convey and critique scientific findings.

To be sure, the lessons that I have described only permitted us to scratch the surface of medieval thought. This seminar suffered from the limitations of all courses with a broad, comparative scope, in that we were able to delve deeply into only a few texts and contexts. However, such limitations may be instructive in themselves if we are honest about them with our students. Studying even a handful of premodern texts reveals the impossibility of condensing the full range of human knowledges into a single course or a singular model. Moreover, comparative approaches encourage us to scrutinize our own preconceptions, including our views of modernity, authority, textual genres, and processes of historical change. Medieval philosophy may be more "livresque" than modern science, but comparing the two highlights the subtle role of rhetoric in modern science writing. Teaching premodern science in the humanities classroom thus prepares students to consider not only what science is and has been—without equating historical change with progress—but also what it might become and how their literary training enables them to participate in ecologies of knowledge production.

Notes

1. The medieval term *scientia* was used more broadly to mean any knowledge acquired through formal education; knowledge acquired through practical training was commonly described as *ars* (art).

2. I begin here because European scholarship changed considerably during and after the twelfth century. In fact, medievalists sometimes (controversially) describe this period as a "renaissance" because of the growth of universities and the spread of Aristotelian science (Burnett, "Twelfth-Century Renaissance").

3. In the first week of class, McKibben provided an example of the argument that quantitative knowledge may be more reliable or persuasive than qualitative knowledge, which students were quick to refute. We also considered Imarisha's claim that "all organizing is science fiction" because activism involves imagining a different social order (3) and Latour's description of how scientific theories become settled as "black boxes" (1–17).

4. The definitive study of the history of objectivity, including its moralization as a form of self-restraint during the nineteenth century, is Daston and Galison's *Objectivity*.

5. We also discussed Ghosh's *Great Derangement*, which argues that modern science is ill-equipped to address discontinuity and disaster, such that society requires fiction to conceptualize climate change. Students found this argument (and its negative view of speculative fiction) somewhat totalizing but useful as a contrast to McKibben.

6. The bestiary entry on wolves (Clark 142–45) is also useful for discussing "Bisclavret."

7. Though I did not assign it in this class, Kiser's "Chaucer and the Politics of Nature" is an important and highly teachable essay on gender, class, and the social construction of nature in *Parliament*. I have generally found that students respond well to readings that relate the medieval animal/human boundary to gender, sexuality, race, or religion (DeVun; Ramey 89–100).

8. Scholars have argued that it is anachronistic to draw sharp distinctions between European and Middle Eastern science during the later Middle Ages. Rather, a continuous intellectual tradition extended across this entire region, supported by translators who transmitted knowledge from Greek to Arabic, Hebrew, and Latin (Burnett, "Translation").

9. Reading *Parliament* in Middle English is not essential but benefits discussions of how the poem depicts (animal) sound and (human) language (Warren).

10. Students had previously encountered historical differences in scientific rhetoric during our unit on early modern astronomy. For instance, we discussed Copernicus's evocations of the Christian principle of a divinely ordered cosmos.

11. It is now thought that premodern writers conflated two modern species, namely the barnacle goose (*Branta leucopsis*) and the goose barnacle (*Lepas anatifera*) (Buckeridge and Watts).

12. See also Roanhorse, which we read later in the term, for a critique from the perspective of a speculative fiction writer.

13. The literature on the complicity of Western academic institutions in colonialism is substantial and includes many accessible options for students (e.g., Collins 251–71; McGregor; Simpson).

14. Other students wrote imitations of Kepler's *Somnium* and Carson's *Silent Spring*, both of which are politically motivated efforts to communicate scientific principles to a broad audience.

Works Cited

Adelard of Bath. *Questiones naturales. Conversations with His Nephew*, by Adelard, edited and translated by Charles Burnett, Cambridge UP, 1998, pp. 81–235.

Albertus Magnus. *Albertus Magnus, On Animals: A Medieval* Summa Zoologica. Translated by Kenneth F. Kitchell, Jr., and Irven Michael Resnick, Ohio State UP, 2018.

Buckeridge, John, and Rob Watts. "Illuminating Our World: An Essay on the Unraveling of the Species Problem, with Assistance from a Barnacle and a Goose." *Humanities*, vol. 1, no. 3, 2012, pp. 145–65.

Burnett, Charles. "Translation and Transmission of Greek and Islamic Science to Latin Christendom." Shank and Lindberg, *Medieval Science*, pp. 341–64.

———. "The Twelfth-Century Renaissance." Shank and Lindberg, *Medieval Science*, pp. 365–84.

Carson, Rachel. *Silent Spring*. 1962. Mariner Books Classics, 2022.

Chaucer, Geoffrey. *The Parliament of Fowls. The Riverside Chaucer*, edited by Larry Benson, 3rd ed., Houghton Mifflin, 1987, pp. 383–94.

Clark, Willene B. *A Medieval Book of Beasts: The Second-Family Bestiary: Commentary, Art, Text and Translation.* Boydell, 2006.

Collins, Patricia Hill. *Black Feminist Thought: Knowledge, Consciousness, and the Politics of Empowerment.* 2nd ed., Routledge, 2002.

Copernicus, Nicolaus. *On the Revolutions of Heavenly Spheres.* Translated by Charles Glenn Wallis, Prometheus, 1995.

Crane, Susan. "'The Lytel Erthe That Here Is': Environmental Thought in Chaucer's *Parliament of Fowls.*" *Studies in the Age of Chaucer*, vol. 39, no. 1, 2017, pp. 1–30.

Daston, Lorraine, and Peter Galison. *Objectivity.* Zone Books, 2007.

DeVun, Leah. "Animal Appetites." *GLQ: A Journal of Lesbian and Gay Studies*, vol. 20, no. 4, 2014, pp. 461–90.

Ghosh, Amitav. *The Great Derangement: Climate Change and the Unthinkable.* U of Chicago P, 2016.

———. *The Hungry Tide.* HarperCollins Publishers, 2004.

Haraway, Donna. "Situated Knowledges: The Science Question in Feminism and the Privilege of Partial Perspective." *Feminist Studies*, vol. 14, no. 3, 1988, pp. 575–99.

Ibn al-Nafis. *The* Theologus Autodidactus *of Ibn al-Nafis.* Edited and translated by Max Meyerhof and Joseph Schacht, Clarendon, 1968.

Imarisha, Walidah. Introduction. *Octavia's Brood: Science Fiction Stories from Social Justice Movements*, edited by adrienne maree brown and Imarisha, AK Press, 2015, pp. 3–6.

Kepler, Johannes. *Kepler's* Somnium*: The Dream; or, Posthumous Work on Lunar Astronomy.* Translated by Edward Rosen, Dover Publications, 2003.

Kiser, Lisa J. "Chaucer and the Politics of Nature." *Beyond Nature Writing: Expanding the Boundaries of Ecocriticism*, edited by Karla Armbruster and Kathleen R. Wallace, U of Virginia P, 2001, pp. 41–56.

Kordecki, Lesley. "Ecofeminism and the Father of English Poetry: Chaucer's *Parliament of Fowls.*" *Interdisciplinary Studies in Literature and Environment*, vol. 10, no. 1, 2003, pp. 97–114.

Langdon, Alison. "La Femme Bisclavret: The Female of the Species?" *Medieval Feminist Forum*, vol. 54, no. 1, 2018, pp. 34–49.

Latour, Bruno. *Science in Action: How to Follow Scientists and Engineers through Society.* Rev. ed., Harvard UP, 1988.

Marie de France. "Bisclavret." *The* Lais *of Marie de France: Text and Translation*, edited and translated by Claire M. Waters, Broadview Press, 2018, pp. 144–61.

McGregor, Deborah. "Traditional Ecological Knowledge: An Anishinabe Woman's Perspective." *Atlantis*, vol. 29, no. 2, 2005, pp. 103–09.

McKibben, Bill. "When Words Fail." *Orion Magazine*, 23 June 2008, orionmagazine.org/article/when-words-fail/.

Murdoch, John E. *Album of Science: Antiquity and the Middle Ages.* Charles Scribner's Sons, 1984.

Ramey, Lynn T. *Black Legacies: Race and the European Middle Ages.* UP of Florida, 2014.

Roanhorse, Rebecca. "Postcards from the Apocalypse." *Uncanny Magazine*, no. 20, 2018, www.uncannymagazine.com/article/postcards-from-the -apocalypse/.
Salisbury, Joyce E. *The Beast Within: Animals in the Middle Ages*. 3rd ed., Routledge, 2022.
Shank, Michael H., and David C. Lindberg. Introduction. Shank and Lindberg, *Medieval Science*, pp. 1–26.
———, editors. *Medieval Science*. Cambridge UP, 2013. Vol. 2 of *The Cambridge History of Science*.
Simpson, Leanne Betasamosake. "Land as Pedagogy: Nishnaabeg Intelligence and Rebellious Transformation." *Decolonization: Indigeneity, Education and Society*, vol. 2, no. 2, 2014, pp. 1–25.
Steel, Karl. *How to Make a Human: Animals and Violence in the Middle Ages*. Ohio State UP, 2011.
VanderMeer, Jeff. *Annihilation*. HarperCollins Publishers, 2014.
Warren, Michael J. "'Kek Kek': Translating Birds in Chaucer's *Parliament of Fowls*." *Studies in the Age of Chaucer*, vol. 38, no. 1, 2016, pp. 109–32.
Whyte, Kyle P. "Indigenous Science (Fiction) for the Anthropocene: Ancestral Dystopias and Fantasies of Climate Change Crises." *Environment and Planning E: Nature and Space*, vol. 1, nos. 1–2, 2018, pp. 224–42.
Yusoff, Kathryn. *A Billion Black Anthropocenes or None*. U of Minnesota P, 2018.

Rosalind Powell

Epistolary Science:
The Early *Philosophical Transactions*

When asked to draw comparisons between literary texts and science writing, students often cite stereotypical dichotomies between subjective and objective knowledge or between creativity and fact. There is often a sense that there are indeed two cultures. As the essays in this volume show, these generalizations and assumptions can be counterbalanced with attention to science writing from any period of study. Science writing of the seventeenth and eighteenth centuries precedes both the professionalization of the discipline and the erection of boundaries demarcating science from other areas of knowledge. This context means that the two-way direction of influence between literature and science—that is, the adoption of new scientific topics into literary discourse, the concept of science as public property, and the use of literary discourse to present new scientific ideas—is all the more visible. This essay makes the argument for using such scientific texts as part of seminars in English literature at the undergraduate level. I present strategies for using letters published in the early *Philosophical Transactions of the Royal Society* to introduce literature students to some key concepts in late-seventeenth-century natural philosophy.[1]

Contemporary pedagogical scholarship on teaching literature at the tertiary level emphasizes the development of skills in addition to communicating and testing content. Patrick Collier discusses how students must learn "advanced reading comprehension" by being confronted with challenging texts, taught to recognize interpretative difficulty, and helped to develop new research skills in order to fill interpretative gaps. Collier explains how, as part of this process, students must be trained in methods of "advanced literacy" in order to decode and interpret complex texts (27). These valuable transferable skills can be applied to analytical reading of any kind. By bringing early science writing into the literature classroom, it is possible to give students new opportunities to practice and develop these skills while also providing a more rounded view of the period's culture. Taking as examples two letters from 1672—one from Robert Boyle outlining his observations on a piece of meat that appeared to glow in the dark and the other from Isaac Newton detailing his new theory of how colors are produced ("Letter")—I show how a literary critical approach to nonscientific texts can develop in students a sense of the role of science in broader society and an understanding of how and why the skills of literary analysis should be applied to a wider range of texts.

The letters are both addressed to the secretary of the Royal Society, Henry Oldenburg. By selecting texts that present new scientific observations through the epistolary form, which is likely familiar to students from prefaces to early novels, epistolary fiction, or even the conventions of formal letter writing, it is possible to draw attention to rules of sociability and authority central to validating the reports of new scientific observations and theories. Another significant similarity between the two texts is the interruption of experimental observations by life events. The morning after surveying the properties of the "shining flesh," Boyle is "hastily called up before day for a Niece, that I am very justly and exceedingly concerned for, who was thought to be upon the point of death" (5113). Whereas Boyle's report covers two days, Newton's letter on optics spans a much greater period, from 1666 to 1671, and he explains midway through the letter how he had to quit his experiments in Cambridge as a result of "the Intervening Plague" (3080). As students will learn, such subjective elements are more than incidental details.

Finally, the two examples that I introduce here show the breadth of early natural philosophy in Britain: Boyle's meat that glows in the dark hardly seems a subject of scientific interest and has been all but forgotten today, whereas Newton's work on light is a foundational text for modern optics. An introduction to the period's science writing can therefore draw attention to the diversity of what the *Philosophical Transactions'* extended title describes as "Labours of the Ingenious."

Boyle's Larder

Boyle's letter on shining flesh offers opportunities for students to get to grips with the nature of the period's scientific writing. The published letter begins as follows:

> Yesternight, when I was about to go to bed, an *Amanuensis* of mine, accustom'd to make Observations, informed me, that one of the Servants of the house, going upon some occasion into the Larder, was frighted by something of Luminous that she saw (notwithstanding the darkness of the place,) where the meat had been hung up before: Whereupon suspending for a while my going to rest, I presently sent for the meat into my Chamber, and caused it to be placed in a corner of the room capable of being made considerably dark, and then I plainly saw, both with wonder and delight, and the joint of meat did in divers places shine like rotten Wood or stinking Fish. (5108)

Boyle proceeds with a numbered list of eighteen investigations into the nature of the glowing meat. The first ten items describe the phenomenon in terms of the size, color, location, and other stable features of the piece of veal and its "Lucid parts" (5109), and the remaining items describe more interactive processes, such as rubbing, pressing, and cutting it.

Spending time on the temporal and spatial framing of Boyle's letter helps students comprehend the porous boundaries of natural philosophy, the kinds of audiences that need to be considered, and the differing strategies needed to present scientific knowledge in this period. Students are often surprised to see that the site and subject of Boyle's observations are domestic. The natural philosopher is interrupted at bedtime by the discovery of the meat, and his investigations are limited by the "accommodations" available at nighttime (5108). The subject of inquiry has been kept in a larder "almost a story lower than the level of the street" (5110); observations are carried out in the adjoining kitchen, in another room without a fire, and in Boyle's own chamber. While the natural philosopher employs a number of instruments, including thermometers and an air pump, he also uses nonspecialist apparatuses such as a china cup (5111) and describes scale by comparison with the size of coins (5110) and his fingernails (5109). Rather than being a rarity, domestic practices of this kind are representative of the period's scientific activities (Werrett; Cooper).

We might note at this point how Boyle frames the initial responses to the unexpected luminosity of meat: whereas the servant is "frighted," the writer himself is struck with "wonder and delight" and states that he had been tempted to invite Oldenburg "to be a sharer in the pleasure of it" (5108). This emotive framing demonstrates a hierarchy of appreciation where the addressed reader and Boyle are placed on an equal level and the elite readers of *Philosophical Transactions* are also encouraged to engage with the piece of shining flesh as an object of scientific inquiry. This discussion of enthusiasm and its import helps model for students how attention to small details in the letter can help us understand what seventeenth-century readers valued in the presentation of natural philosophy. This method is linked to Sherry Lee Linkon's description of apprenticeship in the English literature classroom, which "mak[es] things visible" to students through demonstrating examples of what they should look for (69). Having been primed in this way, students can be prompted to work in groups on the following questions: How does Boyle describe and explain the new concept of shining flesh? What methods does he use to construct evidence about it? These questions encourage students to develop their advanced literacy independently based on this modeling by paying attention to the natural philosopher's sensory observations of the piece of veal in the opening pages to determine the scale of the shining patches, their brightness and color, the fact that they are not warm to the touch, and that the meat smells "very fresh" (5110).

Students can also be encouraged to analyze the significance of statements such as the following: "I *caused* . . . a piece of shining flesh to be compressed betwixt two pieces of glass" and "I *caused* the Pneumatical Engine to be prepared in a room without fire" (5111; emphasis mine). Having noted the letter's early reference to an amanuensis, students may be able to determine that the verb "caused" indicates that Boyle does not act alone in conducting his experiments. There are two elements to unpack here. The first is that others are clearly present to operate the machinery, reflecting the norm that elite natural philosophers preferred not to get their hands dirty (Pumfrey 148). The second is an important concept in early science writing: witnessing.

Witnessing is described in Steven Shapin's foundational article on the authentication of knowledge in Boyle's pneumatics experiments, where Shapin claims that "[m]atters of fact were to be produced in a public space: a particular space in which experiments were collectively performed and directly witnessed and an abstract space constituted through virtual witnessing" (497). Both direct and virtual witnessing can be found in Boyle's descriptions of the shining flesh: the other witnesses present see the processes directly, and readers can access the evidence through the detailed, structured documentation of events. Virtual witnessing is permitted by the invitation of the readers into the experimental space and through references to shared experiences and familiar objects and activities that bring the observations to life. These interactions between the individual observer and experimental matter blur the line between subject and object and publicize private actions that, as Simon Schaffer notes, need to be accredited by the "public community of natural philosophy" (330) to be recognized as evidence.

Newton's Chamber

Boyle's investigation of shining flesh is open-ended: a postscript outlines what is yet to be completed—"I shall willingly leave the Solution of such abstruse *Phenomena* as some of ours, unattempted," he says (5115)—and, crucially, though the letter describes the meat's environment as well as its properties and responses to manipulation, Boyle does not offer any explanations about how the phenomenon has come to be. Instead, the letter documents the cumulative acquisition of knowledge that mirrors other attempts to describe the features of unknown substances. The concept of description is also helpful for understanding our second example, Newton's letter on colors. Newton's letter, which is longer than Boyle's, poses different pedagogical challenges: there are some geometrical explanations and diagrams and elements that will need glossing with notes or a mini-lecture. That being said, the color spectrum will likely be familiar to students, and the opportunity to see how Newton promotes a new description of color as the product of refracted white light can strengthen strategies for reading complex texts and build a stronger conception of how knowledge production and science writing functioned in the period.

This letter provides less in the way of sociable framing than Boyle's does, though Newton does reference an earlier agreement with Oldenburg to account for his experiments. It is written as the experimental report of a single natural philosopher. Newton acknowledges the expertise of members of the Royal Society who are reading his work: he provides direct instructions for how to replicate the experiments that he sets out, and he also includes an invitation for feedback. Students will be familiar with Newton's name, if not his physics, so it is worth turning here to Patricia Fara's reminder that "[b]ecause [Newton] has become an international icon of scientific genius, it can be hard to appreciate that he was scarcely known outside Cambridge before his ground-breaking paper on optics was published in 1672." For this reason, Newton's self-fashioning in this letter invites particular attention, and we might spend some time considering the prevalence of the first-person singular—here there is no reference to "causing" assistants to set up experiments, giving the impression of a singular, hands-on affair of experimental outcomes that have been confirmed by repetition and are soon to be validated by replication.

The natural philosopher's strategic use of surprise at the start of his investigations is comparable to Boyle's expressions of wonder. Students will notice that, as in Boyle's letter, the first experiment involves a domestic framing:

> I procured me a Triangular glass-Prisme, to try therewith the celebrated *Phaenomena* of *Colours*. And in order thereto having darkened my chamber, and made a small hole in my window-shuts, to let in a convenient quantity of the Suns light, I placed my Prisme at his entrance, that it might be thereby refracted to the opposite wall. It was at first a very pleasing divertisement, to view the vivid and intense colours produced thereby; but after a while applying my self to consider them more circumspectly, I became surprised to see them in an *oblong* form; which, according to the received laws of Refraction, I expected should have been *circular*. (3075–76)

While Newton begins here by replicating an already known experiment to test out a prism, his surprise at the oblong shape formed by the refracted rays quickly eclipses his enjoyment of the "vivid and intense colours." A close reading of the succeeding paragraphs takes us through a systematic sequence of tests to determine that this effect is not due to an irregularity in the glass. Given that our focus is on color and light, rather than on Newton's improvement of lenses, we can then move to a consideration of the natural philosopher's "*Experimentum Crucis*" (3078), his proof of the origin of colors, which involves refracting sunlight with one prism to produce a spectrum and then using a second prism (together with a focusing lens) to reconstitute the rays into white light.

For both Boyle and Newton, knowledge can be sought only about the external properties of the phenomena they investigate and how those phenomena react to manipulation. As Newton says, "I shall not mingle conjectures with certainties" (3085). In this final section, I focus on encouraging students to consider the numbered "propositions" in the letter and how this can help them identify how Newton corrects his audience's assumptions about color and its production through the rhetorical framing of experimental evidence. Newton's explanation of the nature of color is a case in point: "Colours are not *Qualifications of Light*, derived from Refractions, or Reflections of natural Bodies (as 'tis generally believed,) but *Original* and *connate properties*, which in divers Rays are divers. Some Rays are disposed to exhibit a red colour and no other; some a yellow and no other, some a green and no other, and so of the rest" (3081).

Gillian Beer's concept of science as "redescribing what is known and taken for granted" (35) is helpful for leading students through the implications of Newton's statement about the production of colored light rays through the refraction of white light. Instructors can encourage students to pay attention to Newton's emphatic language and the larger issue of correcting assumptions by applying the following excerpt from Beer's essay:

> Scientific inquiry constantly revives questions which are answered both in science and literature at changing levels of description. Description must find ways out of the circle of current presumptions if it is to create knowledge or fresh insight. Yet all descriptions draw, often unknowingly, upon shared cultural assumptions which underwrite its neutral and authoritative status and conceal the embedded designs upon which describing depends. (35)

Reminded of the diverse scientific backgrounds and levels of readers of the *Philosophical Transactions*, students can be asked to consider how references to colors might function at different levels of description by discussing the associations carried by these phenomena, such as values attached to certain colors or the description of the rainbow as a divine sign in the book of Genesis. We might also think about how Newton employs personal authority, his experimental evidence, and the prompt to replicate the trials he sets out in order to demonstrate "fresh insight" about the topic.

Newton's description of white light as a "compound[ing]" (3083) of the primary colors demonstrates how readers can test out the evidence for themselves with a simple piece of apparatus:

> I have often with Admiration beheld, that all the Colours of the Prisme being made to converge, and thereby to be again mixed as they were in the light before it was Incident upon the Prisme, reproduced light, in-

tirely and perfectly white, and not at all sensibly differing from a *direct* Light of the Sun, unless when the glasses, I used, were not sufficiently clear; for then they would a little incline it to *their* colour. (3083)

This call to replication is a key element of Newton's science communication. His explanation is simple and could, with the requisite prisms, be modeled in the classroom. Students can also learn from this process to differentiate between explicit instructions and descriptions where details are omitted. Fara also notes that Newton's descriptions of his experiments with the prisms, particularly the *"Experimentum Crucis,"* were deceptively simple and downplayed the level of accuracy needed to replicate his production. The complexity of replicating the experiments can open up two final areas of classroom debate based on encounters that can prompt what Collier calls "the process of grappling collaboratively for meaning" (27). The first is the epistemological role of omission in scientists' self-presentation and descriptions and explanations of phenomena. Although the early stages of engagement with the *Philosophical Transactions* letters highlighted subjectivity and domestic settings, by this point students will be aware that these elements do not equate to a complete lack of selection. The second is the contingency of scientific knowledge: a description of a phenomenon constitutes scientific fact only until it is replaced by a new description. (This is a matter that Newton addresses directly in his fourth rule of reasoning in the *Principia* [*Mathematical Principles* 205].) Newton is readily aware that there may be problems with his account and that his "propositions" are merely suggestions, albeit those of an expert, based upon observation: "if any thing seem to be defective, or to thwart this relation, I may have an opportunity of giving further direction about it, or of acknowledging my errors, if I have committed any" (3087).

Possible Comparisons

Boyle's letter would sit comfortably alongside close readings of early modern literary texts that engage with detailed observations and descriptions of different kinds, such as Anne Finch's "A Nocturnal Rêverie" or Hester Pulter's poem about birds of paradise, "The Manucodiats." Thomas Shadwell's *The Virtuoso* sees Boyle's observations on shining flesh briefly lampooned in Nicholas Gimcrack's catalog of absurd experiments—Gimcrack exclaims that he has "read a Geneva Bible by a leg of pork" (5.2.31–32). This play provides instructive comparisons with the *Philosophical Transactions* articles it parodies and helps explain how the person and presentation of the natural philosopher formed part of the accreditation of science writing.

There are a number of literary texts that package Newton's optics for a broader readership. Poems such as James Thomson's "A Poem Sacred to the Memory of Sir Isaac Newton" and Elizabeth Tollet's "On the Death of Sir Isaac Newton" present descriptions of the spectrum in the context of celebrating Newton's life and achievements and therefore have significant potential in the classroom for comparative discussions of scientific description and the construction of authority. Other texts that translate Newtonian optics for a broader audience, such as Francesco Algarotti's *Sir Isaac Newton's Philosophy Explain'd for the Use of the Ladies* or Benjamin Martin's *The Young Gentleman and Lady's Philosophy*, can be excerpted to good effect as a means of thinking about the longer-term implications of science as description.

Notes

This essay reflects principally on my experience teaching literature and science at the University of Bristol between 2015 and 2022. The majority of English literature students at this institution are products of the English or Welsh school systems, which require specialization from age sixteen (often, though not exclusively, in either the humanities or the sciences).

1. The *Philosophical Transactions* began in 1665 as a monthly journal designed, as its title page claims, to give "some accompt of the present undertakings, studies, and labours of the ingenious in many considerable parts of the world" (*Philosophical Transactions*). Early issues of the journal were made up of letters on a broad range of natural philosophical and associated topics addressed to the journal's founder, Henry Oldenburg, and subsequently to later secretaries of the Royal Society. Their contents reflect the burgeoning scientific ideas and networks of the time. Though it was not owned or distributed by the Royal Society until 1752, it quickly became associated with its activities (Boas Hall 22). The society's online archive provides open access facsimiles of the journal's contents from its founding until 1886.

Works Cited

Algarotti, Francesco. *Sir Isaac Newton's Philosophy Explain'd for the Use of the Ladies.* Translated by Elizabeth Carter, London, 1739. 2 vols. *Gale,* link.gale.com/apps/doc/CW0121785163/ECCO?u=amst&sid=bookmark-ECCO&xid=b3219878.

Beer, Gillian. "Problems of Description in the Language of Discovery." *One Culture: Essays in Science and Literature,* edited by George Levine, U of Wisconsin P, 1987, pp. 35–58.

Boas Hall, Marie. "Oldenburg, the *Philosophical Transactions,* and Technology." *The Uses of Science in the Age of Newton,* edited by John G. Burke, U of Chicago P, 1983, pp. 21–47.

Boyle, Robert. "Some Observations about Shining Flesh." *Philosophical Transactions of the Royal Society*, vol. 7, no. 89, 1672, pp. 5108–16.

Collier, Patrick. *Teaching Literature in the Real World*. Bloomsbury, 2021.

Cooper, Alix. "Homes and Households." *Early Modern Science*, edited by Katherine Park and Lorraine Daston, Cambridge UP, 2006, pp. 224–37. Vol. 3 of *The Cambridge History of Science*.

Fara, Patricia. "Newton Shows the Light: A Commentary on Newton (1672) 'A Letter . . . Containing His New Theory about Light and Colours . . . .'" *Philosophical Transactions of the Royal Society A: Mathematical, Physical and Engineering Sciences*, vol. 373, 2015, royalsocietypublishing.org/doi/10.1098/rsta.2014.0213.

Finch, Anne. "A Nocturnal Rêverie." *Eighteenth-Century Poetry: An Annotated Anthology*, edited by David Fairer and Christine Gerrard, 3rd ed., Wiley-Blackwell, 2015, pp. 33–35.

Linkon, Sherry Lee. *Literary Learning: Teaching the English Major*. Indiana UP, 2011.

Martin, Benjamin. *The Young Gentleman and Lady's Philosophy, in a Continued Survey of the Works of Nature and Art; by Way of Dialogue*. 2nd ed., London, 1759–63. 2 vols. *Gale*, link.gale.com/apps/doc/CW0119952115/ECCO?u=amst&sid=bookmark-ECCO&xid=bd23b697.

Newton, Isaac. "A Letter of Mr. Isaac Newton . . . Containing His New Theory about Light and Colors." *Philosophical Transactions of the Royal Society*, vol. 6, no. 80, 1672, pp. 3075–87.

———. *The Mathematical Principles of Natural Philosophy*. Translated by Andrew Motte, vol. 2, London, 1729. *Gale*, link.gale.com/apps/doc/CW0108169950/ECCO?u=amst&sid=bookmark-ECCO&xid=7efc91c7.

Philosophical Transactions of the Royal Society. Vol. 1, no. 1, 1665, royalsocietypublishing.org/toc/rstl/1665/1/1.

Pulter, Hester. "The Manucodiats." *The Pulter Project*, edited by Leah Knight and Wendy Wall, 2025, pulterproject.northwestern.edu/poems/ee/the-manucodiats-emblem-5/#ctxs.

Pumfrey, Stephen. "Who Did the Work? Experimental Philosophers and Public Demonstrators in Augustan England." *The British Journal for the History of Science*, vol. 28, no. 2, 1995, pp. 131–56.

Schaffer, Simon. "Self Evidence." *Critical Inquiry*, vol. 18, no. 2, 1992, pp. 327–62.

Shadwell, Thomas. *The Virtuoso*. Edited by Marjorie Hope Nicolson and David Stuart Rodes, Edward Arnold, 1966.

Shapin, Steven. "Pump and Circumstance: Robert Boyle's Literary Technology." *Social Studies of Science*, vol. 14, no. 4, 1984, pp. 481–520.

Thomson, James. "A Poem Sacred to the Memory of Sir Isaac Newton." *"Liberty," "The Castle of Indolence," and Other Poems*, by Thomson, edited by James Sambook, Oxford UP, 1986, pp. 1–14.

Tollet, Elizabeth. "On the Death of Sir Isaac Newton." *Poems on Several Occasions*, by Tollet, London, 1755, pp. 128–30. *Gale*, link.gale.com/apps/doc/CW0113468259/ECCO?u=amst&sid=bookmark-ECCO&xid=98c2a96e.

Werrett, Simon. *Thrifty Science: Making the Most of Materials in the History of Experiment*. U of Chicago P, 2019.

Aaron Ottinger

Less Than Nothing in
The Rime of the Ancient Mariner:
Literature, Mathematics, Realism,
and Anti-Realism

This essay suggests that literature can serve as an inroad to teaching science writing on mathematics. In the last decade, we have seen an increase in secondary literature on the intersection of literature and mathematics, which can certainly provide students with opportunities for more robust conversations.[1] Of course, these resources are not always available to instructors at institutions with limited resources, nor are they necessarily written in a way that makes them accessible to students. For these reasons, focusing specifically on historical literature and mathematics can mean greater access to primary sources (through websites such as *Project Gutenberg* and *Google Books*), and popular science writing, such as the freely available articles in *Quanta Magazine*, may provide helpful alternatives to secondary sources. My historical approach has the added advantage of understanding how each discipline developed over time and the stakes involved in their dynamic relationship. Mathematics and literature, I suggest, did not evolve in isolation, or along straight, step-by-step paths, but often hand in hand and recursively, with starts, stops, agreements, and disagreements, some of which endure to this day.

Before proceeding it is worth sketching out my background, which might inspire others to apply the approaches discussed here in a variety of courses not restricted to the science writing classroom. While at the university level I have taught classes on literature and mathematics and literature and the ethics of science (including mathematics), at present I mainly teach first-year writing courses at a community college, with themes that focus on mathematics in culture and society, digital culture, and the decolonization of digital technology. But during the 2023–24 academic year, faculty members at my institution, Highline College, piloted a series of learning communities that allowed instructors to link classes in different fields. Using this model, I have taught research writing courses linked with an introductory statistics course, and in the upcoming school year we will offer English 101 linked with College Algebra. In these classes, I help students explain their mathematical methods or tell a story with their data. In addition, I help students better appreciate their mathematical tools from a humanist perspective, which involves lessons on the rhetoric and history of mathematics (e.g., thinking about audience and genre or thinking about the connections between mathematics and colonialism, etc.). But I also offer students opportunities to write on literary works that integrate mathematical forms, concepts, or debates. Whether it is a science writing class, a writing across the curriculum course, or possibly even a literature course for STEM students, I believe there are many ways we can include conversations and assignments about literature and mathematics that delight and surprise us, teach a variety of generic conventions for a host of audiences, and ultimately prepare us for writing on mathematics, in the context of either science writing or literary criticism.

Through the lenses of literary and historical contexts, students have an opportunity to deconstruct mathematical abstracta, discovering not only that certain things that seem natural today were once considered absurdities but also the converse: what seems outlandish today may have at one time been second nature. To provide an example of how students might enter into an analysis of literature and mathematics, I provide a reading of negative numbers in *The Rime of the Ancient Mariner*, by Samuel Taylor Coleridge. Following this reading I outline how the terms *realism* and *anti-realism* are cross-disciplinary terms and can be used as frameworks through which writers may help larger varieties of audiences appreciate the importance of mathematical and literary developments throughout time.

But are literature and mathematics not old enemies? What could these two domains possibly have to say to each other? Alain Badiou, a French philosopher working since the 1960s but whose work was introduced to readers in the United States beginning only in the 2000s, is one of the few philosophers today writing extensively on the relationship between mathematics, the arts (especially poetry), philosophy, and politics. (The essay I quote below, "What Is a Poem?," is the perfect length for classroom discussion.) While Plato subordinated poetry to mathematics, establishing a hierarchy that endured for almost two thousand years, Badiou points out that in the modern age—beginning with Romanticism—philosophy reverses these roles: "By all appearances, modernity makes the poem ideal and the matheme sophistical" ("What" 21). Badiou means that philosophers started to turn away from mathematics and instead viewed poetry as a window into being, or unmediated reality, which is ordinarily obfuscated by language, habit, and ideology.

According to Badiou's reading, however, both mathematics and poetry are truth procedures. The truths they reveal are just hints of different worlds and what the "universe would be if the total effects" of their respective truths "were limitlessly allowed to unfold within it" ("What" 22). In other words, both mathematics and poetry can be windows into other worlds (e.g., by subtracting the parallel postulate from Euclid, we start to see a non-Euclidean world where parallel lines actually meet). The main difference separating these two truth procedures is that math must be consistent and deductive, while poetry harnesses the endless possibilities of language (24–25). Badiou goes on to describe the role of philosophy as operating under the "double condition of the poem and the matheme," which might mean interpreting a truth revealed in poetry and then following and elucidating this truth through a mathematical (i.e., consistent) outline (26–27). The scientist also aids in the elucidation of these truths but differs from the philosopher in the sense that they need not maintain Badiou's "fidelity" to the truth (26). Here we can add that a science writer's main purpose is communication, and like the philosopher (but, generally speaking, unlike the mathematician), they are free to entertain math and literature under the same umbrella, as exemplified in my reading of Coleridge's *Rime of the Ancient Mariner*.

As the short inquiry above illustrates, one of the joys of teaching the intersection of English and mathematics, even at an introductory level, is the chance to bring up philosophical questions too often neglected in math classes. For starters, what is mathematics? For Proclus, the Ancient Greek term for mathematics, *mathesis* (μάθησις), refers to the "recollection of the eternal ideas in the soul" (38). In my experience, math majors and mathematically oriented students from across STEM fields love these questions because they rarely appear in a practical or applied mathematics course. Students might benefit from a list of questions to guide them in their inquiries, including ontological questions (What is a number?), epistemological questions (Where do mathematical ideas come from?), and even social, ethical, or political questions (How is mathematics used to oppress historically marginalized communities?). The science writing classroom (or lesson) can afford students accustomed to solving proofs a chance to take a step back and develop their metacognitive skills and historical understanding. An understanding *about* math is important for the sake of communicating the human value of mathematics and to help nonspecialists better appreciate the research and accomplishments of mathematicians. At the same time, but from a more critical angle, humanist tools can help us interrogate the history and application of mathematics, from reducing people to numbers in the transatlantic slave trade (McKittrick) to using biometrics to surveil Black bodies today (Browne). The above suggestions are just a short list for inspiration. Hopefully these suggestions and my more developed reading below will convince others that bringing these two disciplines into conversation is far more revealing, productive, and exciting than restricting them to their respective corners.

Negative Numbers in Coleridge's *Ancient Mariner*

Before he was known as a poet, the young Coleridge was largely known for his radical politics. He wrote and lectured on the abolition of slavery, he was vociferously anti-war, and during his undergraduate days, he was sympathetic to the egalitarian ideals of the French Revolution. In 1793, these Jacobite tendencies attracted Coleridge and his circle to the trial of their Cambridge tutor, William Frend, who was charged with religious blasphemy. Coleridge came to Frend's defense, often disrupting the courtroom, while his private rooms "became a centre of the Frend faction" (Holmes 47). Of course, his investment in Frend's trial is important for understanding Coleridge's political frame of mind. But I am emphasizing it here for a different reason: Frend was also an accomplished mathematician.

Frend largely distinguishes himself in the history of mathematics for his view on negative numbers. Countering well-known giants like Gottfried Wilhelm Leibniz and Leonhard Euler and following instead conservative mathematicians, such as Francis Maseres, Frend argues in his preface to *The Principles of Algebra*, "You may put a mark before one, which it will obey: it submits to be taken away from another number greater than itself, but to attempt to take it away from a number less than itself is ridiculous. Yet this is attempted by algebraists, who talk of a number less than nothing" (x). While negative numbers had been used for some time, especially for practical purposes like accounting, according to Frend's reading, they were ontologically dubious. Given Coleridge's enthusiastic defense of Frend, a tacit embrace of his tutor's strong stance on negative numbers would be a reasonable conclusion. And yet the contrary seems to have been the case.

Over the course of the next five years, Coleridge would go on to befriend William Wordsworth; the two of them would write the quintessential text of the Romantic period, *Lyrical Ballads*; and Coleridge's largest contribution, as entitled in the 1798 edition, *The Rime of the Ancyent Marinere, in Seven Parts*, would go on to become one of the most celebrated poems of the English language. It also happens to be the poem where Coleridge explores in detail the mathematical underpinnings of two worlds, one domain adhering to whole numbers (1, 2, 3, and so on), or the set of natural numbers (N), as well as necessity, determinacy, and finitude, and a second domain where negatives, zero, chance, and infinity reign supreme. The takeaway from this story is that these two worlds, positive and negative, rather than mirroring each other (e.g., a Platonic realm and a reflecting material world), appear to be immanent worlds: Neither realm serves as a transcendent determination of the other. Instead, these two worlds touch, and yet they differ in terms of the kinds of beings they contain and the rules they adhere to.

The poem opens with a wedding guest approaching the church where the day's festivities will take place. Before reaching his destination, the guest is interrupted by an ancient mariner, "[a]nd he stoppeth one of three" (line 2). For James Averill, this line speaks to the "mathematics of readership": "Two of three, those unable to throw aside life's business and embrace the 'willing suspension of disbelief . . . ,' will not listen to the Marinere and indeed will likely put the book [*Lyrical Ballads*] aside" (392). The mariner, and the tale he is about to tell, is competing with a mathematics of everyday life. Territories and cities are organized geometrically; the economy is diagrammed; and, as Mary Poovey shows in *A History of the Modern Fact*, even people must be counted—tying who counts to their social stations (120–38). What Averill identifies is an author-reader relationship (analogous to the scientist-tutor relationship) in which the mariner interrupts the wedding guest's well-ordered life, redirecting him not to an anti-mathematical world but to a mathematical world that challenges the natural number system.

Having stopped the wedding guest, the mariner begins his tale, embedding mathematical images in his verse. The best clue that Coleridge had negative numbers in mind appears in the first lines of the mariner's story: "The Ship was cheer'd, the Harbour clear'd / Merrily did we drop / Below the Kirk, below the Hill, / Below the Light-house top" (lines 25–28). Certainly, Coleridge is thinking of the way ships appear to descend as they reach the sea's horizon. But the mariner's ship also "drop[s]" below the positive number line, entering a negative domain. If this reading feels strained, in the following stanza, Coleridge reinforces a geometrical reading of these numbers: "The Sun came up upon the left / Out of the Sea came he: / And he shone bright, and on the right / Went down into the Sea" (29–32). The mariner's description of the sun's apparent rotation mirrors the movements of a weaver, algorithmically constructing texts.[2] The warp is stretched vertically, while the weaver's hand passes the weft through one side and out the other, constructing a geometrical design (consistent, symmetrical, and stable) in the process. In these two stanzas, the ship is still in transition, passing from positive to negative. But it is an overall downward trajectory, and the last signs of a positive unity are about to pass.

With the mainland far behind them, Coleridge now imagines the ship's voyage as a hellish tour through the underworld: a negative domain. The typical shapes determining human life no longer apply ("Ne shapes of men ne beasts we ken" [line 55]), and in their place a vast vacancy subsists ("Ice was all between" [56]). The only sign of hope is an albatross—the poem's most enduring symbol—which the mariner proceeds, inexplicably, to shoot with his bow (79–80). Now, with this last connection to the human realm and the natural number system severed, Coleridge entertains the ultimate image of the negative—death. "Four times fifty men" (208), the mariner recounts, begin to die, "one by one" (211). More terrifying, the crew rises once again, groaning but never speaking or moving their eyes. Instead, they work, raising "their limbs like lifeless tools— / We were a ghastly crew" (331–32). If we tend to associate zero with death, negative numbers function as an analogue to the undead—an image often invoked by British Romantic writers to highlight the extreme suffering of enslaved people, those without homes, and veterans, plus sinners, criminals, and pariahs (e.g., Lord Byron's Giaour, who is both a pirate and a vampire). As representations, they count; they still affect other people. And yet, they are reduced to animate objects, emptied of feelings and memory or positive human subjectivity.

As the poem concludes, there is not a corresponding return to normal—one of the more remarkable points of the poem. Upon telling his tale, the mariner dies, leaving the wedding guest "a sadder and a wiser man" (line 657). He is fundamentally changed by this story, almost as if the mariner's tale is contagious and the auditor has been infected by it. The wedding guest has been made all too aware that beyond the natural numbers lies a negative realm. On some level he seems to embody this idea, and thus his spontaneous relationship to the world is no longer as it seemed. We could compare this realization to more recent examples, such as Neo's awakening in *The Matrix* or Eleven and the gang's unearthing of the Upside Down in *Stranger Things*. Of course, these more contemporary realizations point to more contemporary mathematical ideas and practices (matrices, cryptography, computer programming, and more), while Coleridge's negative numbers have been incorporated into our most basic, everyday worldview. Each generation, it seems, must contend with a new and more complicated shattering of its mathematical reality.

We have by no means exhausted the mathematical references in the poem, but I have charted a pattern that might serve students as a point of entry for writing on the shifting historical understanding with respect to numbers and number systems. Coleridge's poem supports a minority but burgeoning view that embraces numbers beyond the natural and rational numbers. By extension, he advocates, albeit not without certain warnings, for the exploration of any domain beyond what is already known. As the mariner declares, "We were the first that ever burst / Into that silent Sea" (lines 101–02). In this respect, Coleridge shares a bond with those mathematicians and philosophers who believe truths inhere within mathematics, and those truths oftentimes lie outside or beyond the horizon of accepted knowledge.

Even today, some philosophers and mathematicians believe that what lies beyond knowledge is true, perhaps even more so than what is commonly accepted as known. Badiou's "subtractive" philosophy infers from what we already know—variously referred to as knowledge, the encyclopedic, or the finite (*Being* 331–34)—infinities that he equates with truth. And what is true "can never be, has never been, *counted*" (*Number* 9). Badiou takes some of his most important cues from P. J. Cohen's work on set theory in the 1960s. But mathematicians continue to reveal and elucidate new ways of counting and new number systems, completely up-ending our most common and seemingly intuitive understanding of the real number line (which includes the natural numbers as well as negative numbers, rational numbers, and even irrational numbers). For example, using a modular way of counting (like counting around a clock, so that 1:00 and 13:00 are the same), and organized around primes (i.e., 3, 5, 7, and so on), mathematicians show how "[i]n the 3-adics, for instance, 82 is much closer to 1 than to 81" (Houston-Edwards). This alien way of counting reveals an infinite number of number systems. Indeed, as Bianca Viray, professor of mathematics at the University of Washington, says on the subject, "We're all on Earth and we work with the reals, but if you went [anywhere] else, you'd work with the *p*-adics. . . . It's the reals that are the outliers" (qtd. in Houston-Edwards). One cannot help but read this and think that Coleridge, by calling into question the most basic assumptions about the numbers of his time, was genuinely on a path toward new worlds replete with negatives, imaginaries, transcendentals, infinities, and beyond.

Realism and Anti-Realism in Literature and Mathematics

My concluding section on realism may feel out of place, especially because no one who has ever read Coleridge's *Rime of the Ancient Mariner* would associate it with realism. But it would be a good candidate for an anti-realist poem, and "anti-realist" is not a bad way to characterize Romanticism more generally. I am choosing to conclude with these terms because they cut across disciplines, establishing epistemological and ontological criteria and thereby binding together—or severing—ideologies or worldviews. Because science writers must appeal to the common ground of various audiences, they will greatly benefit from such a discussion.

Of course, the suggestion that there are only two camps in mathematics, realism and anti-realism, would be misleading. But these are helpful headings, even if not everyone would select these headings in particular—for instance, Badiou, in a very accessible introduction to philosophy and mathematics, prefers realism and formalism (*In Praise* 29). In any case, under these headings, we find a host of other schools of thought. Under the banner of realism, we find Platonism, intuitionism, naturalism, and perspectival realism. Under the banner of anti-realism, we find nominalism, constructivism, formalism, and fictionalism. These terms are not always categorically distinct. Depending on how an individual defines them, these terms can sometimes overlap with realism and anti-realism (e.g., a formalist could still defer to intuition and thus be a realist). Conveniently, these headings also correlate—again, not perfectly—with analytic philosophy (realism) and continental philosophy (anti-realism). My aim below is to illustrate how this framework can also be mapped onto literature.

For the purposes of a classroom discussion, this binary (realism and anti-realism) can also be a useful organizational device. Imagine providing, or asking students to construct, a Venn diagram or table that parses out these various theories. This exercise would be a particularly versatile one because it is feasible to have this discussion regardless of the historical period—even in ancient Greece there were disputes about the nature of geometrical objects. My suggestion, then, is this: a conversation in class about realism can help us better appreciate historical points of agreement and separation between the arts and humanities and the sciences, especially literature and mathematics, and it can also help us better appreciate competing philosophical frameworks that do indeed inform science writing. (I provide an example from *Quanta Magazine* below.)

Literary realism has been defined many times over. Perhaps the hallmark criterion of literary realism is a correspondence between the story and the world, where "world" usually equates with objects and causal relationships. While "realism" was not a word used to describe literary genres just yet, this correspondence was important for eighteenth-century philosophers and literary theorists (John Locke, Adam Smith, Samuel Johnson, and Henry Home, Lord Kames) because it was thought to encourage a similarly ordered mind, where words correspond with things and happenings in the world (see Ottinger, esp. 442–43).

However, as Elaine Freedgood clarifies—focusing on the Victorian novel—the narrator often complicated this mirror of nature by adding "levels" to the text: the narrator can address the audience, descend into the story itself, and reveal their internal dialogue or even other characters' thoughts, but, and especially noticeable in the nineteenth century, they can also cross-reference literary and nonliterary history, creating a strange, hybrid reality (77–98). These conventions of the so-called realist novel signal an anti-realist tendency, in which there are many worlds and not just one unique world. And yet, as Freedgood points out, the Victorian novel maintains a realist stance because, even within this ontological plurality, there remains the consistency of the form and a correspondence "with an intact world" (113). Coleridge's *Ancient Mariner* serves as an excellent prologue to these tendencies, beginning as it does with the ordered world of the wedding guest and then exploring a negative world, all contained within the story of the mariner (which is not quite *the* intact world because the poem itself is already presented as a tale from another time, featuring, for instance, anachronistic spellings). Accordingly, the eighteenth and nineteenth centuries represent not so much the age of realism's dominance as the testing of realism's boundaries.

Maintaining only the broad strokes of this narrative, we could say that literary history closely parallels the eighteenth- and nineteenth-century story of realism and anti-realism in mathematics. We have already seen how William Frend and others might represent a more conservative, realist wing of mathematicians. A good example of anti-realism can be seen in the rise of algebra and the new reliance on symbols—which created the conditions for a formalist theory of mathematics. From ancient Greece until the nineteenth century, the dominance of Euclidean geometry meant that a concept of a mathematical object had a direct relationship to the construction of its figure. But as algebra spread, it became clear that symbolic terms and other mathematical abstracta, including negative numbers—or, even more alarming, the square roots of negative numbers—lacked a direct correspondence with sensible objects.

Michael Detlefsen begins an outline of formalism's rise with George Berkeley. Detlefsen points to *Alciphron; or, The Minute Philosopher* (1732), where Berkeley uses "counters" in a game of cards as an analogy to illustrate the arbitrariness of the relationship between symbols and their quantitative meaning: "There is an important formalist message in [*Alciphron*]—namely, that reasoning can, at some level, proceed on the basis of syntactically marked regularities of expressions, without adversion to supposed semantic contents" (264). Berkeley's theory of the arbitrariness of signs signaled a strong counter to realism, so that a mathematical concept no longer required a corresponding transcendent ideal (Platonism), or even an intersubjective ideal (Kantianism), but only a non-semantic sign of human convenience (formalism).

This realism/anti-realism debate continues today. In the latter half of the twentieth century, the dominant theories of poststructuralism and postmodernism were largely associated with anti-realism. (Jacques Derrida's work is representative here.) But since the early 2000s, we have seen an uptick in realist philosophy, some of which was inspired by Badiou and some of which runs counter to him, referred to variously as speculative realism, new realism, agential realism, contextual realism . . . the list goes on. And no doubt, some realists represent a reactionary position. We would indeed be wise to remember that, while realism about numbers is one thing, political realism can mean something quite different.[3] But there have also been more coolheaded negotiations. Michela Massimi, in an interview with Philip Ball in *Quanta Magazine*, espouses "perspectival realism," which, she says,

> acknowledges that scientists don't have a God's-eye view of nature: Our conceptual resources, theoretical approaches, methodologies and technological infrastructures are historically and culturally situated. Does that mean we can't reach true knowledge about nature? Certainly not. Does it mean we should give up on the idea that there is an overarching notion of scientific progress? Absolutely not.

Massimi's more moderate approach, and the larger history of realism and anti-realism across the disciplines, reminds us that our present-day mathematical framework is always open to revision—and we should simply embrace this development as part of the larger human career.

If we can agree that the literature of old does not adequately capture all aspects of human experience today, it should not be hard to accept that our math and philosophy also require occasional updating. The science writer of mathematics and the scholar of literature have the privilege of helping audiences understand these changes and how they might help us arrive at truths previously hidden, in some cases because of our own impeding conceptual frameworks (i.e., the various realisms and anti-realisms). Literature is no doubt a powerful tool in this respect, since many of our literary favorites, including Coleridge's *Ancient Mariner*, encourage us to look beyond our inherited truths and ask questions about the gaps, absences, and unknowns in our knowledge.

Notes

1. For a historically comprehensive guide, see Tubbs et al. For the eighteenth century, see Campe (on probability) and Wickman (on calculus). For the nineteenth century, see Jenkins; Henderson; and Kornbluh. On modernism and beyond, see Brits. For a recent publication focusing on Coleridge alone, see Colley.

2. On mathematics and weaving, see Brezine.

3. On the history of the imperialist-colonialist agenda of twentieth-century political realism, see Specter.

Works Cited

Averill, James H. "The Shape of *Lyrical Ballads* (1798)." *Philological Quarterly*, vol. 60, no. 3, 1981, pp. 387–407.

Badiou, Alain. *Being and Event*. Translated by Oliver Feltham, Continuum, 2006.

———. *In Praise of Mathematics*. With Gilles Haéri, translated by Susan Spitzer, Polity Press, 2016.

———. *Number and Numbers*. Translated by Robin Mackay, Polity Press, 2008.

———. "What Is a Poem? or, Philosophy and Poetry at the Point of the Unnamable." *Handbook of Inaesthetics*, by Badiou, translated by Alberto Toscano, Stanford UP, 2005, pp. 16–27.

Brezine, Carrie. "Algorithms and Automation: The Production of Mathematics and Textiles." *The Oxford Handbook of the History of Mathematics*, edited by Eleanor Robson and Jacqueline Stedall, Oxford UP, 2009, pp. 468–92.

Brits, Baylee. *Literary Infinities: Number and Narrative in Modern Fiction*. Bloomsbury Publishing, 2018.

Browne, Simone. *Dark Matters: On the Surveillance of Blackness*. Duke UP, 2015.

Campe, Rüdiger. *The Game of Probability: Literature and Calculation from Pascal to Kleist*. Translated by Ellwood H. Wiggins, Jr., Stanford UP, 2012.

Coleridge, Samuel Taylor. *The Rime of the Ancyent Marinere, in Seven Parts*. Lyrical Ballads: *1798 and 1800*, by Coleridge and William Wordsworth, edited by Michael Gamer and Dahlia Porter, Broadview Press, 2008, pp. 49–72.

Colley, Ann C. *Coleridge and the Geometric Idiom: Walking with Euclid*. Cambridge UP, 2023.

Detlefsen, Michael. "Formalism." *The Oxford Handbook of Philosophy of Mathematics and Logic*, edited by Stewart Shapiro, Oxford UP, 2005, pp. 236–317.

Freedgood, Elaine. *Worlds Enough: The Invention of Realism in the Victorian Novel*. Princeton UP, 2019.

Frend, William. *The Principles of Algebra*. London, 1796. *Google Books*, www.google.com/books/edition/The_Principles_of_Algebra/La02AAAAM AAJ?hl. Accessed 30 Dec. 2023.

Henderson, Andrea K. *Algebraic Art: Mathematical Formalism and Victorian Culture*. Oxford UP, 2018.

Holmes, Richard. *Coleridge: Early Visions, 1772–1804*. Pantheon Books, 1989.

Houston-Edwards, Kelsey. "An Infinite Universe of Number Systems." *Quanta Magazine*, 19 Oct. 2020, www.quantamagazine.org/how-the-towering -p-adic-numbers-work-20201019/.

Jenkins, Alice. *Space and the "March of Mind": Literature and the Physical Sciences in Britain, 1815–1850*. Oxford UP, 2007.

Kornbluh, Anna. *The Order of Forms: Realism, Formalism, and Social Space*. U of Chicago P, 2019.

Massimi, Michela. "Questioning Truth, Reality and the Role of Science: An Interview with Michela Massimi." Conducted by Philip Ball. *Quanta Magazine*, 24 May 2018, www.quantamagazine.org/questioning-truth-reality-and-the -role-of-science-20180524/.

McKittrick, Katherine. "Mathematics Black Life." *The Black Scholar*, vol. 44, no. 2, 2014, pp. 16–28.

Ottinger, Aaron. "The Mathematics of Associationism in Laurence Sterne's *Tristram Shandy*." Tubbs et al., pp. 439–56.

Poovey, Mary. *A History of the Modern Fact: Problems of Knowledge in the Sciences of Wealth and Society.* U of Chicago P, 1998.
Proclus. *A Commentary on the First Book of Euclid's* Elements. Translated by Glenn R. Morrow, Princeton UP, 1970.
Specter, Matthew. *The Atlantic Realists: Empire and International Political Thought between Germany and the United States.* Stanford UP, 2022.
Tubbs, Robert, et al., editors. *The Palgrave Handbook of Literature and Mathematics.* Palgrave Macmillan, 2021.
Wickman, Matthew. *Literature after Euclid: The Geometric Imagination in the Long Scottish Enlightenment.* U of Pennsylvania P, 2016.

Melissa Dickson

The Vampire We Need:
Bram Stoker's *Dracula* and the
Victorian Science of the Mind

"Every age," as Nina Auerbach observes, "embraces the vampire it needs" (145), for the vampire is at once an eternal creature of the past and a manifestation of sociocultural fears and fantasies of the moment. Perpetually relevant to the modern age, each new iteration of the vampire is distinctly reflective of its time—or, to use the words of Bram Stoker, "up to date with a vengeance" (*Dracula* 36)—and the present generation of undergraduates has embraced a host of new, undead monsters. The immensely popular *Twilight Saga* has fueled the vampire romance genre with angst-ridden teenage courtship, and television series such as *What We Do in the Shadows*, *Anne Rice's Interview with the Vampire*, and *First Kill*; the superhero film *Morbius*; Isaac Fellman's novel *Dead Collections*; and Claire Kohda's debut work, *Woman, Eating*, collectively offer very human, youthful vampire figures who tell their own stories, argue with their parents, spend time with their friends, and experience various forms of attraction, desire, and discrimination. Writing of this most recent "invasion" of pop culture by the perennial "monster of choice," Judy Berman notes that "at a time when binaries like insider-outsider, oppressor-oppressed, and us-them have never felt more subjective, these new vampire narratives blur the line separating mortal souls from allegedly soulless immortals."

The undead of today, in other words, provide many readers and viewers with an appealing type of category confusion, one that disrupts prevailing structures of gender, sexuality, race, and politics.

Harnessing the present-day thirst for vampire stories proffers a compelling avenue to delve, first, into discussion of the role of the vampire in the cultural imaginary and, second, into the scientific and psychological underpinnings of Stoker's *Dracula*. *Dracula* is a novel that revels in late Victorian modernity. There are references throughout to phonographs, photographs, Kodak cameras, and portable typewriters as well as to train timetables, elaborate shipping and postal networks, and telegrams sent across Europe. There are up-to-date medical procedures, such as the trephining of an asylum patient, and the series of blood transfusions carried out by Professor Van Helsing in an attempt to preserve the young Lucy Westenra. Notably, however, these latter procedures fail, and we are reminded of Jonathan Harker's fearful realization that "the old centuries had, and have powers of their own which mere 'modernity' cannot kill" (Stoker, *Dracula* 36). Appearing in a historical and cultural moment when definitions of science were extremely malleable and scientific authority was a site of contest, Stoker's figure of the vampire points present-day students to the potential limits of scientific practice and the fundamental instability of the broader nineteenth-century culture of materialist investigation and technological innovation. In particular, it points to the mysterious nature of the self to the self, to the mind's unknown depths, and to the invisible forces operating beneath the thresholds of human consciousness.

The gothic, as Robert Miles has noted, "worries over a problem stirring within the foundations of the self," and it has thus remained "embroiled within a larger, theoretically complex project: the history of the 'subject'" (1–2). In the latter decades of the nineteenth century, gothic writing was deeply enmeshed in the history of psychiatric research. Using *Dracula* as a gothic case study, this essay focuses on the close exchange of ideas and terminologies across literary and psychiatric discourses of nineteenth-century Britain. It seeks to demonstrate practical strategies by which scientific and medical ideas and writing might be introduced into the classroom through their entrance into literary discourse as well as methods for teaching nineteenth-century literature in conjunction with scientific writings of the period. Its central premise is that literature does not simply mirror medical culture and its concerns; rather, it can play a constitutive role in the formation and formulation of medical theories and categories. Guiding students through this dynamic relationship demonstrates to them that medicine is embedded in, and indeed constituted by, language and culture.

Unconscious Cerebration

The burgeoning Victorian science of the mind, with its emphasis on the nature of individual subjectivity and agency, is very deliberately brought to bear on Count Dracula and his operations by Dr. John Seward, a young psychiatrist with "an immense lunatic asylum all under his own care" (Stoker, *Dracula* 55). As Seward questions the increasingly strange behavior of his "zoophagous" (125) patient R. M. Renfield, he draws explicitly upon a concept peculiar to late-nineteenth-century conceptualizations of the mind: "It was evident then that my surmise had been correct. Unconscious cerebration was doing its work, even with the lunatic. I determined to have the matter out. 'What about them yourself?' I asked. He did not reply for a moment but looked all round him, and up and down, as though he expected to find some inspiration for an answer" (270). The terminology Seward uses here demonstrates that he has kept up to date with developments in Victorian psychological practice. Unconscious cerebration was a model of mind developed by the English physiologist William Carpenter, who held in his *Principles of Human Physiology* that "every sensory impression which has once been recognised by the perceptive consciousness is registered (so to speak) in the brain" and, further, that each impression may be "reproduced at some subsequent time, although there may be no consciousness of its existence in the mind during the whole intermediate period" (781). The human mind, in other words, operated as a kind of library, where every sight and every sound that the individual experienced was recorded in the brain, even if it was not accessible to the conscious mind. In *Principles of Mental Physiology*, Carpenter notes that the unconscious mind can produce logical conclusions "below the plane of consciousness, either during profound sleep, or while the attention is wholly engrossed by some entirely different train of thought" (516). "[E]ven with the lunatic" Renfield, then, it is possible that the impressions lurking beneath the conscious mind might be brought forth by a skilled psychiatrist.

Psychiatric and mesmeric studies of the late nineteenth century were increasingly invested in the notion that external stimuli might be registered within, or impress themselves upon, the human mind, even while remaining entirely outside that mind's conscious control. A foray into some of these materials not only enhances readings of *Dracula* as both symptomatic of its age and a testament to the mysterious powers of the human brain but also facilitates the drawing out of connections between gothic fiction and the wider concerns of emerging materialist sciences of the self. *Embodied Selves: An Anthology of Psychological Texts, 1830–1890*, edited by Jenny Bourne Taylor and Sally Shuttleworth, provides an invaluable selection of accessible primary sources relevant to this work, in particular the book's second section, on the unconscious mind and the workings of memory (65–162). For example, in an 1859 lecture on "mental latency," William Hamilton presented recent German theories of the unconscious mind in strikingly prescient terms: "The mind may, and does, contain far more latent furniture than consciousness informs us it possesses. . . . I do not hesitate to maintain, that what we are conscious of is constructed out of what we are not conscious of,—that our whole knowledge, in fact, is made up of the unknown and the incognisable" (81–82). Hamilton's spatial representation of the subconscious as a room filled with furniture is a materialist metaphor of mind typical of the period in that it imagines thoughts and memories as physical objects stored beneath the surface of the mind. It is useful in demonstrating to students the shared language of literary and psychiatric writing of the nineteenth century, resonating as it does with Dr. Seward's speculation that "there is a method in [Renfield's] madness, and the rudimentary idea in my mind is growing. It will be a whole idea soon, and then, oh unconscious cerebration! you will have to give the wall to your conscious brother" (Stoker, *Dracula* 69). Thought becomes matter, which is in the process of growing out from the unconscious into the conscious mind.

Dracula also pairs nicely with the Anglo-Irish writer and philosopher Frances Power Cobbe's influential 1870 essay "Unconscious Cerebration: A Psychological Study," one of a series of articles Cobbe wrote to explore various aspects of the unconscious mind and the state of current mental science.[1] "Unconscious Cerebration," which opens by drawing on the image of the Teraph, the "decapitated head of a child, placed on a pillar and compelled by magic to reply to the questions of the sorcerer" (24), is often surprising to students as a piece of science writing that (not unusually for the period) makes use of mythology, literature, and the creative arts in explicating a case for the automatic or unconscious operations of the mind. The skills of textual analysis and close reading that can be applied to *Dracula* may also be applied to this text. Undertaking this comparative analysis as a classroom exercise is useful for demonstrating to students the shared vocabularies of science and wider culture as well as the ways in which nineteenth-century science writing is infused with individual sub-jectivities and emotions. Writing of "the manner in which we find our mental work of any kind . . . arrange itself in order during an interval either of sleep or wakefulness, during which we had not consciously thought of it at all," Cobbe notes that "it is as if a 'Fairy Order' had come in the night and unravelled the tangled skeins of thought and laid them all neatly on the table" (25). Drawing attention to this language of fairies and enchantment and discussing its implications gives students insight into the sense of wonder and excitement that new theories of the mind and its potentialities were generating.

Wonder, Philip Fisher reminds us, occupies the horizon between the familiar and the unfamiliar. It is an "impassioned state," underpinned by novelty, pleasure, and surprising new facts (12). In the context of the burgeoning British science of the mind, Cobbe's wonder expresses itself through the correlation of an invisible mental operation yet to be fully defined or understood with a force nothing short of magical. Students might be instructed to read this alongside the fictional Professor Van Helsing's ruminations on his own thought processes, which are equally creative in attempting to render consciousness in language. Van Helsing observes to Mina Harker:

> A half-thought has been buzzing often in my brain, but I fear to let him loose his wings. Here now, with more knowledge, I go back to where that half-thought come from and I find that he be no half-thought at all; that be a whole thought, though so young that he is not yet strong to use his little wings. Nay, like the "Ugly Duck" of my friend Hans Andersen, he be no duck-thought at all, but a big swan-thought that sail nobly on big wings, when the time come for him to try them. (Stoker, *Dracula* 340)

In the imaginative construction of his thought process as a bird buzzing within the hidden spaces of the mind, Van Helsing intimates his awareness that he is not fully in control of the mysterious forces that constitute his complex, multilayered self. Latent but active and dynamic thoughts emerge from beyond the threshold of consciousness, and like Cobbe's "Fairy Order," his language invests this construction of the self with a sense of wonder and magical transformation. In both cases, students may be led to observe a new awareness in this period that there is an element of the mind that operates automatically, seemingly by magic, and without conscious mediation. This is critical to analyzing the ways in which the late-nineteenth-century figure of the vampire plays and preys on forces and energies operating beneath the threshold of human consciousness while also fostering debates as to whether a conscious, rational individual might be made to behave in certain ways through unconscious influences.

Psychic Bonds

Mina Harker's psychic connection with Count Dracula can be used in the classroom to bring into focus many of the late Victorian concerns with the capabilities and limits of the human mind. The practice of mesmerism, with its emphasis on the powers of one individual to influence or control the mind and body of another, was taken up somewhat belatedly in Britain, fifty years after the German physician Franz Mesmer had first theorized the existence of a vital magnetic fluid that might be manipulated in order to influence the thoughts, behaviors, and feelings of others and to cure illness. In the autumn of 1837, when the renowned French mesmerist Jules Denis Dupotet arrived in London to demonstrate publicly the art and powers of magnetic healing, his experiments were widely covered in the general and medical press, and the nature and veracity of the mesmeric trance and the advisability of mesmerism became subjects of national debate. These questions filtered through the many colleges and institutes dedicated to technological, medical, and scientific innovation that were being established in London in the 1830s and 1840s and formed a part of broader conversations about the nature and boundaries of legitimate scientific practice.[2] Stoker's own intellectual interest in mesmerism is clear: he included Mesmer as a case study in his 1910 book, *Famous Impostors* (95–106).

Dracula's insistence to Mina that "when my brain says 'Come!' to you, you shall cross land or sea to do my bidding" (288) realizes the inherent vulnerability and penetrability of a human mind open to external forces while drawing on questions of automatism and self-control, which were essential to Victorian studies of the mind, in particular to the burgeoning field of physiological psychology. Students might usefully compare this moment in the novel to short nineteenth-century accounts of mesmeric experiments, such as that described in the *Mirror of Literature, Amusement, and Instruction* in 1837, when Dupotet, "spreading forth his hand with the fingers closed . . . moved it gently, with a downward motion, over the patient's face" in a series of mesmeric passes, reportedly establishing a psychic connection so profound that "it would be impossible for the magnetized to resist following him to whatever part of the room he went" ("Animal Magnetism" 185). Indeed, the patient "struggled with himself for some time, but yielded to the influence, and cried out for us to hold him, or he must follow, as if he were dragged by a strong chain" (185). Examining passages like these underscores for students the nature of the threat posed by the vampire in this period, who represents a destabilizing influence on notions of the coherent, stable self. They may recognize ways in which this threat is imaginatively realized throughout Stoker's novel: Lucy's somnambulism renders her susceptible to Dracula, Renfield finds himself emotionally and mentally manipulated by the Count from a distance, Jonathan recalls a struggle to awaken his instincts at Castle Dracula as he realizes that "I was becoming hypnotised!" (44), and Dracula uses his mesmeric powers to entrance his victims and satisfy his thirst for human blood. Each of these instances points to the alarming openness to manipulation of a subject who has lost their self-control.

Mesmerism is central to the struggle between the Transylvanian vampire and the British men of science, and it is the mind and body of Mina Harker that operate as the primary site of conflict. Placed in a hypnotic state by Professor Van Helsing, Mina is able to enter the Count's mind just as he can access hers, allowing the vampire hunters to track his movements across Europe and ultimately destroy him. Jonathan recounts the means by which Mina is entranced:

> Looking fixedly at her, [Professor Van Helsing] commenced to make passes in front of her, from over the top of her head downward, with each hand in turn. Mina gazed at him fixedly for a few minutes, during which my own heart beat like a trip hammer, for I felt that some crisis was at hand. Gradually her eyes closed, and she sat, stock still; only by the gentle heaving of her bosom could one know that she was alive. The Professor made a few more passes and then stopped, and I could see that his forehead was covered with great beads of perspiration. Mina opened her eyes; but she did not seem the same woman. There was a far-away look in her eyes, and her voice had a sad dreaminess which was new to me. (312)

The relationship between Van Helsing and Mina in these moments is best illuminated by comparison to the experiments of the British physician John Elliotson on a young woman named Elizabeth O'Key. An 1838 report from *The Lancet*, a major medical journal of the period that is still running today, states that the young woman was put into a trance by way of mesmeric pass and subsequently lost all individual volition:

> [T]he Doctor drew his hand, pointed towards hers, upwards and outwards in the air. In a few seconds her hand and arm began to move up in the same direction. While ceasing, for a short time, in order to talk to someone near, he produced a motion with his fingers, which those of the girl immediately imitated. "See," said the Doctor, "my fingers were moved involuntarily; I did not mean to influence hers."
> ("University College Hospital" 284–85)

The mesmeric pass is a gesture at once intimate and public, and it transforms the female subject into an instrument for the doctor to utilize and control. We see in this passage that the young woman's physical movements are made to mirror those of the doctor. At the same time, the passage registers the inherent vulnerability and penetrability of a female body understood to palpitate, vibrate, and tremble involuntarily in response to the desires of the male mesmerist.

The Lancet, which is fully digitized and keyword searchable, contains a series of articles covering Elliotson's mesmeric experiments. It is thus a useful resource in guiding students through online searches of medical journals and encourages them to read more of the science writing that was produced during this period. Such comparisons lend insight into the ways both Dracula and Van Helsing use Mina's body and mind. While mesmerism was popularly believed to connect minds, inculcate sympathies, and distribute energies across new corporeal networks and therefore offered great hope in the treatment of disease and alleviation of suffering, Stoker's novel demonstrates the ways that it also inculcated deep-seated fears of an individual's being stretched, contorted, lost, or reduced to a mere echo of a powerful mesmerist. The female body emerges from these analyses as the site of the novel's central struggle between science and the supernatural.

Stoker's Dr. Seward explicitly declares himself a follower of Jean-Martin Charcot, the leading neurologist of the nineteenth century, who, Seward claims, has proved the existence of hypnotism. Charcot's school for the study of hypnotism, established at the Salpêtrière Hospital in Paris in 1878, belonged to a wave of new psychologists who turned to the trance states induced by Mesmer's mesmeric practice as an objective physiological condition but rejected the theory that a magnetic fluid existed between doctor and patient. Rather, the effects of the hypnotist were understood to be produced by setting certain ideas in motion in the mind of the individual. In response to Seward's declaration, Van Helsing questions him: "Then tell me—for I am student of the brain—how you accept the hypnotism and reject the thought reading" (191). Here the modern medical practitioner and illustrious expert in "obscure diseases" (111) reveals the fundamental instability of definitions and categories within late Victorian paradigms of psychology. To some, like Professor Van Helsing, the possibility that thought patterns might pass in a current between two minds is no less worthy of contemplation and investigation than the largely invisible operations of steam or electricity or experiments with automatons and galvanism. If, as Van Helsing insists, "there are things done to-day in electrical science which would have been deemed unholy by the very men who discovered electricity" (191), then constructions of the material and the immaterial, the natural and the unnatural, are far more fluid than a scientific materialist like Seward will acknowledge. Ultimately, drawing science writing into the humanities classroom allows Count Dracula to emerge as the vampire that the late Victorian age needed, a vampire who brought into relief the period's ongoing explorations of the mind, its operations, and its hitherto untapped potential.

Notes

1. Cobbe was a well-known social reformer, philosopher, anti-vivisectionist, and women's suffrage campaigner in the latter decades of the nineteenth century. Her work lends significant depth to discussions of both the role of women and the role of animals in Stoker's text.

2. A short but detailed and very accessible account of the arrival and reception of mesmeric practice in Victorian London is available in Winter 32–59. This excerpt might be set alongside *Dracula* to facilitate discussion of mesmerism in the classroom.

Works Cited

"Animal Magnetism in London, in 1837." *Mirror of Literature, Amusement, and Instruction*, vol. 30, no. 853, 16 Sept. 1837, pp. 185–86.

Auerbach, Nina. *Our Vampires, Ourselves.* U of Chicago P, 1995.

Berman, Judy. "Vampires Are Taking Over Pop Culture Again—but This Time, the Monster Is Us." *Time*, 11 Oct. 2022, time.com/6220602/vampires -pop-culture-2022/.

Bourne Taylor, Jenny, and Sally Shuttleworth, editors. *Embodied Selves: An Anthology of Psychological Texts, 1830–1890.* Clarendon Press, 1998.

Carpenter, William. *Principles of Human Physiology*. 5th American ed., Philadelphia, 1853.

———. *Principles of Mental Physiology*. London, 1874.

Cobbe, Frances Power. "Unconscious Cerebration: A Psychological Study." *Macmillan's Magazine*, vol. 133, 1870, pp. 24–37.

Fisher, Philip. *The Vehement Passions*. Princeton UP, 2002.

Hamilton, William. "Three Degrees of Mental Latency." Bourne Taylor and Shuttleworth, pp. 80–83.

Miles, Robert. *Gothic Writing, 1750–1820: A Genealogy*. Routledge, 1993.

Stoker, Bram. *Dracula*. Edited by A. N. Wilson, Oxford UP, 1983.

———. *Famous Impostors*. Sturgis and Walton, 1910.

"University College Hospital, Animal Magnetism." *The Lancet*, vol. 30, no. 769, 26 May 1838, pp. 282–86.

Winter, Alison. *Mesmerized: Powers of Mind in Victorian Britain*. U of Chicago P, 1998.

Julia Dauer

Botany in the American Literature Classroom: Emily Dickinson and Amy Matilda Cassey

As a student in Amherst, Massachusetts, in the late 1830s and early 1840s, the poet Emily Dickinson learned to keep an herbarium, collecting botanical specimens in a bound book alongside other girls her age. Around the same time, Amy Matilda Cassey, a young Black woman living in Philadelphia, began keeping a friendship album, where she displayed her penmanship and invited her friends to contribute poems, notes, and occasional botanical drawings reflecting their education and shared sensibility. This essay argues that nineteenth-century women botanists' texts and images, including Dickinson's and Cassey's, belong in literature classrooms. Teaching Dickinson and Cassey opens up an exploration of which texts and whose labor count as "science" in this period. This is especially valuable in a nineteenth-century American literature course because these works raise questions about gendered access to knowledge, collaborative bookmaking as a scientific endeavor, and the significance of semipublic texts.

Teaching Early American Botany

I have taught Dickinson and Cassey in two institutional contexts, as a postdoc at the University of Virginia, a large public research university in

Charlottesville, Virginia, and as a faculty member at Saint Mary's College, a small Catholic women's liberal arts college in Notre Dame, Indiana. At both institutions, I have taught these works to English and environmental studies students, and at the University of Virginia, my classes also included American studies students.

I teach Dickinson and Cassey as a sequential pair in a course called American Natures, which examines competing representations of the natural world in American literature before 1900. American Natures begins with texts from the late eighteenth century. We start with an introduction to important ways of thinking about the natural world in the United States, including through the binomial Latinate taxonomic system developed by the Swedish botanist Carl Linnaeus. My most successful approach to introducing colonial natural history and its significance has been to give students excerpts from scholarship that illuminates the ways claims about plants are connected to ideas about racial, gender, and sexual difference in humans. I utilize Susan Scott Parrish's analysis of Anglo-colonial women's participation in imperial networks of specimen collecting to introduce students to the history of female practitioners of natural science and the relationship of this work to Anglo-colonial projects in the seventeenth and eighteenth centuries (174–214). I also excerpt a few pages from Greta LaFleur, who connects Linnaeus's botany to his theorization of racial and sexual difference (2–5). I assign a review I wrote of LaFleur's book, which gives context for thinking about botanical sexuality, as an optional additional reading (Dauer). This approach gives students a framework for understanding gendered and racialized ideas about the natural world in the early United States and prepares them to think critically about the role of botany in nineteenth-century girls' and women's education.

As we discuss botanical specimens and images in Dickinson and Cassey, I also introduce students to the idea that "objectivity," as Lorraine Daston and Peter Galison argue, is a specific set of scientific virtues that emerged unevenly in European and US scientific traditions in the first half of the nineteenth century. The epistemic and visual paradigms of objectivity, which are often naturalized in contemporary scientific discourse, emerged gradually over time and interacted with earlier representational modes, including the truth-to-nature model of producing idealized specimens that predominated in eighteenth-century natural history (Daston and Galison 60). As they encounter the visual culture of natural history and learn about how these visual representations have changed over time, students also begin to consider the ways scientific and ornamental representational practices overlap in this period.

Dickinson's Herbarium and Botanical Politics

In American Natures, we begin a unit titled Women and Vital Plants with Dickinson's herbarium. We start by reading Mary Kuhn's article "Dickinson and the Politics of Plant Sensibility," which describes Dickinson's life as a gardener and examines the circulation of plants in Dickinson's poetry and botanical practices. Kuhn's reading of Dickinson's poetry tracks the poet's acute awareness "that flowers simultaneously comprised the local garden and circumnavigated the globe" and examines Dickinson poems that "can suggest how middle-class horticultural enterprises were facilitated by colonial botanical pursuits, and how the projects of the home gardener were tied to imperial designs" (144). In American Natures, we connect Kuhn's analysis to the colonial botanical frameworks established in the first weeks of class. We also talk about Kuhn's focus on the materiality of plants, which could "challenge human efforts to understand or control them" (141). Students sometimes respond to this claim with confidence that human beings can control plant life, but more often, they are curious about this proposition and its stakes. Digging into Kuhn's argument and Dickinson's writing challenges ideas about the passivity of plant life.[1]

Dickinson's herbarium is held and has been digitized by the Houghton Library at Harvard University and is readily available for use in classrooms (Dickinson, Herbarium). The online interface is intuitive for my students. They find it unclear, however, what it means to read or engage with a book like this one, given that its content is primarily visual and consists of specimens students sometimes struggle to describe and analyze.[2] The kinds of books used to participate in scientific discourse in this period differ greatly from the contemporary paperbacks students often encounter in literature courses. Digitized objects like these can help students develop a more capacious understanding of scientific books and their circulation, even as they also present new interpretive challenges. While I have sometimes taken students to special collections to view natural historical materials, these free online resources allow me to engage questions of form, production, and audience in the botanical book without relying on local archival holdings.

Because Dickinson's herbarium can seem opaque, we begin by working with it together in class. An herbarium is a collection of dried plant specimens, sometimes in the form of a book. Dickinson's herbarium consists of sixty-six pages of pressed herbal specimens bound between embossed green covers. The blank herbarium was purchased, and Dickinson filled its pages between around 1839 and 1846. Assembling an herbarium was a central component of botanical education in the nineteenth-century United States. Botanical education was deemed particularly suitable and important for girls, as widely circulated botanical textbooks written by women, including the British writer Priscilla Wakefield's *An Introduction to Botany, in a Series of Familiar Lectures* (1796) and the US writer Almira Phelps's *Familiar Lectures on Botany* (1831), make clear.

I share Virginia Jackson's view that Dickinson's herbarium is best engaged as an "ordinary object, the result of an ordinary domestic practice," one of many created by "rich white girls in New England" for whom "the pressing, pasting, and labeling of garden varieties was a generic pastime" (108). While we may wish to read it in relationship to Dickinson's poems and the concepts of global nature and material disruption central to our initial discussion of Dickinson, I present the herbarium as a representative object that can help us understand nineteenth-century botany.

As we get a handle on Dickinson's herbarium, I encourage students to browse its contents, getting a sense of the whole. Then I direct our attention to sequence 29,[3] where we find a plant that many students quickly recognize: a dandelion.[4] This page contains five specimens, each of which has been pressed, dried, and affixed to the page with small strips of paper. The specimens are arranged in two rows, with two larger specimens in the top row and three smaller specimens in the bottom row. Like many of Dickinson's pages, this page mixes plants from different taxonomic groups and contexts: yellow clintonia (misidentified as white clintonia), common horse chestnut, common dandelion, spiked lobelia (misidentified as pukeweed), and common yellow daylily (misidentified as Madonna lily). As the Houghton's corrections make clear, Dickinson misidentifies three of the five plants on this page. Noticing Dickinson's frequent misidentification and periodic lack of labeling allows our class to see the herbarium as a learning document in which Dickinson makes mistakes.

Discussing Dickinson's misidentification can also lead students to reflect on the specimens they themselves do and do not recognize. The dandelion, which most of my students quickly recognize, invites students into the herbarium. Sometimes students are drawn to other plants they recognize, but more often, students express surprise that Dickinson could have identified so many specimens and reflect that they themselves do not know the names of nearly so many plants. Here it is important to remind them that Dickinson is an avid observer of nature but not an exceptional specialist in her own time. We talk about why Dickinson was trained as a child to develop botanical expertise and why children in our own time may not be. I assign optional additional readings that invite students to reflect on everyday knowledge about the natural world, including Daegan Miller's essay on the changing vocabulary of children's texts and Aimee Nezhukumatathil's essays about her students' inability to recognize common North American plants and animals like maple trees and fireflies.

Starting with the dandelion, a familiar plant often treated as a weed in the contemporary United States, also draws attention to the questions about value inherent in an herbarium. The herbarium suggests that its specimens are valuable, but the species represented are not necessarily rare. Comparing the dandelion with other specimens on this page and noting their dissimilarities deepens conversation about the range of plants Dickinson gathers in her herbarium as a whole and on this page specifically. The discrepancy between the dandelion and the horse chestnut is especially striking. While they look comparable grouped on the page, horse chestnuts are large trees with grandiose peaking blooms, dramatically larger than the dandelions that might cluster at their base. Zooming in on the horse chestnut specimen reveals that it is a combination of a leaf and stem, assembled to depict its significant parts, despite the fact that the plant in its entirety and large scale cannot be captured in this format. Discussing the challenges of representing a large tree like the horse chestnut helps students more concretely understand the process of selecting and producing a representative specimen.

I've taken different approaches to other parts of the album, sometimes structuring discussion around Dickinson's taxonomically organized pages. Sequence 49, for example, is the page of violets, another familiar and often beloved plant group. Dickinson displays eleven specimens in three neat rows. Nine of the specimens are in the genus *Viola*. The remaining two specimens, a trumpet creeper, in the genus *Bignonia*, and a type of cucumber, in the genus *Sicyos*, visually echo the flowers and leaves of the violets but are taxonomic outliers. This page demonstrates the collision between taxonomic organization and other visual and aesthetic patterns, foregrounding the relationship between aesthetics and scientific learning. Other fruitful avenues might include exploring the presence of algal specimens in an herbarium consisting almost entirely of land plants (sequence 33 and sequence 37) or considering specimens not local to Dickinson's region, like the Japanese honeysuckle (sequence 55) and the dwarf Japanese quince (sequence 30), whose possible path to Dickinson Hiroko Uno examines.

Sometimes I ask students to independently choose additional pages for analysis, tasking them with choosing a page, describing it, and making connections to concepts from our class. I've had mixed results with this approach. The strongest independent student analysis of herbarium pages has raised questions about the materiality of the herbarium, including the unusually bright colors of some specimens (cypress vine [sequence 19]) and the particularly three-dimensional quality of others (tall cotton grass [sequence 50]).

Cassey's Album, Feminine Florals, and Scientific Education

In American Natures we turn to Cassey's album the week after we examine Dickinson's herbarium. The herbarium helps students understand the culture of amateur botanical collecting and its role in education. This exploration continues as we discuss Cassey's album and its botanical illustrations.

Cassey's album was purchased as a book of blank signatures of plain and colored paper bound in an embossed morocco leather cover. The album, which is held and has been digitized by the Library Company of Philadelphia, opens with a hand-lettered page that reads "Original and selected poetry, & c" and includes Cassey's name (Amy Matilda Cassey friendship album). The seventy-five pages that follow contain poems by Cassey's friends and acquaintances, essays on abolitionist activism, and floral drawings and watercolors. Unlike Dickinson's herbarium, which is the collection of a schoolgirl, Cassey's album is an artifact of an adult social world, begun when Cassey was twenty-five in 1833 and continuing until her death in 1856. Cassey was an abolitionist, activist, and member of Philadelphia's Black elite. Her album displays the botanical illustrations of middle-class and elite Black women, demonstrating the role of scientific knowledge in these women's social and political lives.[5]

As with the herbarium, my students and I begin looking at Cassey's album together in class to get some interpretive tools on the table. We talk on this first day about some of the album's floral illustrations, which students are immediately drawn to, and the poetry that goes with them.

For example, we might look at page 9 of Cassey's album, which depicts a pink rose and pair of rosebuds above a poem that begins "I love a flower!" and goes on to describe the feelings a flower imparts to the speaker. We consider together the role of this kind of sentimental content in Cassey's album and social circle.

In my experience students intuitively understand that floral culture has historically been feminized in the United States. Introducing students to the nineteenth-century popularity of the language of flowers and floral illustration in women's education helps ground students' expectations in the historical specificity of the period. Friendship albums like Cassey's were semipublic texts that allowed Black women to circulate personal writing and commentary on political concerns and social norms (Armstrong 83, 87, 94). They were sites of exhibition in which women demonstrated their talents and affirmed their respectability, and using conventional floral motifs facilitated this (Cobb 28). In Cassey's circle, contributing "flowers to friendship albums asserted black womanhood as legible by the terms of this popular convention" (39).

To expand our initial class discussion, I ask students to turn all the pages of the album, closely reading at least three pages, carefully examining at least one image, and considering the album as a collectively written text. Students love turning the pages of this album. I consistently receive comments about how the album makes its community of contributors seem dimensional, real, and engaging. At the end of the semester, students regularly choose the Cassey album as their favorite course text. Students are quick to engage with the album's sentimental poetry and images, and they often make strong claims about its representation of Cassey's social world and literary practices. All of it, though, can seem to them a far cry from science. But the album records connections between the culture of sentiment—of proper feeling and sympathy—and the culture of empirical observation and scientific illustration.

To bring botany and natural historical images back into our conversations, I have students read Britt Rusert's chapter on the Philadelphia educator Sarah Mapps Douglass's contributions to the Cassey album (181–218). Rusert argues that friendship albums broadly, and Douglass's contributions specifically, "register the important intersections between women's sentimental flower culture and the science of botany in the nineteenth century" (206). Douglass was a teacher and lecturer who made science central to girls' education. Kabria Baumgartner characterizes Douglass as an educational activist, one of a group of African American girls and women who "engaged in concerted efforts to procure advanced schooling (beyond the primary level) and teaching opportunities for themselves and their communities" (2). Douglass made several contributions to Cassey's album.[6] Indeed, she contributed the album's first illustration, which depicts a black butterfly perched on a branch above the inscription "'A token of love from me, to thee.' S.M. Douglass" (Amy Matilda Cassey friendship album 5). This gorgeous image comes early in the album, and it always catches students' attention in our initial discussions of Cassey. Douglass also produced the floral image and poem "I love a flower!" mentioned above.

Douglass's watercolors have received consistent critical attention. Given the near total absence of human forms and the total absence of Black female bodies in Cassey's album, flowers, including those depicted by Douglass, "often stand in for depictions of black women and female forms" in this context (Cobb 40). The butterfly in particular, in its striking blackness and feminine coding, reads as a stand-in for Black women.[7] Rather than discounting readings of the butterfly as a beautiful decorative image or representation of Black femininity, reading the image as a scientific production can deepen these initial readings. The butterfly image echoes an image from a natural historical textbook at Douglass's school and evinces "technical specificity," linking the image to Black women's scientific knowledge and practice (Rusert 213). Details like these help students begin to consider the parlors in which friendship albums were displayed as sites of scientific practice.

We go back to the black butterfly image after our discussion of Rusert, and I ask students to look at the image closely again and think about it as a botanical and natural historical illustration, considering how reading about Douglass changes their views. This progression of the conversation can also fruitfully lead to other entries in the Cassey album, including other floral illustrations and textual entries that include botanical language. On this last point, Daniel Alexander Payne's entry "The Rose and the Rose-Bud," in which Payne mourns his wife and daughter through an extended metaphor that includes technical botanical terms like "corolla," "stamen," "pistil," "anther," and "stigma," is particularly rich for discussion (Amy Matilda Cassey friendship album 64–68).

As I conclude teaching the Cassey album, I ask students to describe relationships they see between the album and other course texts. I want them to think about how the album connects to Dickinson's herbarium and other texts we've read, from Leonora Sansay's *Secret History*, a novel about the Haitian Revolution in which nature seems to act on the side of Black rebellion, to Nathaniel Hawthorne's "Rappaccini's Daughter," in which women and plants coexist in venomous sorority. Throughout the semester, students learn about the idea of feminized ornamental nature and how traditions of ornament coexist with and shape traditions of empirical observational science. Engaging with Cassey and Dickinson as both botanical practitioners and literary figures expands students' understanding of science, literature, and the book form.

Notes

1. I've paired the herbarium and Kuhn with different Dickinson poems in different years. Most recently, I decided to spend our time with Dickinson's "The Birds reported from the South—." Kuhn reads this poem for its depiction of an autonomously animated natural world (159–61), and it's helpful to ask students why we may wish to attend to autonomous natures and the value of depicting ideas about human dominance. This sets up a robust discussion of Dickinson's herbarium by introducing Dickinson's botanical practices as well as the ways formal botanical endeavors might be disrupted by the material realities of plants themselves.

2. Gillian Osborne's application of lyrical reading to some of Dickinson's pointedly "un-lyric, even unliterary" texts (58), in which accumulation and variation become formal patterns of significance, helpfully connects Dickinson's poetry and the herbarium, which some students experience as redundant or even boring.

3. I use sequence numbers, which match the Houghton scan's labels and differ from the internal page count because of the inclusion of images of the album's covers and endsheets in the count.

4. I refer to Dickinson's specimens by their common names for ease of understanding. Dickinson identifies most specimens by their binomial Latinate names, following Linnaean taxonomic norms.

5. The Library Company of Philadelphia holds and has digitized two other albums belonging to Black women in Philadelphia (lcpalbumproject.org). The albums, created by Cassey's neighbors Martina and Mary Anne Dickerson, also contain botanical drawings, poetry, and essays. I most often teach Cassey's album, in part because the digital scan is available in an interface that allows students to flip through its pages like a book.

6. Douglass also contributed to the albums of Martina and Mary Anne Dickerson, who were students at Douglass's school.

7. Katherine Bondy's article about the butterfly's relationship to its surroundings and contextualization of the image in relationship to religious botany take this comparison in a surprising new direction, linking the solitary butterfly to interior reflection and the value of invisible social networks.

Works Cited

Amy Matilda Cassey friendship album, 1833–56. *The Library Company of Philadelphia*, digital.librarycompany.org/islandora/object/Islandora%3A64815.

Armstrong, Erica R. "A Mental and Moral Feast: Reading, Writing, and Senti-
mentality in Black Philadelphia." *Journal of Women's History*, vol. 16, no. 1,
spring 2004, pp. 78–102.

Baumgartner, Kabria. *In Pursuit of Knowledge: Black Women and Educational
Activism in Early America*. New York UP, 2019.

Bondy, Katherine Isabel. "Freedom Flora: Botanical Revision and Community in
African American Friendship Albums." *J19: The Journal of Nineteenth-
Century Americanists*, vol. 10, no. 3, spring 2022, pp. 49–76.

Cobb, Jasmine Nichole. "'Forget Me Not': Free Black Women and Sentimental-
ity." *MELUS: Multi-Ethnic Literature of the U.S.*, vol. 40, no. 3, fall 2015,
pp. 28–46.

Daston, Lorraine, and Peter Galison. *Objectivity*. Zone Books, 2007.

Dauer, Julia. "The Environmental Histories of Desire." *Edge Effects*, 16 Apr.
2019, edgeeffects.net/greta-lafleur/.

Dickinson, Emily. "The Birds reported from the South—." *The Collected Poems
of Emily Dickinson*, edited by Thomas H. Johnson, Little, Brown, 1961,
pp. 364–65.

———. Herbarium, circa 1839–46. Harvard U, Houghton Library, MS Am
1118.11, nrs.lib.harvard.edu/urn-3:fhcl.hough:883158.

Hawthorne, Nathaniel. "Rappaccini's Daughter." *Mosses from an Old Manse*,
edited by William Charvat et al., Ohio State UP, 1974, pp. 91–128.

Jackson, Virginia. "Emily Dickinson's Herbarium: A Facsimile Edition." *The Emily Dickinson Journal*, vol. 16, no. 1, 2007, pp. 105–08.

Kuhn, Mary. "Dickinson and the Politics of Plant Sensibility." *ELH*, vol. 85, no. 1,
spring 2018, pp. 141–70.

LaFleur, Greta. *The Natural History of Sexuality in Early America*. Johns Hopkins UP, 2018.

Miller, Daegan. "Reading to Children to Save Ourselves." *Public Books*, 13 Mar.
2018, www.publicbooks.org/reading-to-children-to-save-ourselves/.

Nezhukumatathil, Aimee. *World of Wonders: In Praise of Fireflies, Whale Sharks,
and Other Astonishments*. Milkweed Editions, 2020.

Osborne, Gillian. "Dickinson's Lyric Materialism." *The Emily Dickinson Journal*,
vol. 21, no. 1, 2012, pp. 57–78.

Parrish, Susan Scott. *American Curiosity: Cultures of Natural History in the Colonial British Atlantic World*. U of North Carolina P, 2006.

Rusert, Britt. *Fugitive Science: Empiricism and Freedom in Early African American Culture*. New York UP, 2017.

Sansay, Leonora. *Secret History; or, The Horrors of St. Domingo*. Secret History;
or, The Horrors of St. Domingo *and* Laura, edited by Michael J. Drexler,
Broadview Editions, 2007, pp. 59–154.

Uno, Hiroko. "Emily Dickinson and Japanese Flowers: Her Herbarium and
Perry's Expedition to Japan." *The Emily Dickinson Journal*, vol. 26, no. 1,
2017, pp. 51–79.

Susanna Lee

Experiments with the Science of Alcoholism

The physiologist Claude Bernard wrote in the 1865 *Introduction à l'étude de la médecine expérimentale* (*Introduction to Experimental Medicine*), "L'art, c'est moi; la science, c'est nous" ("Art is me, science is us"; 96). This phrase underscores not just the broadly shared utility of science but also, ideally, its detachment from individual bias and egotism: "Pour les arts et les lettres, la personnalité domine tout" ("In arts and letters, personality dominates everything"; 95), writes Bernard, whereas "la méthode expérimentale est la méthode scientifique qui proclame la liberté de l'esprit et de la pensée. . . . L'expérimenteur fait acte d'humilité en niant l'autorité personnelle" ("the experimental method proclaims the liberty of mind and thought. . . . The experimenter acts humbly by denying personal authority"; 96). At the same time, while science may be "us," science writing—which communicates scientific understanding to the reader—contains indisputable elements of "me." Science writing, like fiction writing, may convey meaning through metaphor, imagery, and tone. Bernard notes that while observation must be free of preconceived ideas, experimentation depends upon them (80). And yet, reading science writing generates preconceived ideas, especially for readers who will not do their own experiments: this is part of the reason why science writing from any era is usefully read as a cultural document.

This essay examines late-nineteenth-century French scientific writings about alcoholism and discusses the pairing of those writings with fiction in advanced undergraduate courses on French literature and culture. One such course that I teach concentrates on illness in nineteenth-century France; it is taught in French and is cross-listed with medical humanities. The principal focus of the course is canonical fiction; however, we also read excerpts of scientific articles about illnesses that were prevalent either during the specific historical period in which the novels were written or within the plots of the fiction itself. For instance, while reading texts that reference the cholera epidemic and use metaphors of contagion, we consult articles about cholera. While reading texts that feature neurasthenic and agoraphobic protagonists, we consult articles about neurasthenia. Even in some more general nineteenth-century novel courses that do not have an explicitly medical humanities focus, we consult scientific articles as contextual material. During one iteration of this late-nineteenth-century novel course, toward the end of the semester, we read Émile Zola's *L'Assommoir*. Belonging to a series of twenty novels entitled the Rougon-Macquart, which chronicles the various fortunes and misfortunes of a French family under the Second Empire, this particular text recounts a working-class couple's slide into alcoholism, degradation, and death.

Zola, known as the father of the naturalist school of French fiction, saw his characters—and all people—as being organically connected to their milieu: "Notre héros . . . est le sujet physiologique de notre science actuelle, un être qui est composé d'organes et qui trempe dans un milieu dont il est pénétré à chaque heure" ("Our hero . . . is the physiological subject of our current science, a being who is composed of organs and who steeps in a milieu with which he is constantly infused"; *Œuvres complètes illustrées* 262). In class, discussions of this novel focus frequently on questions of fault, accountability, and the boundaries of agency. How does the phenomenon of heredity determine whether we judge or pity? We investigate how the novel's narrative voice, word choice, and intertextual references shape reader response to the character in question and encourage compassion, judgment, or aversion. To see where others have placed responsibility and accorded empathy, and how others have understood the phenomenon of problem drinking, we consult science writing.

Late-nineteenth-century French science writing on out-of-control drinking does not resolve but rather complicates the question of accountability. We know that Zola consulted various scientific works in the process of writing the Rougon-Macquart. One of these was a work on alcoholism by Valentin Magnan, the principal psychiatrist at St. Anne's Hospital in Paris from 1867 to 1912. Magnan's monograph, *De l'alcoolisme, des diverses formes du délire alcoolique et de leur traitement* (*On Alcoholism, on the Diverse Forms of Alcoholic Delirium and Their Treatment*), was published in 1874, three years before the publication of *L'Assommoir*. Zola borrowed heavily from that book in his portrait of the male protagonist Coupeau's alcoholic death at St. Anne's Hospital. In fact, Zola wrote:

> Je m'étonne surtout que le docteur V. Magnan ne m'ait pas fait un procès pour avoir emprunté tant de passages à son beau livre *De l'alcoolisme*. Mon Dieu, oui! j'ai pris dans ce livre tout le *delirium tremens* de Coupeau; j'ai copié des phrases que le docteur a entendues dans la bouche de certains alcoolisés; j'ai suivi ses observations de savant pas à pas, et certes, si vous voulez bien comparer *L'Assommoir* à son ouvrage, vous trouverez la matière d'un nouveau réquisitoire.
> (*Les Rougon-Macquart* 1563)

> I am amazed that Doctor V. Magnan has not taken me to court for borrowing so many passages from his fine book, *On Alcoholism*. My God, yes! I took from that book Coupeau's entire *delirium tremens*; I copied phrases the doctor heard from certain alcoholics; I followed his learned observations step-by-step, and if you wish to compare *L'Assommoir* to his work, you'll find the basis for a new lawsuit.

But Zola did not just borrow science writers' descriptions of delirium tremens: he also imagined (and in some cases replicated) their disdainful tone. At the end of the novel, when Coupeau is perishing from alcoholism, the attending doctor at St. Anne's Hospital—read as an avatar for Magnan himself—converses with the patient's wife, Gervaise, and learns with disapproval that the unfortunate man comes from an alcoholic family: "Puis, le vieux monsieur chauve, pas très-poli d'ailleurs, parut enfin s'apercevoir de sa présence; et, quand l'interne lui eut dit qu'elle était la femme du malade, il se mit à l'interroger, d'un air méchant de commissaire de police.—Est-ce que le père de cet homme buvait?" ("Then the elderly bald-headed gentleman, who was not very polite, seemed at last to become aware of her presence; and when the intern had informed him that this was the patient's wife, he began to interrogate her in the harsh manner of a police commissioner. 'Did this man's father drink?'"; 786).[1] In this scene, the judgmental doctor is himself a character, one to whom the reader can respond as such. Readers can wonder at his detached and police-like voice. This is important because it provides a lead-in to discussions of science writing itself as having a narrative voice and employing narrative voice and character development. We therefore consult contemporaneous science writing to explore what kind of understanding dominated during the period in question: Was alcoholism understood to be an inescapable hereditary curse? Was it connected with immorality, even sin, or was it read as a social scourge, concentrated in the working class? As Zola understood, and as various critics of his have pointed out, symptomology that wanders into the dramatic and disastrous can underscore a topic's social importance and draw readers (see, e.g., Rollins). Science writing of the late nineteenth century, especially in the domain of alcoholism and hereditary mental illnesses, alternated between the theatrical, the accusatory, the dispassionate, and the compassionate, depending on the writerly bent of the author. In the next section, I trace the precise ways in which science writing—long before Zola's fiction—contributed to creating the character of the brutal, savage, and violent alcoholic.

Building a Ferocious Beast

The *Dictionaire des sciences médicales* (*Dictionary of Medical Sciences*), published in 1818, contains a lengthy entry on the topic of drunkenness, or *ivresse* ("Ivresse"). To this entry is appended a somewhat shorter subsection written by Percy and Laurent titled "Ivresse convulsive" ("Convulsive Drunkenness"), which states, "On a dit que l'ivresse faisait descendre l'homme au rang de la brute: l'ivresse convulsive est plus affreuse; elle le rend semblable aux bêtes féroces; elle lui en donne la force, les agitations, l'aspect, et jusqu'à la cruauté. Il faut enchaîner, comme elles, celui qu'elle attaque, pour se mettre à l'abri de se fureurs" ("They have said that drunkenness made man descend to the level of the brute: convulsive drunkenness is more frightful; it makes him resemble ferocious beasts; it gives him their strength, their agitations, their aspect, even their cruelty. One must shackle, like those beasts, the man that it attacks, to protect oneself from his furies"; "Ivresse convulsive" 249). In this formulation, drunkenness is the aggressor, and the individual the victim ("the man that it attacks"), but it is the comparison to "ferocious beasts" that dominates the entry: "Son regard est farouche, ses yeux étincelants, ses cheveux se hérissent, ses gestes sont menaçants; il grince des dents, crache à la figure des assistants, et ce qui rend ce tableau plus hideux encore, il essaye de mordre ceux qui l'approchent" ("His look is wild, his eyes shine, his hair stands on end, his gestures threaten. He grinds his teeth, spits in the face of assistants and, making the tableau even more hideous, tries to bite those who approach him"; 249).

The tone of the Percy and Laurent's entry is dramatic, and their images alarming, all the more so in their evocation of animal savagery.[2] After presenting this portrait, though, the authors then note that they have seen eighteen such patients. It is not a very large number, but the description they give has proven durable and eminently quotable. Magnan remarks in his 1874 book that it would be wrong to rank this sort of drunkenness, with its "fureur maniaque" ("maniacal fury") alongside "ivresse commune" ("common drunkenness"; 116). He does not say that he himself has observed any such cases. But he nonetheless repeats the citation at length, as do numerous other science writers of the late nineteenth century, including Henri Legrand du Saulle, in *L'Abeille médicale* (*Medical Bee*; 456); Charles-Claude Brillaud-Laujardière, in *De l'ivresse considérée dans ses conséquences médico-légales* (*Of Drunkenness Considered in Its Medical and Legal Consequences*; 127); and Clément Ollivier, in *Pathologie morale* (*Moral Pathology*; 180). In an article on drunkenness in an 1871 issue of the *Revue pratique de droit français* (*Practical Review of French Law*), Charles Muteau cites Percy and Laurent's entry and states that drunkenness is the source "non-seulement des délits, mais des plus effroyables crimes" ("not just of misdemeanors but of the most frightful crimes"; 313).

The term *alcoholism* was introduced in the mid–nineteenth century, about thirty years after the dictionary entry, in Magnus Huss's *Alcoholismus chronicus eller chronisk alkoholssjukdom* (*Chronic Alcoholism or Chronic Alcohol Disease*). The specter of out-of-control brutality then appeared commonly in French writing in connection with alcoholism (though not in Huss's own writing). To cite only a few examples, in his 1874 *Dangers de l'abus des boissons alcooliques* (*Dangers of Abusing Alcoholic Beverages*), Eugène Picard, a doctor, says that the alcoholic is "l'homme moins l'intelligence et la conscience, c'est à dire c'est la pire des brutes" ("man without intelligence, without conscience, which is to say the worst of brutes"; 99). An 1890 treatment of the same topic by Paul Garnier casts the alcoholic as a hopeless victim: "Dans son délire, l'alcoolique est avant tout un tragique; dans ses conceptions fantaisistes, c'est un dramaturge qui édifie de toutes pieces un roman où tout est horrible, terrifiant . . ." ("The alcoholic is above all a tragic figure: in his fantastical conceptions, he is a dramatist constructing around him a novel in which everything is horrible, terrifying . . ."; 123). Shown this series of citations, students understand that a character is building. Zola uses this character outline in his portrait of Bijard, an abusive alcoholic and "bête brute" ("brutal beast"; *Les Rougon-Macquart* 556).[3] And where once Zola had copied, other science writers borrow from him. In *Les dangers de l'alcoolisme* (*The Dangers of Alcoholism*), a book destined for schoolchildren, Jules Steeg reproduces almost verbatim the scenes of Bijard's murderous madness, though his description is meant to be generic and documentary in nature: "L'ivrogne se rue sur sa femme comme une bête féroce, il l'accable de coups, dans sa fureur alcoolique, il brise les quelques meubles qu'il n'a pas vendus" ("The drunken man rushes at his wife like a furious beast, he bombards her with blows; in his alcoholic fury, he breaks the furniture he hasn't yet sold for drink"; 104). Science writing and fiction work together to create a type, though—to return to Bernard—less through observation than through citation and paraphrase. To be clear, there is no doubt that violent alcoholics can certainly be terrible domestic abusers: this is not a meaningless stereotype. What I want to point out is the reinforcement of bestial descriptions through collaboration (even unintentional collaboration) between fiction and science writing and the ways in which such descriptions overcome the search for solutions.

Observation and Compassion

In a recent iteration of the course focusing on illness in the nineteenth century, one taught during the COVID-19 pandemic, students were assigned to write a poetic or prose description of an illness. I asked them also to reflect on the process of that writing and recount what obstacles arose. Finally, students were asked to consider whether one can write beautifully about something painful and whether the response would be different for physical illness than for mental illness. In some cases, students wrote about an illness they themselves had experienced. In other cases, they wrote about illnesses that their loved ones had experienced. When students wrote about their own experiences, I noticed that they described the illness (sometimes in the third person, sometimes in the second person) as a separate entity, an actor, an antagonist. This was the case whether they were writing about a physical or a mental ailment: it was described as a familiar companion or an aggressive intruder, given agency and even a personality. When students wrote about the afflictions of other people, though, they described that person's feelings and reactions, their sufferings and their courage. The illness was not the dominant agent in the writing; the patient was. This was creative writing, not science writing. But it was striking to note the contrast between student descriptions of people with illnesses, which foregrounded the experience of sickness without erasing the humanity of the person having the experience, and nineteenth-century science writing, which used accounts of alcoholic poisoning to describe lurid and monstrous metamorphoses.

To return to Bernard's notion of observation and experimentation, and his insistence that observation should be free of preconceived ideas, it seems that observation, rendered into writing, nonetheless activates and instrumentalizes—indeed relies upon—preconceived ideas. When Percy and Laurent write that drunken ferocity "rend ce tableau plus hideux encore" ("mak[es] the tableau even more hideous"), they underscore the visual presentation of the patient as spectacle, almost as theater. Science writing can subtly become creative writing, and it often did in the nineteenth century: it leaned heavily into the melodramatic in ways that serious science writing of the present day is less likely to do. Theatrical or hyperbolic representations may seem to be anachronistic, old-fashioned choices. This is all the more so because in teaching science writing of centuries past, it is common to come upon facts that are no longer accepted. (Magnan's endorsement of arsenic as a reasonable treatment for alcoholic paralysis, a neurological symptom of long-term heavy drinking, is one such example.) Students are sometimes tempted to dismiss outmoded theories, and by extension the scientific text containing them, out of hand. But to call something "old-fashioned" is of course to underestimate its simultaneous modernity or its similarities to characterizations that persist today. The repeated use of hyperbole and alarmism in the texts described above is instructive for understanding the powerful draw of such rhetorical devices, a draw that acted on fiction writers and science writers alike.

In Germain Marty's *Contribution à l'étude de l'alcoolisme* (*Contribution to the Study of Alcoholism*), Percy and Laurent's entry appears again, with the following comment: "Quelques auteurs décrivent sous ce nom une quatrième forme d'ivresse" ("Some authors include under this name [of convulsive or furious alcoholism] a fourth form of drunkenness"), to which Marty adds the now familiar chestnut "qui rend l'homme semblable à une bête féroce" ("which makes a person resemble a ferocious beast"; 28). However, Marty notes that in the more than eighty years intervening between the dictionary's publication and his own writing in 1899, in addition to the eighteen cases that Percy and Laurent had observed, another doctor had observed "des cas" ("some"), and two others had noted "plusieurs" ("several"; 28). Marty does not report having observed any cases himself. The verbatim description (complete with references to ferocious beasts) had been cited, it seems, almost as many times as the phenomenon had been observed, not counting in fiction, but a character outline had nonetheless been produced.

The Harm in Melodrama

Friedlander, the author of the entry on drunkenness in the *Dictionnaire*, had insisted that drunkenness would make a person's inherent characteristics emerge but not that it would turn a person into something they were not: "L'homme brut se montre tel qu'il est, et l'homme civilisé, tant qu'il le peut, tel qu'il a été formé par l'éducation tel qu'il voudrait paraître" ("The person in the rough shows himself as he is, and the civilized man, so far as he is able, shows himself as his education has formed him"; "Ivresse" 243). Despite this observation that "in vino veritas," as it were, the subsequent statement that the victims of "ivresse convulsive" ("convulsive drunkenness") became like "bêtes féroces" ("ferocious beasts"; "Ivresse convulsive" 249), when combined with Friedlander's statement, implies that those who become brutal were brutes to begin with. The doctor in Zola's novel takes up this same ambiguity when he accusingly raises the specter of heredity. At the same time, the contrast between "the person in the rough" and "the civilized man" has nothing to do with nature and much to do with nurture. Here, also, attention to standards of observation is crucial to noticing where pontification and preconceived ideas replace—or appear dressed as—observation.[4]

References to a brutal or bestial nature appear frequently in writing about alcoholism and other mental disorders. Some of this comparison is literary in nature (e.g., Percy and Laurent's observation that "it makes him resemble ferocious beasts") and is not based on direct observation. Some of it is methodological and is based on observation. Magnan, for instance, spends the first half of *On Alcoholism* talking about his experiments on dogs. Émile Galtier-Boissière notes in his 1896 anti-alcoholism pamphlet that becoming "extrêmement brutal, féroce" ("extremely brutal, ferocious") can happen to individuals "qui boivent chaque jour un verre ou deux d'absinthe" ("who drink one or two glasses of absinthe a day") and that "[i]l suffit d'un an d'un tel régime pour voir apparaître l'empoisonnement" ("one year of such a regime is enough to produce poisoning"), adding, "On ne peut s'étonner d'une marche aussi rapide lorsqu'on sait que le docteur Magnan a provoqué une attaque violente d'épilepsie chez un cheval en lui injectant un gramme d'essence d'absinthe" ("One cannot be surprised by this progression when one knows that Doctor Magnan provoked an epileptic attack in a horse by injecting him with one gram of absinthe essence"; 21). In none of these experiments did a drunken animal become savage, but the comparison of drunk people to wild animals had considerable rhetorical staying power. Science writing had a symbiotic relationship to fiction; when comparing Zola's work to science writing, students noted their numerous shared metaphors. When reading *L'Assommoir*, they remarked on Gervaise's comparisons of her alcoholic husband to a pig, a metaphor that echoed science texts in its evocation of unpleasant animals.[5] And in their coursework, students grasped the ethical problems of confusing imagination and observation. Drawing on Zola's use of free indirect discourse, for instance, where the third-person narrator openly channels the voice of a character, they observed in science writing those moments when documentation and invention were blended for dramatic effect.

Science writing about alcoholism also points to stakes far beyond that particular illness. In 1881 the *Bulletin de l'Association française contre l'abus du tabac et des boissons alcooliques* (*Bulletin of the French Association against the Abuse of Tobacco and Alcoholic Beverages*) describes an individual who, "dans l'enivrement de l'ivresse du combat et de l'ivresse alcoolique, devient plus féroce que les farouches habitants des forêts du nouveau monde, lesquels ne peuvent apaiser leur fureur que dans le sang de leurs victimes" ("intoxicated by the drunkenness of combat and the drunkenness of alcohol, becomes more ferocious than the wild inhabitants of the forests of the New World, who can quench their fury only with the blood of their victims"; Dr. Mora 68). The author takes the bestial nature of the human "inhabitants of the forests" as a given and cites it to illustrate the wildness of the alcoholic. The combination of repulsion and alarm is overtly racialized, in ways that immediately draw student attention and comment. If I present such writing, I present it as racist pseudoscience that has been thoroughly taken apart by the numerous scholars working on racism in science (see, e.g., Fuentes; Saini; Poskett). All the while, though, its rhetorical influence continues to hold sway. Remembering the supposed reliance of observation on the absence of preconceived ideas is instructive in examining such writings and evaluating their stakes.

Science writing on alcoholism encourages literature students to consider the relationships between observation, preconceived ideas, and creativity. It invites them to consider issues of bias and projection within science and to examine the role of science writing itself in creating what then become preconceived ideas. Nineteenth-century science writing is itself a fluid category, encompassing texts for popular interest (often with a melodramatic tone) as well as those for medical specialists. Writing on alcoholism uses and even activates that fluidity. Analyzing the science of alcoholism reminds students that to create lurid spectacles—and to move from observation into theatricality—is a narrative choice, one made by scientists and authors alike.

Notes

All translations in this essay are my own.

1. See Hewitt on "the portrayal of medical men as unfeeling and disinterested" (150).

2. While Percy and Laurent open their entry by writing, "They have said that drunkenness made man descend to the level of the brute," the preceding entry on simple drunkenness does not in fact say this.

3. Jared Wenger calls the death of Bijard's daughter "a height of poignancy" and "a story quite English in its brutality" (1155). In this way, brutality, by its very intensity, is rendered distant and fictional. See also Cummins on the use of *L'Assommoir* in English temperance movements.

4. Paul-Maurice Legrain represents one notable ideological and stylistic outlier in the anti-alcoholism field of late-nineteenth-century France. Legrain distinguished himself from his colleagues by advocating complete abstinence from all alcohol, including wine: "A un homme qui se tue par la morphine on ne dit pas: Modérez-vous, soyez tempérant! On lui dit: Abstenez-vous! L'alcool est un poison à l'égal de la morphine; il est plus dangereux que la morphine, parce qu'il est d'un usage plus répandu et fait plus de victimes" ("To a man killing himself with morphine, one doesn't say 'be temperant!' One tells him: 'Abstain!' Alcohol is a poison equal to morphine; it is more dangerous than morphine, because its usage is more widespread and its victims more numerous"; 2). The style here is flowery, the presentation of hypothetical urgings similar to that in other temperance writings, but there are two points of difference. First, Legrain directly casts alcohol as the problem and drinkers as victims. Second, he takes an epidemiological perspective ("more widespread") rather than casting the alcohol problem as a lurid spectacle centered on one person.

5. When reading Zola's *Germinal* in another course, students observed the narrator's comparison of miners to dogs and horses, a comparison facilitated by the presence of actual animals in the mine.

Works Cited

Bernard, Claude. *Introduction à l'étude de la médecine expérimentale.* Flammarion, 1984.

Brillaud-Laujardière, Charles-Claude. *De l'ivresse considérée dans ses conséquences médico-légales.* Paris, 1866.

Cummins, Anthony. "From *L'Assommoir* to 'Let's Ha' Some More': Émile Zola's Early Circulation on the Late-Victorian Stage." *Victorian Review,* vol. 34, no. 1, 2008, pp. 155–70.

Dr. Mora. "L'abus de alcooliques." *Bulletin de l'Association française contre l'abus du tabac et des boissons alcooliques.* No. 1, 1881, pp. 66–72.

Fuentes, Agustín. "Systemic Racism in Science: Reactions Matter." *Science,* vol. 381, no. 6655, 20 July 2023, https://doi.org/10.1126/science.adj7675.

Galtier-Boissière, Émile. *Livret d'anti-alcoolisme: Application à l'hygiène des notions de sciences.* Armand Colin, 1896.

Garnier, Paul. "Le délire alcoolique et ses modalités réactionnelles." *La France médicale,* vol. 3, Jan. 1890, pp. 121–29.

Hewitt, Jessie. *Institutionalizing Gender: Madness, the Family, and Psychiatric Power in Nineteenth-Century France.* Cornell UP, 2020.

Huss, Magnus. *Alcoholismus chronicus eller chronisk alkoholssjukdom.* Stockholm, 1849.

"Ivresse." *Dictionaire des sciences médicales.* Vol. 26, Paris, 1818, pp. 232–49.

"Ivresse convulsive." *Dictionaire des sciences médicales.* Vol. 26, Paris, 1818, pp. 249–57.

Legrain, Paul-Maurice. "La Société contre l'usage des boissons spiritueuses." *L'Alcool: Bulletin de la société contre l'usages des boissons spiritueuses,* no. 1, 20 Jan. 1896, pp. 2–5.

Legrand du Saulle, Henri. "Le délire alcoolique étudié au point de vue médico-légal." *L'Abeille médicale: Revue des journaux et des ouvrages de médecine, de chirurgie, de pharmacie,* vol. 26, 1869, pp. 453–58.

Magnan, Valentin. *De l'alcoolisme, des diverses formes du délire alcoolique et de leur traitement.* Delahaye, 1874.

Marty, Germain. *Contribution à l'étude de l'alcoolisme.* Paris, 1873.

Muteau, Charles. "Ivrognerie." *Revue pratique de droit français: Jurisprudence, doctrine, législation,* vol. 31, 1871, pp. 305–24.

Ollivier, Clément. *Pathologie morale.* Paris, 1867.

Picard, Eugène. *Dangers de l'abus des boissons alcooliques, manuel d'instruction populaire à l'usage des instituteurs.* Paris, 1874.

Poskett, James. *Materials of the Mind: Phrenology, Race, and the Global History of Science, 1815–1920.* U of Chicago P, 2019.

Rollins, Yvonne Bargues. "Une 'Danse Macabre': *L'Assommoir* de Zola." *Nineteenth-Century French Studies,* vol. 9, nos. 3–4, 1981, pp. 233–46.

Saini, Angela. *Superior: The Return of Race Science.* Beacon Press, 2019.

Steeg, Jules. *Les dangers de l'alcoolisme.* Paris, 1896.

Wenger, Jared. "The Art of the Flashlight: Violent Technique in *Les Rougon-Macquart.*" *PMLA,* vol. 57, no. 4, part 1, Dec. 1942, pp. 1137–59.

Zola, Émile. *Germinal.* Pocket, 2018.

———. *Œuvres complètes illustrées.* Vol. 19, Charpentier, 1906.

———. *Les Rougon-Macquart.* Vol. 2, Gallimard, 1961.

Part II

General Education and Writing Courses

Laura McGrath

Digital Science Communication in Rhetoric and Writing Courses

From COVID-19 to climate change, college students in all majors are stakeholders in conversations about science, technology, and society—conversations that are increasingly taking place on social media. Many students engage with digital science communication to learn about topics important to them, to increase their understanding of academic course content, or to be entertained. They are certainly among those who, as the Pew Research Center indicates, are increasingly turning to social media and online news platforms for scientific information (Hitlin and Olmstead; Saks and Tyson). By the time they enroll in my rhetoric and writing courses, students have been exposed to dozens of sometimes conflicting perspectives on the value, authority, and promises of science, often without having had the opportunity to engage critically with questions about the rhetorical and ethical dimensions of digital science communication.

In *Composition and the Rhetoric of Science*, Michael Zerbe argues that "[b]ecause scientific rhetoric influences students so profoundly . . . it is incumbent upon rhetoric and composition studies to provide an opportunity to students to develop or hone the requisite intellectual skills to engage this discourse in a fully informed way" (7). Whereas Zerbe focuses on scientific discourse—"discourse in which science is actually *performed*"

(3)—my teaching centers another important element of professional practice: the public communication of science. Critical engagement with digital science communication demands what Emily Howell and Dominique Brossard refer to as "digital media science literacy": the ability to "access science information" online, understand how it "travels through media systems," and "evaluate individual pieces of science information in media messages" (3). As I demonstrate in this essay, a humanities-based digital rhetoric course provides an ideal context for analyzing contemporary digital science communication practices and developing digital media science literacy.

As a rhetoric and digital media specialist, I teach in the Department of English at a large suburban comprehensive university. Although I have also taught science-related topics in first-year composition, this essay focuses on Topics in Digital Rhetoric, an advanced course in our writing curriculum that I have offered in both hybrid and fully online formats. I describe the hybrid version elsewhere (McGrath and Guglielmo), and here I focus on the online asynchronous version. The standard course description for Topics in Digital Rhetoric (now titled Writing and Digital Culture) reads as follows: "This course explores rhetorical practices in electronic environments and provides an examination of major works on digital reading, writing, and culture framed by contemporary rhetorical theories. Students plan, design, and compose a variety of rhetorically effective digital texts" ("WRIT 3150"). In addition to English majors and a variety of students who are minoring in professional writing, the course enrolls a significant number of media and entertainment majors from the School of Communication and Media because the course is an option for fulfilling that degree's writing competency requirement. I find that students sometimes enroll in the course not because they are interested in the topic but rather because they need to fulfill a requirement or want an online option; this is something I address by building student choice and flexibility into my assignment designs.

When planning how the section of the course focused on digital science communication would work, I consulted publications from rhetoric and composition, media studies, technical communication, and science and environmental communication. My own research also informed the course design. Specifically, insights from interviews I conducted with thirteen individuals working around the world in biodiversity conservation shaped my decisions about everything from learning objectives to instructional content. The individuals I interviewed offered perspectives on the role social media plays in their efforts to communicate science, engage publics, and promote the kind of understanding that leads to action, allowing me to provide students with real-world examples of rhetoric in action. The interviewees also shared information about their formal or experiential training in science communication, the techniques they employ when crafting content for specific audiences and contexts, and the challenges and successes they have faced. For the most part, they take what I would describe as a rhetorical approach to science communication, considering audience, context, and genre; thinking about the visuals and examples audiences are likely to connect with emotionally and find most compelling; and matching their goals to their strategies. Additionally, all the individuals I interviewed, without prompting, used "story" or "storytelling" in their responses, which influenced how I connected the humanities to science communication.

I wrote course learning objectives that emphasize analysis as well as production:

Students will be able to

use rhetorical terms and concepts to explain how specific textual, visual, and auditory choices create rhetorical effects in examples of digital science communication;

identify examples of persuasive intent in digital science communication and evaluate those examples for evidence of the communicators' motivations as well as any logical fallacies or biases;

describe and provide examples of how science communicators attempt to establish credibility and promote trust in digital contexts;

analyze digital science communicators' use of narratives, metaphors, explanatory chains, and other techniques;

make observations about how publics interact with digital science communication through shares, likes, comments, tagging, and so on, and consider the role interactivity plays in supporting or subverting communicators' goals; and

apply science communication strategies to the planning and creation of digital content about science-related topics, providing a rationale for their rhetorical choices.

To achieve these outcomes, students completed three carefully scaffolded and sequenced units that began with modeling and discussion and moved to practice and formative assessment. Units 2 and 3 included mid-unit and end-of-unit summative assessments, one focused on analysis and the second focused on production and reflection. Before describing these units and the assignments, I share an overview of the instructional material that provided students with foundational concepts and frameworks.

To introduce students to the concepts, examples, and frameworks we use in the course, I created media-rich lessons in the SoftChalk content-authoring program, incorporating written information and guiding questions, mouse-over definitions, my own instructional videos, other relevant videos, and screenshots from examples of digital science communication. These lessons served as the primary text for the course, but I also assigned a range of readings, including the following texts, which were often cited by my students in their writing: Laura Gurak's "Ethos, Trust, and the Rhetoric of Digital Writing in Scientific and Technical Discourse," Ben Lillie's "Science and the Art of Personal Storytelling," Michael Dahlstrom's "Using Narratives and Storytelling to Communicate Science with Nonexpert Audiences," and Birte Fähnrich's "Conceptualizing Science Communication in Flux—a Framework for Analyzing Science Communication in a Digital Media Environment."

Gurak's essay explores "the question of how the rhetorical appeal of ethos functions in digital settings and how credibility is created, established, and reified" in those contexts (124) while drawing attention to concepts and elements of digital science communication that I explore with students: trust, deception, misinformation, confirmation bias, and the influence of visual information and appeals. Gurak ends by reflecting on how studying digital scientific and technical discourses requires "interdisciplinary approach[es]," which those who are trained in "motivated, symbolic uses of language and images" are well positioned to contribute to (129); because a number of my students—as I anticipated—struggled with their own ethos as nonscience majors in a course on science communication, Gurak's essay helped illustrate the value of their analytical skills.

Lillie's and Dahlstrom's texts both focus on storytelling in science communication, supplementing my instruction on how programs like those offered by the Alan Alda Center for Communicating Science at Stony Brook University and National Geographic's Sciencetelling Bootcamp emphasize storytelling when training scientists. Lillie founded The Story Collider, which invites people—in person or on a podcast—to "tell true, personal stories about science in their lives" (97). His essay, which is geared toward science communicators interested in blogging, touches on narrative theory and emphasizes the value of narratives and personal experiences for engaging audiences and connecting with them emotionally. He distinguishes between "science first" and "story first" approaches. In "science first" storytelling, anecdotes offer metaphors or illustrations that help the audience understand a scientific concept. In "story first" approaches, which Lillie devotes the most attention to, the story takes the audience "on a journey" and is "the whole point of the piece" (99). My students used "science first" versus "story first" as a frame for analysis, considered the pros and cons of narrative approaches (e.g., potential for oversimplification or emotional manipulation), and were also able to apply Lillie's advice on technique to their own digital science communication content.

Although Dahlstrom's academic writing style is less accessible to students than Lillie's conversational approach, Dahlstrom's article nonetheless provides valuable information about "the potential persuasive impacts of narrative communication and the ethical considerations of using narrative to communicate science" (13614). Dahlstrom offers students a theoretically grounded discussion of how narrative works in science communication, prompting discussions about how accuracy differs from "authenticity and plausibility," how various values and biases shape digital science communication, and the extent to which "persuasive intent" is obvious or concealed in particular examples of digital science communication (13616).

Finally, Fähnrich's article reminds readers that not only "universities and researchers but also activist groups, corporations, political actors, bloggers, vloggers, science enthusiasts, science sceptics, and many more communicate about science-related content, and thus they contribute to the overall public perception of science" (4), demonstrating that social media broadens participation in science communication and foregrounds a complex range of motivations and perspectives. Fähnrich also provides a table of categories that researchers can use when studying science communication in digital contexts: "actors involved, underlying intentions, aspects of content and framing, level of controversy, and media-specific aspects such as directions of communication, modes of presentation, and types of effects" (6); this table, with Fähnrich's helpful categories, explanations, and examples, provided my students with a framework for analyzing digital science communication in units 2 and 3 of the course. This reading also complements instruction on explanatory chains (causal descriptions) and message framing, which ties presentational choices to the way audiences come to understand a science topic.

In unit 1, Introduction to Digital Rhetoric, I covered rhetorical terminology and definitions of digital rhetoric from chapter 1 of Douglas

Eyman's *Digital Rhetoric: Theory, Method, Practice* (12–55), discussed unique features of digital communication (e.g., interactivity), and provided heuristics for analysis: a SOAPStone handout (speaker, occasion, audience, purpose, subject, tone) and guiding questions from Jodie Nicotra's *Becoming Rhetorical* for analyzing textual, visual, auditory, and haptic modalities. We also read Gurak's essay and discussed ethos. Next, using examples of digital science communication, I modeled rhetorical analysis. Students then completed mini-analyses and participated in a related discussion board activity.

With a strengthened foundation in rhetorical terminology and approaches to analysis, we moved into unit 2, Digital Rhetoric and Science Communication. Among other readings, students studied Lillie's, Dahlstrom's, and Fähnrich's texts along with examples of digital science communication—social media posts, podcasts, websites, video content—that illustrated the concepts covered. Analysis-focused discussion board activities prepared students for the mid-unit summative assessment: a rhetorical analysis project that challenged them to apply course concepts related to digital rhetoric, social media, and science communication. Some students analyzed the use of narrative techniques in multiplatform social media content created by a specific science communicator or organization. Others compared the rhetorical techniques used by two science communicators. Although students had the option to write a traditional academic paper, I also invited them to consider alternative formats. For example, several students incorporated their analyses into multimodal guides for scientists on how to use social media for science communication.

In the second half of unit 2, students used their enhanced understanding of concepts associated with the first five learning objectives to take on a new challenge: planning and creating their own original digital science content. This project offered two options, both of which align with the final learning objective: Students could write a social media plan focused on science communication that included sample content, or they could create a portfolio of original science communication content about a topic of their choosing. Regardless of their project selection, all students needed to think critically about establishing credibility and trust and to aim for accuracy, meaning that the project also involved some research and source evaluation. All students also wrote reflectively about their goals, choices, and techniques, highlighting how they applied concepts from our readings as well as knowledge gained from their rhetorical analysis project.

Unit 3, Environmental Writing on Digital Platforms, was structured identically to unit 2, with a mid-unit rhetorical analysis project and an end-of-unit content creation assignment. The focus of this unit narrowed from science communication broadly to environmental communication in particular. Although the course could certainly have moved from narrow to broad, I believe broad to narrow worked well, with the added kairotic element of unit 3 aligning with Earth Day, which resulted in a corresponding increase in the number of environment-related social media posts available for analysis. The zoomed-in approach in unit 3 allowed us to devote attention to a thematically connected set of case studies with similar rhetorical goals and communicative challenges. Because my own interview research focused on biodiversity conservation communication, I could also draw on that to a greater extent than I could in unit 2. Through their rhetorical analysis project, students connected course concepts to digital content about local and regional environmental issues or pressing global concerns (e.g., climate change, biodiversity loss, plastic pollution). Most students were quite familiar with how these issues are presented and debated on social media, which proved beneficial in terms of identifying accounts, podcasts, or websites to analyze and feeling invested in the subject matter. Still, science communication about environmental issues on social media is incredibly complex and multilayered, presenting students with analytical challenges.

For example, a 2023 post on the *Washington Post*'s @postclimate *Instagram* account shares the results of a *Washington Post*–University of Maryland poll on Americans' perceptions of the "individual actions" that are most likely to "reduce the effects of climate change," promising that the associated article will show why "climate experts say they're wrong." The *Instagram* post's headline reads "Recycling isn't a climate solution. Here's what is" in bold white text over a photo of cardboard boxes stacked up on a city street (*Washington Post* climate coverage). As of this writing there were 332 responses, many presenting alternative viewpoints, sharing statistics, or taking the *Post* to task on problematic aspects of its reporting. Aside from some blue check marks indicating that certain commenters' accounts have been verified as authentic by *Instagram*, there is very little for readers to go on when assessing which claims are most accurate. To analyze an example like this, students would need to consider numerous elements of the rhetorical context, including the reputation and goals of the content creator, what that creator knows or assumes about their audience, the identities and motivations of commenters, the rhetorical strategies and choices evident in the text (headline, description, associated article) and visuals, the rhetorical strategies employed by commenters, the significance of the fact that this is posted on a climate-focused news account (e.g., who is or isn't likely to see the information), and the role the platform's algorithms might play in the visibility of this content. Unit 3 provides a space for doing this sort of work.

At the end of unit 3, students completed the production-focused end-of-unit assignment, informed by greater critical awareness of how environmental communicators and others (as listed in Fähnrich's article) use textual, visual, and auditory modes and specific rhetorical and explanatory techniques to achieve their goals. The project also emphasized the application of techniques for communicating ethos, establishing trust, and using sources ethically. Project options included social media posts, podcast episodes or scripts, blog posts, or multimodal digital essays similar to examples we studied from the Center for Humans and Nature and *Orion*'s online offerings: Frankie Gerraty's "Intertidal Entanglements" and Sandra Steingraber's "The Fracking of Rachel Carson." Student projects focused on a range of topics, including urban nature initiatives, water pollution, wildfire prevention for campers, deforestation, and climate change. I encouraged students to connect with environment-focused student organizations or area environmental organizations about contributing content, but only one took that optional step. (In contrast, I established community partnerships before teaching the earlier hybrid version of this course, and public dissemination was a project requirement—an approach that can be difficult to sustain but is ultimately worthwhile.)

Overall, I believe the course design successfully supported the stated learning objectives, increased students' digital media science literacy, and enhanced their awareness of the rhetorical and ethical dimensions of digital science communication. According to course evaluations, students "learned useful analytical and critical thinking skills" and found the assignments "creative, fun, and informative." They performed particularly well on the analysis assignments, arriving at insights that would be of interest to audiences beyond the course. Students' literate lives already intersect with science in important ways, so making science communication the focus of a humanities-based digital rhetoric course promotes desirable outcomes. As I anticipated, flexibility and student choice are essential in such a course.

As I prepare to teach the course again, I have planned some adjustments. First, I will continue to refine the production assignments. Although many students crafted excellent work and wrote thoughtful reflections about how they applied course concepts to meet their goals, some struggled to construct their own rhetorical situations and take on the role of science communicators. Although I had introduced examples including Fähnrich to illustrate that many people—not just scientists—participate in science communication in digital contexts, a handful of students still could not imagine themselves having something worthwhile to contribute because of limited experience with or interest in scientific topics.

Second, instead of including rhetorical analysis and content production assignments in both unit 2 and unit 3, I intend to focus exclusively on rhetorical analysis in unit 2 and on production in unit 3. This will allow for improved scaffolding, with lower-stakes mid-unit assignments creating the foundation for higher-stakes end-of-unit assessments within instead of across units. By focusing exclusively on production in unit 3, I can also include some additional checkpoints that will allow me to intervene if a student seems to be struggling.

This change would also make more room for community-engaged or other public-facing work, which I value and want to prioritize in future course revisions, in part because this would help students more readily understand the exigence to which they are responding. On campus, it would be wonderful if my students could present their science communication strategy knowledge to science majors. Partnering with the writing center and other academic support units may also be an option. I am also considering the advantages and drawbacks of using a single thematic focus for the entire course, such as sustainability. My college has made sustainability the theme of a yearlong program called 365 Days of Service and Learning, and I have communicated with faculty and staff members who lead campus sustainability initiatives about potential partnerships. Although it can be challenging to coordinate such opportunities for students enrolled in fully online courses, it is certainly possible and worth pursuing.

I designed this digital rhetoric and writing course to provide a context for analyzing contemporary digital science communication practices and developing digital media science literacy. This is necessary, timely work and an endeavor that a humanities course is particularly well suited to support. In "The Relevance and Resiliency of the Humanities," Stephen Behrendt states that "[e]thics lies at the center of the humanities, both as an academic subject and as an intellectual engine of social thought in the broader culture," and goes on to claim that "[t]he humanities and the STEM disciplines are fundamentally necessary to each other, both in academia and in our broad contemporary culture." By emphasizing the rhetorical and ethical dimensions of current science communication practices, especially on social media, the course opens critical conversations about integrity, accuracy, authority, persuasive intent, and the strengths and limitations of strategies communicators use to make science engaging and understandable to nonscientists. Ultimately, I hope that students who complete the course will do the work of holding science communicators accountable and upholding ethical communication principles in their own contributions to these discourses.

Works Cited

Behrendt, Stephen C. "The Relevance and Resiliency of the Humanities." *Profession*, Dec. 2017, profession.mla.org/the-relevance-and-resiliency-of-the -humanities/.

Dahlstrom, Michael F. "Using Narratives and Storytelling to Communicate Science with Nonexpert Audiences." *PNAS*, vol. 111. no. 4, 2014, pp. 13614–20.

Eyman, Douglas. *Digital Rhetoric: Theory, Method, Practice.* U of Michigan P, 2015.

Fähnrich, Birte. "Conceptualizing Science Communication in Flux—a Framework for Analyzing Science Communication in a Digital Media Environment." *JCOM*, vol. 20, no. 3, 2021, pp. 1–13.

Gerraty, Frankie. "Intertidal Entanglements." *Center for Humans and Nature*, 23 June 2020, humansandnature.org/intertidal-entanglements/.

Gurak, Laura J. "Ethos, Trust, and the Rhetoric of Digital Writing in Scientific and Technical Discourse." *The Routledge Handbook of Digital Writing and Rhetoric*, edited by Jonathan Alexander and Jacqueline Rhodes, Routledge, 2018, pp. 124–31.

Hitlin, Paul, and Kenneth Olmstead. *The Science People See on Social Media.* Pew Research Center, Mar. 2018, www.pewresearch.org/internet/wp-content/up loads/sites/9/2018/03/PS_2018.03.21_Facebook-and-Science_FINAL.pdf.

Howell, Emily L., and Dominique Brossard. "(Mis)Informed about What? What It Means to Be a Science-Literate Citizen in a Digital World." *PNAS*, vol. 118, no. 15, 2021, pp. 1–8.

Lillie, Ben. "Science and the Art of Personal Storytelling." *Science Blogging: The Essential Guide*, edited by Christie Wilcox et al., Yale UP, 2016, pp. 96–103.

McGrath, Laura, and Letizia Guglielmo. "Communities of Practice and Makerspaces: DMAC's Influence on Technological Professional Development and Teaching Multimodal Composing." *Computers and Composition*, vol. 36, no. 1, 2015, pp. 44–53.

Nicotra, Jodie. *Becoming Rhetorical: Analyzing and Composing in a Multimedia World.* Cengage, 2019.

Saks, Emily, and Alec Tyson. "Americans Report More Engagement with Science News than in 2017." *Pew Research Center*, 10 Nov. 2022, www.pewresearch.org/short-reads/2022/11/10/americans-report-more-engagement-with-science-news-than-in-2017/.

Steingraber, Sandra. "The Fracking of Rachel Carson." *Orion*, 23 Aug. 2012, orionmagazine.org/article/the-fracking-of-rachel-carson/.

Washington Post climate coverage [@postclimate]. "Recycling isn't a climate solution. Here's what is." *Instagram*, 28 Aug. 2023, www.instagram.com/p/CwgisLDMsTU/.

"WRIT 3150: Writing and Digital Culture." *Kennesaw State University*, 2021, catalog.kennesaw.edu/preview_course_nopop.php?catoid=72&coid=117536.

Zerbe, Michael J. *Composition and the Rhetoric of Science: Engaging the Dominant Discourse.* Southern Illinois UP, 2007.

Marissa Kopp

Science, Stories, and Academic Ecology

My first draft curriculum for teaching writing to ecology undergraduates read much like a battle plan: I anticipated toiling to convince burgeoning scientists that writing was as worthy of their time as chemistry and statistics were. To my (pleasant) surprise, I was proved wrong. In introductory surveys, students overwhelmingly named writing as a linchpin of success in their degrees, careers, and lives. Yet, simultaneously, they confessed their dread at taking a writing class. Many delayed until the last possible semester despite knowing that they needed, and wanted, to improve their writing.[1] My plan shifted from battle to treatment: students needed a therapeutic space to reimagine their relationship with writing.

This scene was familiar. In the years that I tutored at a college writing center, humanities students stumbled to me—the lone scientist—with a data-dense journal article clutched in their hands and desperation in their eyes. They wanted to supplement their arguments with "the science," yet it seemed locked beyond reach, the story hidden amid labyrinths of P values and six-syllable jargon.

Both situations exemplify the same cycle of frustration: students reach toward knowledge from another discipline, find themselves ill-equipped to comprehend (let alone implement) this knowledge, then receive poor grades for their struggle. This cycle creates negative self-perceptions ("I'm a bad writer" or "I don't get the science") that become self-fulfilling prophecies: my ecology students struggle to write the kind of paper that my English students struggle to read.

No one panacea will break the cycle; however, a starting point is to use our classrooms as spaces to heal from the lingering myth of a science/humanities dichotomy. A step in this direction is to uncover, and celebrate, the often hidden synergies between literature, rhetoric, and the science writing crafted *by* experts *for* experts. I use US scientific ecology as a case study to assert that *all* science writing (even a data-dense story) is inextricably entangled with humanistic theories and legacies. Working from this expanded notion of science writing, I turn to the matter of cultivating classrooms—led by scientists, humanists, or both—that facilitate students' access to the underexploited wealth of inter-expert scientific texts and spaces.

Expanding the Notion of Science Writing

Ecology—the study of relationships between the living and nonliving—is a discipline shaped by leaders who could be called writers as readily as they could be called scientists. Modern US environmentalism is as readily traced to Aldo Leopold's pen as it is to any pipette; similarly, the US Environmental Protection Agency has called itself the "extended shadow" of Rachel Carson's *Silent Spring* (Lewis). Contemporary practitioners discussed within this collection, such as Robin Wall Kimmerer, epitomize the tradition of moving science from a private laboratory to the public library. Yet few of the more than nine thousand ecology students trained annually will become science popularizers ("Environmental Science"). Most science stories never escape the ivory tower—instead, they hang in posters pinned to university halls, echo in closed conference rooms, or join the ever-expanding body of disciplinary knowledge (Baron 3). This insularity, in turn, perpetuates the illusion that such inter-expert science communications are isolated from the humanistic influences self-evident in popular science writing.

Examining how we teach US ecologists shatters this illusion. The humanities appear in our scientific textbooks: *The Princeton Guide to Ecology*, an authoritative textbook in the field, highlights publications by William Wordsworth and Henry David Thoreau as "milestones in ecology"

(Morris 764–65). The humanities appear in our conferences: the 2022 Tri-Societies international conference (celebrating agronomy, crop science, and soil science) featured readings from Virgil's *Georgics* and open-mic poetry slams. Humanists themselves appear in our journals, with calls for "deeper integration between the two fields" (Druschke and McGreavy 51). Evidently, the humanities haunt most purportedly scientific spaces.

Yet merely highlighting these appearances undersells humanistic influence on ecological sciences, particularly the influence of writing. I teach from the text *Writing Science*, by the ecologist Joshua Schimel, which he bookends with a simple claim: "As a scientist, you are a professional writer" (3, 204). Truthfully, every step of the scientific process requires us to write, and those who write well shape scientific exploration. New scientific ideas are born in grant writing, where successful writers must convince funders that problems merit investigation. We write protocols to define our investigative approach, and we chart our progress in written activity reports. We write academic articles to decipher this progress, and the act of writing with coauthors distills and refines our conclusions. Our final products are stories about our data that must be good enough for others to read, share, and amplify, because we measure scientific impact not just by how many papers we publish but also by how often others cite them (e.g., the h-index). None of these written products are intended for the public. Yet they are persuasive, rhetorical acts, which supports Schimel's claim that successful ecologists are those who shift perspectives from "treating writing as something a scientist *does*" to "treating *being a writer* as something a scientist *is*" (6).

Still, my examples of inter-expert writing likely conjure the image of dry, data-dense reports far diverged from Kimmerer's best-selling *Braiding Sweetgrass*. To continue shattering the illusion, we might consider one of the most competitive and prestigious grants for ecology students. The US National Science Foundation's Graduate Research Fellowship Program draws over ten thousand applicants each year, and of those applicants about three in twenty are successful (Hu). Their success hinges on two core components: a research statement (the story of the science) and a personal statement (the story of the scientist). According to the foundation, personal statements are a call to "[w]eave together your personal story with your academic and career plans and past experiences" ("Personal, Relevant Background"). Skimming hundreds of successful examples unveils classic storytelling elements (Lang). Scientists-turned-narrators shed the royal pronouns and passive voice to reclaim the personal "I." Some write love letters—where they first bumped into science, how they fell in love with science, and why they've committed for the long haul. Some write memoirs. My own proposal opened with a childhood spent catching blue crabs along Assawoman Bay, where I witnessed an ecosystem's decline that drives my research today. Others write eulogies—a mourning for species they tried, and failed, to save. All employ elements of mystery, ending on the tantalizing cliff-hanger of knowledge yet to be discovered. It is fitting, then, that we call these our grant *narratives.*

Thus, scientists *are* writers and must be trained as such. However, scientists invest most of their energy into writing not intended for a general public. This investment creates a vast yet relatively untapped pool of inter-expert science stories, and science writing classrooms have the potential to welcome practices that tap into this resource.

Bringing an Expanded Notion of Science Writing into the Humanities Classroom

Science writing educators have an opportunity to ask, How can we help students activate the energy trapped in inter-expert science writing? The sections that follow offer strategies for three approaches to answering this question: teaching science students to tell better stories, teaching humanities students to access inter-expert science writing, and collocating scientists and humanists to explore existing science stories and cocreate new ones.

Teaching Science Students to Tell Better Stories

Helping students access the knowledge trapped in inter-expert science writing begins with making such writing more accessible, a feat accomplished by teaching scientists to tell better stories about their data. While humanists devote ample time to teaching (and practicing) storytelling, scientists stepping into the role of writing instructor may find that their own writing training has been informal. Since many scientists are not formally trained communicators (Ritchie et al.), our writing practices may be shaped by personal anecdotes, trial and error, or inheritances from our mentors rather than theory-driven writing pedagogy. However, scientists can readily deploy rhetorically informed teaching models by adopting three vetted tenets: making writing a habit, writing in multiple genres, and reviewing others' work frequently (Druschke et al., "Better Science"

178–80). These methods improve STEM students' writing behaviors and confidence after just two writing workshops (Druschke et al., "Low-Investment, High-Impact Approach" 5).

For science students to tell better stories, they must begin by telling any story—that is, writing must become a habit. Yet putting pen to paper proves challenging for many science students. One common challenge is a lack of time to write. Another challenge is an inability to reckon with the emotions that hinder writing, such as perfectionism and fear of criticism. These emotions feel taboo to acknowledge in scientific spaces, which emphasize rationality. In class I address both challenges through frequent low-stakes (e.g., short or ungraded) reflections. I assign weekly journaling on writing successes and anxieties paired with a reading from *The Scientist's Guide to Writing* (Heard 22–29), which normalizes the practice of acknowledging and reflecting on our writing behaviors. Recurring low-stakes writing lowers the activation energy needed to spur students into forming positive writing habits, and these habits render revising and refining our science stories a less burdensome task.

Once students begin to write, they must write "early and often," in multiple genres, for real audiences (Druschke et al., "Better Science" 179). Though a scientist's audience is rarely a general public, neither is it uniformly made up of academics within their niche area of expertise. Readers of top journals (e.g., *Nature* or *Science*) are diverse global experts, and expertise transcends scientists: ecologists engage local practitioners with lived expertise (foresters, Indigenous land stewards, and beyond), whom scientists risk alienating if they assume that their language and values completely overlap. This assumption fails even for the seemingly homogenous audience of scientific ecologists: I study soil carbon dioxide efflux, and I never assume that my peers who study salamander movements or cacao genetics are more familiar with this process, or why it matters, than a local farmer or a journalist reading *Nature* is. As such, any benefits of perpetuating less generally accessible writing practices (underdefining jargon, burying the lede, etc.), even in inter-expert writing, do not outweigh the risk—namely, that we lose our reader altogether (Schimel 149). Thus, *all* science writing encompasses genres improved by the adage "know thy audience," a skill that STEM students themselves recognize as vital (Ritchie et al.). To hone this skill, my students trace transformations of primary scientific writing to new genres—for instance, academically rigorous journalism, such as *The Conversation*—to learn how writers recycle and repackage information for different audiences. Students then transform their own inter-expert writing through a project in which they write in a new genre (which has ranged from fact sheets to social media posts) and reflect on their rhetorical choices. These activities build critical translational writing skills (Beaufort 17–21) and increase students' motivation by giving students agency to choose genres that reflect their interests.[2]

Students learn to fine-tune writing (of all genres) through feedback from readers with diverse experiences and interests; consequently, frequent reviews are vital in science writing classrooms. Rather than wait to review completed drafts, I incorporate reviews throughout the writing process (outlines, figures, or a single thesis statement). Early feedback reorients students before they submit assignments that may miss guidelines or develop illogical arguments. While reviews can occur asynchronously, students enjoy talking about writing with their peers and the instructor. In fall 2022, thirty percent of my students' end-of-semester reviews named feedback through discussion as an aspect of the course that helped them learn. Since one-on-one instructor conferences are time-consuming, I supplement these with self-reviews, in which students target and submit evidence of specific revisions (e.g., through tracked changes in Microsoft Word).[3] Overall, these experiences improve students' writing during class and prepare them to engage in formal peer review during their careers, both as reviewees writing and as reviewers assessing inter-expert science writing with the goal of creating more accessible stories.

Teaching Humanities Students to Access Inter-Expert Science Writing

Some of the best writing educators whom I have had the pleasure of working alongside have found working with science students an intimidating task—if instructors struggle to pronounce *phytate mineralization*, could they critique a paper on it? It is unreasonable for humanists to extend themselves into niche areas of scientific expertise; instead, those tasked with teaching writing that incorporates science can encourage students to access inter-expert science writing by finding writing worth reading, then reading like a scientist.

Humanities students struggle to find relevant sources in scientific journals because the quantity and specificity of articles render sifting for relevant knowledge overwhelming. To mitigate these issues, I offer two suggestions. First, direct students to journals that require what are referred to as "plain language summaries"—a second abstract stripped of jargon to reach broader audiences. These simplified abstracts allow for rapid sorting of materials to identify papers worth reading closely. Second, direct students to syntheses on a current state of knowledge, such as literature reviews or meta-analyses, to glean trends and knowledge gaps. These genres speak holistically while maintaining the rigor of scientific peer review, which popular science books often lack.[4]

After finding writing worth reading, it is necessary to teach students to read science stories like a scientist. Students learn critical reading strategies in a literary context, and while activating prior knowledge is generally helpful, when students misapply that knowledge in a new disciplinary context, it obstructs their learning and performance (Ambrose et al. 21). Humanities students have likely learned to carefully read papers from start to finish, but few scientists read papers this way (Pain). Rather, most skip to the discussion for key takeaways (Pain). I find that students get stuck amid technical details of methods that scientists themselves rarely read unless they plan to replicate an experiment. Instead, humanities students can critique science papers through credibility assessments suited for any primary literature source (the journal's legitimacy, the authors' vested interests, etc.). Moreover, students from "nonscience, nonquantitative backgrounds" will find that most flawed science falls prey to logical fallacies that are the backbone of argumentation: "the data are flawed or unrepresentative, or the conclusions and interpretation are unjustified. Students do not need a great deal of technical training to spot these problems."[5] Without opening the "black box" that is performing a technical method, students can still critique the data that go into science stories and the conclusions that come out (West and Bergstrom).

Together, these strategies encourage humanities students to find, read, and critique science papers as a scientist would. By engaging with inter-expert science writing, students can access cutting-edge knowledge with countless applications: enriching literary interpretations with the biophysical context from which a piece arose, confirming translations of species' names, complicating representations of environmental disasters in contemporary texts, contesting "hard" science fiction, and more. Beyond their scholarship, students need these skills in their lives: accessing primary scientific knowledge is essential for critical thinking and rational decision-making in an era of mounting misinformation (West and Bergstrom).

Collocating Scientists and Humanists

The previous strategies envisage classrooms with instructors of one expertise teaching students about another area of expertise. However, such disciplinary divides may not apply to today's increasingly transdisciplinary humanities classrooms. One way to lean into this transdisciplinarity is to collocate scientists and humanists—that is, to help humanities students access not only scientific texts but also the spaces where science happens. Accessing such spaces bypasses the issue of knowledge captive in inter-expert science writing by empowering students to uncover it themselves, to experience their own encounters with and within ecosystems, and to record their reflections alongside scientists.

Such efforts are not new. Scattered across the United States are ecological research programs dedicated to centuries-long, place-based observations in which scholars spanning disciplines congregate to explore their own questions and to enrich others' explorations. Perhaps the most well-known is the Long-Term Ecological Reflections Project, which has supported partnerships between literary and scientific writers, for example, as they untangle over two hundred years of change at the H. J. Andrews Experimental Forest in Oregon (Brodie et al.). These collaborations between the arts, the humanities, and science increase participants' knowledge of, attitudes toward, and motivations to learn about ecological processes while also increasing empathetic awareness of more-than-human others (Goralnik et al.). Yet this network is only one of many such opportunities for humanities' instructors to access scientific spaces.[6] The National Ecological Observatory Network, the Critical Zone Collaborative Network, and countless others present opportunities for educators to visit local sites with students alongside ecologists, craft writing inspired by students' observations, and preserve this writing in long-term records.[7]

Collocating science and humanities students is mutually enriching. Humanities students learn the "why" behind their observations and how mechanistic explanations for ecological phenomena arise from these very acts of observation.[8] In essence, they learn how "science" happens and can use it to inform interpretations of others' writing, to inspire their own writing, or both. Simultaneously, science students learn the "how to" for new and improved ways to express these data and processes in their own stories.

Teaching ecology and English students has taught me that both share common frustrations: one group wants to share their knowledge but dreads the act of writing about it; the other wants to gain that knowledge but dreads wading through jargon to find it. This fear factor shapes students' careers and lives (Baron 103–04). Science students who fear writing risk telling stories read by few or misunderstood by many, and humanities students who fear engaging with science risk misunderstanding it or, worse, never encountering it at all. My goal as an instructor is to move students from this place of fear to one of discovery, even joy, and the humanities classroom is an excellent vehicle. Positive, lasting encounters with science writing in the humanities classroom take many forms. For science students, it may be when they first tell a story that makes their science matter to a new audience; for humanities students, it may be when they first wield data to clinch their claim. Popular science writing facilitates these encounters, but we can complement such efforts with the communications in which scientists are most invested—inter-expert science writing.

Notes

Teaching experiences referenced throughout this essay were made possible through funds from a US Agriculture and Food Research Initiative predoctoral fellowship (2022-67011-36460).

1. Though I highlight my anecdotal experience, it is echoed across universities (see, e.g., Druschke et al., "Better Science" 184).

2. "Optimiz[ing] individual choice and autonomy" is a key strategy for encouraging students' interest under recent Universal Design for Learning guidelines ("UDL Guidelines").

3. I use Schimel's end-of-chapter exercises.

4. Consider *The Hidden Life of Trees*, by Peter Wohlleben, a book that is publicly popular yet so scientifically controversial that scientists started a petition "about how we represent scientific knowledge to the lay public," which garnered over 4,500 signatures (Kingsland).

5. See Bergstrom and West for free curricular resources.

6. By "scientific spaces," I mean physical spaces where science happens, not that such spaces belong to scientists. Rather, humanist collaborations may help scientists reckon with the (often fraught) histories of these spaces in hopes that we might decolonize and reimagine them.

7. While I encourage using scientific spaces to collocate humanists' and scientists' research, students can experience rich observational encounters in any outdoor spaces (see Miller's essay in this collection).

8. A classic example is how the ecologist Robert MacArthur observed birds feeding in a forest in order to elucidate the ecological niche, an invaluable insight formed without the technological assistance of so much as a stopwatch (603).

Works Cited

Ambrose, Susan A., et al. *How Learning Works: Seven Research-Based Principles for Smart Teaching*. John Wiley and Sons, 2010.

Baron, Nancy. *Escape from the Ivory Tower: A Guide to Making Your Science Matter*. Island Press, 2010.

Beaufort, Anne. *College Writing and Beyond: A New Framework for University Writing Instruction*. Utah State UP, 2007.

Bergstrom, Carl T., and Jevin West. Syllabus for Calling Bullshit: Data Reasoning in a Digital World. *Calling Bullshit*, 2017–19, www.callingbullshit.org/sylla bus.html.

Brodie, Nathaniel, et al., editors. *Forest Under Story: Creative Inquiry in an Old-Growth Forest*. U of Washington P, 2018.

Druschke, Caroline Gottschalk, and Bridie McGreavy. "Why Rhetoric Matters for Ecology." *Frontiers in Ecology and the Environment*, vol. 14, no. 1, 2016, pp. 46–52, https://doi.org/10.1002/16-0113.1.

Druschke, Caroline Gottschalk, et al. "Better Science through Rhetoric: A New Model and Pilot Program for Training Graduate Student Science Writers." *Technical Communication Quarterly*, vol. 27, no. 2, 2018, pp. 175–90, https://doi.org/10.1080/10572252.2018.1425735.

Druschke, Caroline Gottschalk, et al. "A Low-Investment, High-Impact Approach for Training Stronger and More Confident Graduate Student Science Writers." *Conservation Science and Practice*, vol. 4, no. 1, 2022, article no. e573, https://doi.org/10.1111/csp2.573.

"Environmental Science." *Data USA*, datausa.io/profile/cip/environmental -science. Accessed 14 Mar. 2025.

Goralnik, Lissy, et al. "Arts and Humanities Inquiry in the Long-Term Ecological Research Network: Empathy, Relationships, and Interdisciplinary Collaborations." *Journal of Environmental Studies and Sciences*, vol. 7, 2017, pp. 361–73, https://doi.org/10.1007/s13412-016-0415-4.

Heard, Stephen B. *The Scientist's Guide to Writing*. Princeton UP, 2016.

Hu, Jane C. "NSF Graduate Fellowships Disproportionately Go to Students at a Few Top Schools." *Science*, 26 Aug. 2019, www.science.org/content/article/ nsf-graduate-fellowships-disproportionately-go-students-few-top-schools.

Kingsland, Sharon Elizabeth. "Facts or Fairy Tales? Peter Wohlleben and the Hidden Life of Trees." *Bulletin of the Ecological Society of America*, vol. 99, no. 4, 2018, article no. e01443, https://doi.org/10.1002/bes2.1443.

Lang, Alex. "NSF GRFP Examples." 2022, docs.google.com/spreadsheets/ d/1xoezGhbtcpg3BvNdag2F5dTQM-Xl2EELUgAfG1eUg0s/edit#gid=0.

Lewis, Jack. "The Birth of EPA." *EPA Journal*, Nov. 1985. *US Environmental Protection Agency*, 6 Sept. 2016, www.epa.gov/archive/epa/aboutepa/birth -epa.html.

MacArthur, Robert H. "Population Ecology of Some Warblers of Northeastern Coniferous Forests." *Ecology*, vol. 39, no. 4, 1958, pp. 599–619.

Morris, Christopher. "Milestones in Ecology." *The Princeton Guide to Ecology*, edited by Simon A. Levin, Princeton UP, 2009, pp. 761–73.

Pain, Elisabeth. "How to (Seriously) Read a Scientific Paper." *Science*, 21 Mar. 2016, www.science.org/content/article/how-seriously-read-scientific-paper.

"Personal, Relevant Background and Future Goals Statement and Graduate Research Plan Statements." *NSF GRFP*, www.nsfgrfp.org/applicants/state ments/. Accessed 21 Apr. 2023.

Ritchie, Tessy S., et al. "How Do STEM Graduate Students Perceive Science Communication? Understanding Science Communication Perceptions of

Future Scientists." *PLOS One*, vol. 17, no. 10, 2022, article no. e0274840, https://doi.org/10.1371/journal.pone.0274840.

Schimel, Joshua. *Writing Science: How to Write Papers That Get Cited and Proposals That Get Funded*. Oxford UP, 2012.

"The UDL Guidelines." *UDL Guidelines*, version 2.2, 2018, udlguidelines.cast .org/more/downloads/#v2.

West, Jevin D., and Carl T. Bergstrom. "Misinformation in and about Science." *PNAS*, vol. 118, no. 15, 2021, article no. e1912444117, https://doi.org/ 10.1073/pnas.1912444117.

Luke Rodewald

Environmental Science Communication as Storytelling

In an article for *PNAS*, the official journal of the National Academy of Sciences, Michael F. Dahlstrom argues for narrative writing's unique ability to transform technical-based scientific communication into compelling, comprehensible, and persuasive texts capable of engaging a broad public readership. Concluding his broad literature review about narrative communication and its potential for scientific research, he remarks, "[N]arratives are easier to process and generate more attention and engagement than traditional logical-scientific communication" (13617). Dahlstrom's assertion echoes other sentiments by science communication scholars, including those of the geoscientist Scott L. Montgomery in *The Scientific Voice*, an influential examination of the historic yet evolving relationship between science and discourse. Identifying the field's heavy reliance on technical language, which "sets up a barrier between those who can speak and understand and those who cannot" (7), Montgomery argues, not unproblematically, that "[t]he language of science is the tongue of foreigners, equally exotic whether spoken in the narrative hut of the laboratory or the villages and cliff-dwellings of the professional meeting" (8–9). Such scholarship reflects a growing recognition by scientific researchers of the need to incorporate communicative strategies that

115

allow their research to transcend obscurity and become accessible to a wider audience.[1]

In a similar vein, the environmental education scholar David Orr has famously claimed, regarding efforts to confront ongoing global ecological crises, "The plain fact is that the planet does not need more successful people. But it does desperately need more peacemakers, healers, restorers, storytellers, and lovers of every kind" (12). To this end, recent nonfiction bestsellers such as Elizabeth Kolbert's *The Sixth Extinction*, Helen Macdonald's *H Is for Hawk*, Sy Montgomery's *The Soul of an Octopus*, Suzanne Simard's *Finding the Mother Tree*, and Aimee Nezhukumatathil's *World of Wonders* reveal an expanding cultural appetite not only for more accessible environmental science writing but also for works that emphasize and embrace the value of story and narrative in articulating scientific research. For example, in her review of Simard's *Finding the Mother Tree* for *The Guardian*, Tiffany Francis-Baker praises Simard's ability to situate her groundbreaking research on forest communication within a personal journey of self-discovery, ultimately claiming that the book "demonstrates how storytelling can ignite something science alone cannot." These works transcend conventional genre borders, emerging as environmental memoirs where personal history, scientific research, and environmental advocacy are braided together through widely comprehensible prose or anecdotes. In doing so, environmental memoirs and other long-form personal essays complicate perceived boundaries between object and subject, putting hard data into the context of individual experience. Collectively, such writing—and its increasing popularity—signifies the critical role of storytelling for successful environmental science communication today.

Recognizing the value of narrative both as an object of study and as a mode of writing in a college composition classroom, this essay advocates for teaching environmental science communication through and as storytelling. In alignment with a growing field of science communicators who call for a wider embrace of creative writing techniques when articulating insights from scientific research, I consider teaching such content through popular works of environmental memoir. Moreover, while narrative has long been a familiar genre for composition pedagogy—for example, in the form of first-year writing literacy narratives and other reflective self-life writing opportunities—less attention has been focused on the possibility of its being transferred to other forms of composition, such as scientific and technical communication (Goldman). This essay situates narrative, storytelling, and self-life writing as forms that can scaffold student success in other compositional genres. After broadly surveying the environmental memoir's unique literary and pedagogical qualities, I zoom in on exemplary works by Robin Wall Kimmerer, Michael Pollan, and Barbara Kingsolver that seek to illuminate issues related to contemporary global food systems and industrial agriculture practices yet are also written primarily as narrative accounts of each author's firsthand observations and experiences. I demonstrate how a close study of such scientific rhetoric grounded in personal experience illustrates to students the nuances of argument and persuasion within contemporary environmental science writing and underscores how an author's use of individual experience can captivate a reader. Ultimately, this essay avers that by braiding principles of storytelling, narrative, and science research into their composition pedagogy, instructors can broaden their students' imaginations regarding what constitutes effective science communication and also lead them to understand that their own personal stories hold great rhetorical power.

Science, Narrative, and the Environmental Memoir

Conveying scientific information using communicative styles beyond technical genres is ultimately an exercise in foregrounding accessibility and comprehensibility. Such a task, however, requires a familiarization with writing techniques traditionally considered taboo for scientific discourse. While recognizing this disciplinary hesitancy, Bethann Garramon Merkle, the director of the Wyoming Science Communication Initiative, suggests that techniques from creative nonfiction writing can resonate with scientific communication objectives because "creativity is fundamental to scientific process and progress" (1). To this end, genres that emphasize narrative and storytelling—such as the memoir and long-form personal essay—emerge as ripe terrain for experimenting with structure, voice, and language as they relate to science. Inversely, integrating science research, content, and their writing into the composition classroom—and, in particular, first-year writing curricula—offers alternative ways of thinking about research and positionality for students and models an inquiry-based rhetorical approach that better facilitates knowledge and skill transfer into other STEM courses and endeavors (Thaiss and Wade 373). The stakes of such an instructional move can also, as Tonya Train and Yuko Miyamoto's study suggests, enhance students' confidence in their communication skills and their understanding of research as it relates to writing (76).

For the purposes of this pedagogy-focused essay, my understanding of narrative draws on Jerome Bruner's landmark consideration of the concept,[2] situating it as a method for organizing and making sense—a cognitive "cultural tool kit" for comprehending information and articulating that understanding to others (20). For Merkle, such an understanding of what constitutes successful narrative storytelling reveals its intrinsic connection to traditional forms of scientific communication: "a popular article, a science essay, and the reporting of scientific inquiry are all fundamentally, justifiably, and necessarily a story" (1). Merkle's emphasis on "story" here—which she justifies because of the genre's traits of sequential events, characters, and setting—parallels scholarship on the possibilities of fusion between narrative and science writing instruction. In their overview of the potential intersections between narrative and science writing, Lucy Avraamidou and Jonathan Osborne identify common trademarks of narratives: advancing an overarching purpose and featuring a recognizable chain of events, temporal structure, sense of agency, and some inferred sense of a "narrator" presenting the content to a reader (1693). Avraamidou and Osborne point to Carola Conle's research on narrative-based instructional approaches, which argued that such practices yield a range of benefits for students, including increased comprehension, heightened critical thinking skills, and more meaningful connections with course content. Likewise, Karen Meyer cites her integration of storytelling as a means for facilitating more active student participation—particularly by female students—in her science courses, a move that allowed her class to "trespass within science discourse" through its centering of personal experience (467).

While Avraamidou and Osborne focus on the potential of fictional narratives and short stories for communicating scientific concepts, I have found the burgeoning genres of environmental and nature memoirs to also be especially valuable in offering students accessible entry points for both analyzing and creating environmental science composition. While not a new genre by any means—Rachel Carson's *Under the Sea Wind* (1941), Annie Dillard's *Pilgrim at Tinker Creek* (1974), and Barry Lopez's *Arctic Dreams* (1986) remain iconic milestones for nonfiction writing as a whole—such works have found increasing relevance in our current age of escalating ecological crisis. Kimmerer's *Braiding Sweetgrass*, for example, has remained near the top of the *New York Times* bestseller list for over 180 weeks, with more than 1.5 million copies in print and audio (Heller). Through the weaving together of either original or established research with accounts of memory, witness, and firsthand experience, works of environmental memoir illustrate how scientific insights about more-than-human life can resonate on a personal level. Moreover, with their attention to literary flourishes—an emphasis on the aesthetic use of imagery, figurative language, and other creative writing trademarks—such pieces facilitate not only the reader's increased familiarity with natural science information but also a deepened emotional engagement with this subject matter. For the pedagogical objectives of the composition classroom, the genre also provides an opportunity for students to approach scientific and technical writing through a personal lens and facilitates critical thinking about the dynamics of environmental science research, rhetoric, and communication.

I have incorporated works of environmental memoir into a variety of composition courses, ranging from first-year writing courses to seminars focused on environmental nonfiction. In addition to the rhetorical qualities listed above, the genre's utilization of narrative and storytelling devices—and, consequently, its usefulness as an introduction for students to integrating research into personal writing—further warrants its ongoing inclusion in my curricula. For example, Nezhukumatathil's *World of Wonders*—a collection of vignettes on flora and fauna—situates scientific insights about natural phenomena within the author's memories of growing up in different regions of the United States. In one standout essay titled "Vampire Squid," Nezhukumatathil highlights the creatures' brilliant ability to avoid likely predators through acts of speed, deception, and disorientation. The author considers such biological faculties in light of the displacement she felt when moving from New York to Ohio during high school. Recalling her perceived alienation from her new classmates, Nezhukumatathil writes, "This was my cephalopod year, the closest I ever came to wanting to disappear or sneak away into the deep sea" (55). While the rest of the essay details the author's transition from this period of loneliness to one of confidence in her writing and social skills, she returns to this parallel and considers its impact on her, now from a distance, as a college professor who attempts to connect with a wide range of student personalities: "I emerged from my cephalopod year, exited my midnight zone. But I'm grateful for my time there. If not for that shadow year, how would I know how to search the faces of my own students?" (57). Other essays similarly juxtapose scientific research on more-than-human life—narwhals, corpse flowers, axolotls, cassowaries—with Nezhukumatathil's anecdotal reflections on childhood, adolescence, and eventually parenting.

I have used excerpts from *World of Wonders*, as well as the book as a whole, in both first-year writing seminars and environmentally themed literature and composition courses. The brevity of Nezhukumatathil's essays—most falling between four and six pages—renders them ideal texts for classroom analysis and discussion and as models for students' own composition. In an essay assignment mimicking Nezhukumatathil's structure, students select a natural object, creature, or phenomenon; research its properties; and ultimately establish a connection to their life through the creation of an extended metaphor. The project not only allows students to consider how to highlight particular aspects of scientific information about more-than-human life—a subject's physical characteristics, traits, habits, or life cycle—but also requires them to think deeply about intersections between their own lived experiences and those of beings seemingly unlike themselves. Moreover, such essays invite students to experiment with creative nonfiction techniques, including the use of "I," the construction of metaphors, and the embrace of sensory-based imagery and language—all devices that expand traditional modes of scientific discourse and rhetoric. My students' final pieces demonstrate their understanding of how scientific research—whether on backyard fruit trees or mosquitoes or hermit crabs—can be integrated into the larger canvas of nonfiction composition as well as how they can artfully convey otherwise technical information to a nonexpert reader.

Thinking and Writing about Food, Science, and Stories

While such a singular assignment and unit may fit within a spectrum of humanities courses, the remainder of this essay reflects on an extended study of environmental memoir in a focused upper-level composition seminar. In this course, categorized under the larger thematic umbrella of environmental nonfiction, students considered a number of prolonged narrative engagements with food and contemporary agricultural practices, including Pollan's *The Omnivore's Dilemma*, Kingsolver's cowritten *Animal, Vegetable, Miracle*, and Kimmerer's *Braiding Sweetgrass*. Compared with other significant works of expository composition that students examined—such as Jonathan Safran Foer's *Eating Animals*, Vandana Shiva's *Stolen Harvest*, and essays by Wendell Berry, Anthony Bourdain, and Andrea Nguyen—these three texts offered a sustained consideration of how mainstream narrative writing could meaningfully contribute to environmental science discourse. The science and industrial practices behind food, I have found, is an especially compelling topic for students because so much of what we explore hides in plain sight—at the grocery store, in their dining halls, and inside their dorm room's mini-fridge. Furthermore, as students' robust engagement with these three environmental memoirs demonstrates, food can also emerge as an enticing channel to creating narrative composition projects that articulate environmental science information alongside engrossing narratives of personal experience.

Kingsolver's and Pollan's books serve as particularly dynamic companion texts, in that their explicit and implicit critiques of contemporary food systems unsettle much of what students and I see as the status quo. *Animal, Vegetable, Miracle*—which Kingsolver cowrote with her husband and two daughters—chronicles one year of the family's efforts to exist on an entirely local diet, largely derived directly from their 4.5-acre farm in southwestern Virginia. Kingsolver records the fluctuations of the growing season and her family's struggles and triumphs to live outside industrial food systems while also emphasizing the importance of supporting local agriculture, reducing carbon footprints, and spiritually reconnecting with the land. Meanwhile, Pollan's *The Omnivore's Dilemma* traces four different food chains—industrial, organic, local, and hunter-gatherer—with each representing a distinct way of obtaining sustenance. While much of the book is dedicated to illuminating concealed dimensions of the sources of familiar meal options, Pollan also contextualizes this research with his firsthand experience of visiting numerous farms, feedlots, and industrial facilities. At the heart of this inquiry is Pollan's pursuit of the "perfect meal," an idealized image wherein the author can dine "in full consciousness of everything involved in feeding [himself]" (9).

While both Kingsolver's and Pollan's memoirs exemplify how narrative can work in tandem with environmental science research to successfully inform, the books also present students with intriguing, distinct approaches for advancing an argumentative stance through personal rhetoric. Kingsolver frames her family's collaborative memoir as an explicit case for the benefits of local agricultural practices, especially those that reject the unsustainable turbo speed of familiar factory models. In a chapter on asparagus—the first crop to ripen on their farm—Kingsolver not only details the plant's natural and cultural history but also situates its growing and harvest—a relatively small window each year—as part of a willful act by an eater to reject the ecological malpractices of today's industrial food systems. Directly critiquing the "fuel economy" and extensive oil consumption underlying the bulk of out-of-season produce found at most domestic grocery stores, she avers, "Respecting the dignity of a spectacular food means enjoying it at its best," an endeavor that requires waiting—something she also sees as "part of most value equations"—for foods to come into their natural seasons (Kingsolver et al. 30). Further condemning what she considers a national diet of "instant gratification," Kingsolver states, "The main barrier standing between ourselves and a local-food culture is not price, but attitude. The most difficult requirements are patience and a pinch of restraint" (31). Throughout the rest of the memoir, Kingsolver records her family's attempt to embody this subversive understanding of food, highlighting the extreme nutritional and ethical disparities between the produce and animals raised on their farm and those readers can locate in most supermarket chains.

As an acclaimed novelist and essayist—and recent cowinner of the Pulitzer Prize for Fiction—Kingsolver illustrates how embracing creative writing methods can transform technical information into artful, captivating prose. Beyond her own writing, each chapter's inclusion of tangential asides by Kingsolver's husband, the environmental scientist Steven L. Hopp, further contextualizes the family's story by offering accessible morsels of information on topics like seed sovereignty, pesticides, community gardens, and fair-trade legislation. As such, Kingsolver's memoir provides students with an understanding of the multiple ways in which scientific research can augment personal narrative in positing an explicit argument.

In this regard, Pollan's book diverges from Kingsolver's in that Pollan's rhetoric is significantly more nuanced—even ambiguous at times. In my course, students consider excerpts from *Animal, Vegetable, Miracle* before turning to Pollan's visit to an industrial feedlot (65–84), where the author seeks direct contact with a steer he purchased from a South Dakota cattle ranch. Pollan describes the creature's journey from birth to branding to castration to the feedlot pen, where such cattle are fed unnatural diets of corn and exist largely within a confined space that is a breeding ground for bacterial mutagens. Along the way, Pollan incorporates extensive research on the science behind animal antibiotics, cattle feed, and human-animal gut health—all of which render his visit as an altogether disturbing look at the behind-the-scenes happenings of national meat production. Yet unlike Kingsolver's explicit rhetoric against such practices,

Pollan largely avoids explicit, brazen condemnations.[3] Rather, he often frames such information as material for an individual's future ethical debates about what to eat:

> Standing there in the pen alongside my steer, I couldn't imagine ever wanting to eat the flesh of one of these protein machines. Hungry was the last thing I felt. Yet I'm sure that after enough time goes by, and the stink of this place is gone from my nostrils, I will eat feedlot beef again. Eating industrial meat takes an almost heroic act of not knowing or, now, forgetting. (84)

As students consider Pollan's and Kingsolver's works side by side, they also interrogate this last sentence: How do these texts foreground urgent, provocative scientific information alongside compelling personal narratives so that they might thwart such "not knowing" or "forgetting" in the future? While noting that both authors perform such compositional braiding, students also discuss the merits and pitfalls of their differing approaches and rhetorical strategies. Consequently, this comparative analysis offers them an even deeper tool kit for crafting nonfiction pieces informed by scientific research and personal experience.

Finally, my students and I turn to Kimmerer's *Braiding Sweetgrass*, which helps us envision alternative relationships with food, science, and writing altogether. Drawing from traditional ecological knowledge and Indigenous understandings of the natural environment, Kimmerer contrasts prevailing notions about food and espouses a philosophy that centers sustainable consumption, generosity, and respect.[4] Highlighting her own botanical research on edible plants such as pecans, corn, leeks, and squash, Kimmerer—like Pollan and Kingsolver—contextualizes this content with personal memories and firsthand experiences. After describing her family's cross-generational harvests of wild strawberries, for instance, the author imagines what it might mean—morally and scientifically—to view such a fruit as a "gift" rather than a commodified resource: "When we view the world this way, strawberries and humans alike are transformed. The relationship of gratitude and reciprocity thus developed can increase the evolutionary fitness of both plant and animal" (30). As this brief passage indicates, Kimmerer advocates for a more holistic "scientific" understanding of the earth, one in which Western research correlates with Indigenous forms of knowledge to promote "mutual flourishing" (139).

Moreover, Kimmerer draws attention to the significance of terminology when communicating such information, questioning the ability of

Western European languages to account for animacy in most nonhuman beings. Considering how English conceptualizes the essence of a maple tree, for instance, Kimmerer claims, if "the tree is not a *who*, but an *it*, we make that maple an object; we put a barrier between us, absolving ourselves of moral responsibility and opening the door to exploitation. Saying *it* makes a living land into 'natural resources.' If a maple is an *it*, we can take up the chain saw. If a maple is a *her*, we think twice" (57). As such, reading *Braiding Sweetgrass* offers students an opportunity to further complicate perceived understandings of what constitutes effective science communication in terms of both content and rhetoric. When taught in tandem with Kingsolver's and Pollan's work, Kimmerer's writing offers students yet another lens for reconsidering their relationship to food and environmental science research. At the same time, it allows them to consider how they might use narrative composition, language, and other creative writing techniques to express such understanding of these dynamics.

With such models in mind, my students' works of environmental memoir take shape through a variety of forms and rhetorical approaches. Projects have explored family food traditions, shopping lists, and on-campus dining experiences, integrating research on supply chain dynamics, nutritional issues, and the ecological costs of exported produce into scenes of reflection or dialogue. Students' work has ranged from traditional personal essays to more creative approaches, such as annotated Thanksgiving dinner menus that highlight the potential environmental benefits of eating a spread of local cuisine rather than the conventional holiday fare. Because students are writing about a subject they find particularly accessible—food—and because they are drawing from personal experience and memory to ground their research, their projects are often exceptionally compelling and robust in their articulations of why such information is important for their readers to consider. Applying environmental science research to personal experience generates new understandings for students about the rhetorical significance of situating their voice amid the established work of others and models how to create a braided dialogue between these accounts within a singular piece. In the aforementioned review of Simard's tree memoir, Francis-Baker suggests that "[i]n order to bridge the emotional chasm between the science and our ability to act, we must take what we know and reshape it into something more palatable." In the spirit of this pursuit of "palatability," reading, researching, and eventually writing about food through the environmental memoir genre opens students to enticing new ways of thinking about science communication and empowers them to recognize the rhetorical power found in their own stories.

Notes

1. See, for example, Bray et al., which identifies an emerging trend among science communication instructors of emphasizing courses focused on audience, accessibility, and, consequently, a broader understanding of rhetoric beyond technical, discipline-specific language. See also materials from the 2018 conference of the Public Communication of Science and Technology Network, which met under the theme "Science, Stories, and Society" (Miller and Kimura).

2. As do Merkle and Avraamidou and Osborne.

3. Indeed, Pollan's ambiguity toward such information is explicitly criticized by Safran Foer in *Eating Animals* (207–08).

4. See also Orielle Lake's *The Story Is in Our Bones*, which similarly offers a radical revisioning of contemporary human-nature-sustainability dynamics that are grounded in traditional Indigenous ecological knowledge.

Works Cited

Avraamidou, Lucy, and Jonathan Osborne. "The Role of Narrative in Communicating Science." *International Journal of Science Education*, vol. 31, no. 12, 2009, pp. 1683–707.

Berry, Wendell. "The Pleasures of Eating." *What Are People For?*, by Berry, Counterpoint Press, 1990, pp. 145–52.

Bourdain, Anthony. "Don't Eat before Reading This." *The New Yorker*, 12 Apr. 1999, www.newyorker.com/magazine/1999/04/19/dont-eat-before-reading-this.

Bray, Belinda, et al. "Identifying the Essential Elements of Effective Science Communication: What Do the Experts Say?" *International Journal of Science Education, Part B: Communication and Public Engagement*, vol. 2, no. 1, 2012, pp. 23–41.

Bruner, Jerome. "The Narrative Construction of Reality." *Critical Inquiry*, vol. 18, 1991, pp. 1–21.

Conle, Carola. "An Anatomy of Narrative Curricula." *Educational Researcher*, vol. 32, no. 3, 2003, pp. 3–15.

Dahlstrom, Michael F. "Using Narratives and Storytelling to Communicate Science with Nonexpert Audiences." *PNAS: Proceedings of the National Academy of Sciences of the United States of America*, vol. 111, no. 4, 2014, pp. 13614–20.

Francis-Baker, Tiffany. "*Finding the Mother Tree* by Suzanne Simard Review: A Journey of Passion and Introspection." *The Guardian*, 8 May 2021, www.theguardian.com/books/2021/may/08/finding-the-mother-tree-by-suzanne-simard-review-a-journey-of-passion-and-introspection.

Goldman, Denise. "'The Hidden Door That Leads to Several Moments More': Finding Context for the Literacy Narrative in First Year Writing." *The Journal of the Assembly for Expanded Perspectives on Learning*, vol. 26, 2021, pp. 83–98, https://doi.org/10.7290/jaepl263l9h.

Heller, Karen. "'Braiding Sweetgrass' Has Gone from Surprise Hit to Juggernaut Bestseller." *The Washington Post*, 12 Oct. 2022, www.washingtonpost.com/books/2022/10/12/braiding-sweetgrass-robin-wall-kimmerer/.

Kimmerer, Robin Wall. *Braiding Sweetgrass: Indigenous Wisdom, Scientific Knowledge, and the Teachings of Plants.* Milkweed Editions, 2013.

Kingsolver, Barbara, et al. *Animal, Vegetable, Miracle: A Year of Food Life.* HarperCollins Publishers, 2007.

Merkle, Bethann Garramon. "Writing Science: Leveraging a Few Techniques from Creative Writing toward Writing More Effectively." *Bulletin of the Ecological Society of America*, vol. 101, no. 2, 2020, pp. 1–4.

Meyer, Karen. "Reflections on Being Female in School Science: Toward a Praxis of Teaching Science." *Journal of Research in Science Teaching*, vol. 35, no. 4, 1998, pp. 463–71.

Miller, Steve, and Ka'iu Kimura. "The PCST 2018 Sessions on 'Communicating Science across Cultures': An Overview by the Session Chairs." *JCOM: Journal of Science Communication*, vol. 17, no. 4, 2018, pp. 1–3.

Montgomery, Scott L. *The Scientific Voice.* Guilford Press, 1996.

Nezhukumatathil, Aimee. "Vampire Squid." Nezhukumatathil, *World*, pp. 53–57.

———. *World of Wonders: In Praise of Fireflies, Whale Sharks, and Other Astonishments.* Milkweed Editions, 2020.

Nguyen, Andrea. "What I Learned from Loving Mapo Tofu." *The New York Times*, 5 Oct. 2020, www.nytimes.com/2020/10/05/dining/mapo-tofu-recipes.html.

Orielle Lake, Osprey. *The Story Is in Our Bones: How Worldviews and Climate Justice Can Remake a World in Crisis.* New Society Publishers, 2024.

Orr, David. *Earth in Mind: On Education, Environment, and the Human Prospect.* Island Press, 1994.

Pollan, Michael. *The Omnivore's Dilemma: A Natural History of Four Meals.* Penguin Books, 2006.

Safran Foer, Jonathan. *Eating Animals.* Little, Brown, 2009.

Shiva, Vandana. *Stolen Harvest: The Hijacking of the Global Food Supply.* UP of Kentucky, 2016.

Thaiss, Chris, and Stephanie Wade. "Writing Science in the First Year of College: Why It Matters to STEM Students and How STEM Students Benefit from It." *Writing Spaces: Readings on Writing*, edited by Trace Daniels-Lerberg et al., vol. 5, Parlor Press, 2023, pp. 372–91.

Train, Tonya L., and Yuko J. Miyamoto. "Encouraging Science Communication in an Undergraduate Curriculum Improves Students' Perceptions and Confidence." *Journal of College Science Teaching*, vol. 46, no. 4, 2017, pp. 76–83.

Scott C. Thompson

Embracing Subjectivity: Humanizing and Historicizing Science Writing in the Post-Pandemic Classroom

In the spring semester of 2020, I taught a course titled Science Writing for the English department at Temple University. Science writing—by which Temple's curriculum means "science journalism"—is the discipline of communicating scientific knowledge and discoveries to the public by combining journalistic storytelling principles with scientific research, methods, and concepts. My course was billed as a science journalism class designed for upper-level English majors interested in journalism and science. I went into the course with the idea that some non-STEM undergraduate students might be slightly intimidated by the prospect of reading, digesting, and communicating scientific research. I was also concerned that my students would be unpracticed in thinking critically about Science (with a capital S)[1] and might simply take all scientific claims at face value. I wanted them to understand that science is a human endeavor, open to all the genius and ineptitude humans are capable of, and that it is the science writer's responsibility to separate the wheat from the chaff. My solution was to spend the first couple weeks of the class giving a crash course in the history and philosophy of science. My goal was to unsettle, to disrupt my students' trust in Science (there's that capital S again) by showing them that the discipline has a human-made history and by introducing them to ways of thinking that would allow them to critically examine science's epistemological and ontological claims. I wanted to train them to be investigative science writers—sleuths following up on the facts—and skeptics of any claims made by people in positions of power without first seeing the receipts.

Then the pandemic happened. Suddenly and unexpectedly, the public eye turned its piercing gaze onto the practitioners and practice of science writing; the channels of communication responsible for delivering scientific information to the public came under fire. Suddenly, science was widely seen as politicized, untrustworthy—conspiratorial, even. I found myself backtracking, spending precious class time (on Zoom) articulating that even though I had wanted to "shake up" my students' faith in Science, I had done so with the intention of eventually rebuilding their trust in science (with a small *s*) by giving them the skills to interrogate discrete projects—to find value in good science and expose bad science. I think my students understood. But I realized the way I taught science writing moving forward would have to take into account this new public perception.

Science writers have always relied on narrative techniques, literary devices, and so-called thin descriptions of science to craft compelling stories and make their subjects comprehensible to general audiences. However, these rhetorical maneuvers also signal the constructedness of their work to readers: the practice of epistemological translation from specialized discourse to more accessible language reveals a glaring subjectivity in a profession that values the appearance of objectivity. These moments of discursive synthesis between the sciences and the humanities are strengths, but they also open science writing to criticism from science deniers and skeptics, especially in our post-pandemic present, and this necessarily affects the way we teach science writing in the classroom. It is my belief and this essay's argument that the humanist is equipped with ready-made tools to address the criticisms leveled against the discipline of science writing. After all, thinking with nuance about story, subjectivity, and constructedness is the bread and butter of the humanities. As a professionally trained humanist, I approach science writing through a humanities lens, historicizing the discipline and the problems plaguing the field. Divided into four sections, this essay outlines my approach to teaching science writing to undergraduate students, modeled on a course titled Writing in Public Health that I now teach at the University of Florida. My goal is to identify and contextualize problems facing the discipline in the wake of the pandemic and, by doing so, to begin the process of creating solutions.

The History: From Cheerleader to Watchdog

The gap between the general public and the scientific community is nothing new; in fact, this fracture is at the heart of science writing's modern-day history. Science writing emerged in Victorian England out of the burgeoning need for the new professional scientists to stimulate the public's interest in and understanding of science. Since the nineteenth century, science writing has grown into its own fully-fledged field, and it enjoyed a disciplinary high-water-mark moment in the twentieth century. In "Science Journalism: Too Close for Comfort," Boyce Rensberger frames this disciplinary trajectory as the development of the science writer from cheerleader of science to its watchdog. Rensberger argues that science writing began with the goal of building the public's trust in scientific practice, but over the course of the subsequent century science writers developed a more antagonistic posture in response to misuses of science by corporate industry, becoming the watchdogs and whistleblowers protecting against abuses by big business. In my class I have students read Rensberger's article to introduce them to science writing and its relationship to the public and assign exemplary readings from key periods in the discipline's history.

Our first stop is Victorian England. At the beginning of the nineteenth century, science was the game of interested amateurs, the so-called gentleman scientists with education and leisure enough to spend time examining, collecting, organizing, and labeling the natural world; by the close of the century, science was relegated to trained professionals in sanctioned laboratories using established protocols to conduct experiments. This shift from amateurism to institutionalization required public resources, meaning that scientific inquiry, practice, and methods had to be popularized with the general public.[2] I assign a reading from one of the mid-century popularizers of science attempting to inform and interest the public in science-related pursuits. My personal favorite is George Henry Lewes.[3] We read the first forty pages of his *Seaside Studies at Ilfracombe, Tenby, the Scilly Isles, and Jersey*. On the surface, Lewes is narrating a simple account of his vacation in Ilfracombe and his natural history pastime.

Just below the surface, though, Lewes skillfully interweaves into his story the questions and methods of scientific pursuit in order to interest and instruct his reader on how to think and act like a scientist. For example, when Lewes's narrator comes across an unknown specimen in a tide pool, he states, "You want to know what is that jelly-like globule no bigger than a pea? I can't answer; but probably the ovum of some fish. At any rate, the rule is to carry home whatever one does not know, and identify there, if possible; so pop the globule into a phial" (25). This short quotation illustrates well Lewes's subtle rhetorical maneuvering: he speaks directly to the reader, encouraging imaginative participation, and he models the process of scientific inquiry—curiosity, questioning, extraction, identification—in a step-by-step format.

I end my tour of the nineteenth century with H. G. Wells's now famous article "Popularising Science," published in *Nature* in 1894. Wells makes a compelling argument about the necessity of educating the voting public on the inner workings of science as the state becomes more financially involved in scientific projects; the more science becomes a public endeavor (and not the hobby of private citizens), the more the common people need to understand how their money is being spent. Wells then outlines expected characteristics of science writing, including speaking the language of the readers and not writing down to them, but he also characterizes science writing in unexpected ways, such as its needing to model itself on detective fiction of the likes of Edgar Allan Poe and Arthur Conan Doyle. He argues that detective fiction's "ingenious unravelling of evidence" and presentation of "[f]irst the problem, then the gradual piecing together of the solution" should be the formula for the science writing of the future (301).

My short historical overview comes to a close in the mid–twentieth century with Rachel Carson's *Silent Spring*. Carson's famous book about the damages of the pesticide DDT is a great example of where science writing ended up after becoming an autonomous discipline in its own right. Rather than being a cheerleader for science and attempting to popularize it among the public, Carson is a watchdog of science, guarding against hubristic or greed-inspired overstepping. Trained in both science and the humanities, Carson embodies the modern-day science writer who has a foot in both worlds: she combines her knowledge of science and storytelling to take to task the misuse of science by corporate industry. *Silent Spring* also pairs well with Wells's piece because it opens with a mystery (the famous first chapter depicts a fictional American town afflicted by the environmental side effects of DDT), and the rest of the book is spent unraveling the evidence and "piecing together" the solution.

This brief historical survey allows the students to understand the larger cultural context of science writing as a practice. I then introduce them to a three-pronged problem plaguing present-day science communication.

Science's Problem: Unity and Disunity

"Science is a liar . . . sometimes" ("*It's Always Sunny*" 14:46). This is the comical refrain from the infamous science-religion debate scene between the characters Mac and Dennis in the television show *It's Always Sunny in Philadelphia*. I show the debate scene in class because Mac, an ardent religious believer, provides an oversimplified yet insightful history of science, beginning with Aristotle, moving to Galileo, and concluding with Isaac Newton. For each, he notes things these scientists claimed to know about the world that were later proven to be incorrect. His overarching conclusion is that "[t]hese were all the smartest scientists on the planet; only problem is they kept being wrong, sometimes" (15:51–16:00). This clip not only demonstrates how the history of science can be easily misunderstood or deliberately misconstrued by those with only cursory knowledge of the topic but also posits a genuine question: If what scientists purport to know about the universe can change radically over time, how do we know that what scientists claim to know in the present is true and will not be discredited by future generations of scientists?

This question sets the stage for the course unit on the history and philosophy of science. I consider the inclusion of this unit to be one of the most important aspects of my course. My goal is to get students to think about Science not as a monolith of truth but as a human endeavor with a history, consisting of choices and perspectives, limitations and affordances, biases and brilliance. I begin with some of the foundational texts in the history of science and end with a selection of readings on the unity and disunity of the sciences.

I assign sections of Thomas Kuhn's *The Structure of Scientific Revolutions* (1–22) to begin a conversation about what it means that scientific knowledge continues to change over time. I briefly cover positivist science's concept of linear progress before turning to Kuhn's paradigm shift theory, focusing on what Kuhn calls "normal science" (10). I like to spend time discussing normal science—the day-to-day science that uses the prevailing paradigmatic theory as a guide to the types of questions it can and should ask of the universe. Normal science, for Kuhn, is both good and bad: good in that it allows scientists to speak a common language and pursue common research goals; bad in that it amounts to puzzle-solving or fill-in-the-blank science, where unquestioned assumptions about the nature of the universe are allowed to guide scientific research. I like to end our discussion of Kuhn here because normal science is the type of science most science writers will be investigating and writing about, and Kuhn reminds us that normal science is necessary but limited in the types of truth claims it can make.

The second section of this unit includes a series of readings on the disunity of the sciences. I explain scientific disunity and its importance as follows: Science consists of multiple branches (natural, social, physical, chemical, etc.); each branch has its own internal set of theories, methods, models, and interests; because of this, the scientific knowledge produced by each branch is different from that produced by the others, and it is difficult—and perhaps impossible—to create an overarching, unified theory of Science that accounts for all these variations. Further, this disunity exists inside each of the branches as well. Every scientist brings different interests, assumptions, training, and experiences to their studies. Thus, even within scientific disciplines, there is not always a unified and universally accepted interpretation of the world.

I frame our ensuing class discussion as an attempt to answer the following question: What is good science? I assign readings from Isabelle Stengers, John Dupré, and Hilary Putnam.[4] In "The Thousand and One Sexes of Science," Stengers redefines "theories" as consistent systems, akin to Kuhn's "normal science," and "propositions" as flexible approaches, allowing different questions and answers by scientists. Dupré's "Metaphysical Disorder and Scientific Disunity" argues that "good science" requires case-by-case justification and that it's just one perspective among many, similar to how individuals have different identities in various contexts. In "What Is Realism?," Putnam argues for a "correspondence theory of truth" (141), where truth is confined to a theoretical system that does not necessarily reflect objective reality. Putnam asserts that our descriptions of the real world are limited by our conceptual systems, constrained by human-made language. These readings demonstrate that science can help us understand the world, but science writers must keep in mind that science, like any human-made practice, comes with an internal history and philosophical framework that directs and limits the types of knowledge it can produce.

The Public's Problem: Anti-Science and Conspiracy

There are a variety of factors that have contributed to the quietly rising tide of anti-intellectualism and science skepticism in the United States over the last half century: the proliferation of misinformation, the politicization of science, the historical precedents that warrant a healthy dose of mistrust,[5] the increasing oversimplification of science for public consumption, the general science illiteracy in the United States, and the poor public health messaging by those in positions of influence and power. The last of these—poor public health messaging—is what I focus on in the penultimate portion of my course. To better understand the rhetorical choices that go into public health messaging, and to learn more about the landscape of conspiratorial thinking, we read an academic article and a pop culture article on vaccine skepticism and compare them in terms of content and rhetoric.

The academic article I assign is "An Epidemic of Uncertainty: Rumors, Conspiracy Theories and Vaccine Hesitancy," by Ed Pertwee, Clarissa Simas, and Heidi J. Larson. They argue that conspiracy theories express oversimplified popular beliefs and anxieties (such as the vaccine-microchip claim and its association with real concerns of biodata and surveillance) and are easily spread through social media. Their proposed solutions include leveraging local community networks, approaching public health measures cautiously, and implementing proactive measures to combat misinformation. The popular culture counterpoint is "How the Anti-Vaxxers Got Red-Pilled," a *Rolling Stone* piece by Tim Dickinson. He examines how individuals can become susceptible to misinformation and the phenomenon of "red-pilling" (from *The Matrix*), which refers to the process by which individuals who were once skeptical of a particular conspiracy theory become fully immersed in a network of like-minded individuals who share increasingly extreme beliefs.

After we get a sense of the argument of each text, we switch lenses and analyze the articles' rhetorical strategies. We note that the academic piece considers both perspectives (pro-vaccine and anti-vaccine) in a balanced and nonjudgmental way, using language that does not alienate its audience; it considers the historical context of the conspiratorial thinking; it forwards a clear argument, grounded in numerous citations; and it provides clear solutions to the problems raised. The pop culture piece works within a different rhetorical register. It uses polarizing language, immediately alienating a large swath of readers; it relies on a wide range of sources to make its case, from scholars to movie references; it cites other popular sources as references; and it draws on memorable imagery and figures of speech to complement its argument. Both pieces make arguments and historicize their topic. However, the differences in the rhetoric far outweigh the similarities. The concluding sentiment of our discussion is that while the pop culture piece is a much easier and entertaining read, when examined closely, it clearly falls short of achieving what good science writing should do: provide sound information and potential solutions to problems, not contribute to them.

Ultimately, the focus of this section in terms of writerly skill is on the different rhetorical techniques used by writers to communicate with different audiences in different genres; the philosophical focus is the unsettlingly frayed pathways of effective communication between scientists and the general public. There are no easy answers here about how to reconnect the lines of communication between these two groups, but we discuss in class some of the potential options. My students often suggest things like improving the US education system so that the general public has a better grasp of how science works; bolstering the standard, practice, and expectations of science writing; and encouraging more scientists to become social media influencers.[6] This conversation, though, continually returns to the issue of public comprehension, and until there is some sort of systemic overhaul of how we teach and talk about science, the most tangible solution to how to communicate effectively and efficiently remains in the hands of the science writer.

The Writer's Problem: Thin Descriptions of Science

The final section of my course centers on the dilemma of thin description in science writing. I draw my definition of thin description—and its correlative, thick description—from the recent methodological debates in the social sciences and humanities about the ethical interpretation of an object of study.[7] Thin and thick description are two different approaches to describing one's object. Thin description is surface-level observation that provides an empirical account of an event or behavior, and thick description infuses empirical observation with the observer's analysis and contextual interpretation. The choice between using thin or thick description is an ethical one: thin description attempts to allow the object of study to speak for itself, as it were, while thick description privileges the interpreter as an expert whose insider knowledge is needed to understand fully the object of study. In the context of science writing, thin and thick description and their ethical implications take on new meaning. The science writer must necessarily use thin description to describe scientific practice for the audience in order to communicate the science and its implications in a way that is understandable to the nonscientist. Yet this act of translation comes at a cost: all the nuance, detail, and complexity that underpins scientific practice must be sacrificed on the altar of mass accessibility. This, too, is an ethical problem. Is the price of easily understood science worth the loss of intellectual complexity? What are the social ramifications of discussing science in absolutes, of painting in broad strokes?[8]

To help my students begin to understand these issues, I assign an in-class activity in which they perform and reflect on thin and thick description. In the activity, participants choose a subject they possess insider knowledge about, such as an activity, community, discourse community, or practice, and focus on a specific event within that domain. Initially they describe the chosen event using thin description, which involves providing a surface-level observation without interpretation or context. Then students provide thick descriptions, which involve insider interpretation and context. They reflect on the differences between the two approaches. I have them consider which approach is more useful for conveying meaning and why, the limitations and affordances of each, and the ethical considerations of presenting information without interpretation or context in contrast to providing a description interwoven with both observation and interpretation.

This activity is simple enough, but I find that it really helps students understand just how much interpretation goes into the way they understand the world. Once they recognize this, it becomes clearer how much subjectivity goes into things that are seemingly very objective, such as scientific practice and communication.

In a rapidly evolving world where science, information, and public discourse intersect with unprecedented complexity, teaching scientific writing as a human and historical practice takes on greater importance. In the wake of the pandemic, science writing has been criticized, critiqued, and exposed, with surprising brutality, for being what it has always been—an art, not a science. My goal in bringing together historical insights, philosophical reflections, and ethical considerations is to train students to be active and informed participants in the ecosystem of scientific communication and to help them understand the humanistic side of science. It is only by embracing the subjectivity of science and the art of science writing that the disconnect between practitioners and the general public can begin to be repaired.

Notes

1. Throughout this essay I distinguish between "Science," with a capital *S*, and "science," with a lowercase *s*. "Science," with a capital *S*, refers to the idealized conception of science as an objective, unified, and authoritative body of knowledge—a cultural institution that has come to represent rationality and truth in the Western imagination. In contrast, "science" denotes the everyday, situated practices of empirical investigation carried out by working scientists, shaped by methodological limitations, disciplinary norms, and human judgment.

2. For more on this history, see Lightman 1–38.

3. Charles Darwin's *On the Origin of Species* is another good option that can be assigned as an example of mid-Victorian science writing.

4. Admittedly, these readings are difficult. I usually pick one to have students read in full and provide key excerpts or just summarize in class the takeaways from the other two. Despite the difficultly of these thinkers and texts, I really do believe that what they offer intellectually is important. The juice is worth the squeeze.

5. An infamous example is the Tuskegee syphilis study, conducted between 1932 and 1972 by the US Public Health Service. The study examined the effects of untreated syphilis in Black men in the Tuskegee community without their informed consent.

6. Depending on how much one might want to lean into the nuances of the scientist-as-influencer argument, there are articles on the topic one could assign. For one example, see Shah.

7. For a history of these debates and their recent application to the humanities, see Love.

8. The implications extend further. Theodore Porter argues that the practice of science itself is altered by the push for easily communicated conclusions; scientists are subtly altering the types of questions they ask of the universe in order to produce answers that can be neatly packaged for public consumption.

Works Cited

Carson, Rachel. *Silent Spring*. 1962. Mariner Books Classics, 2022.

Darwin, Charles. *On the Origin of Species by Means of Natural Selection; or, The Preservation of Favoured Races in the Struggle for Life*. D. Appleton, 1861.

Dickinson, Tim. "How the Anti-Vaxxers Got Red-Pilled." *Rolling Stone*, 10 Feb. 2021, www.rollingstone.com/culture/culture-features/qanon-anti-vax -covid-vaccine-conspiracy-theory-1125197/.

Dupré, John. "Metaphysical Disorder and Scientific Disunity." *The Disunity of Science: Boundaries, Contexts, and Power*, edited by Peter Galison and David J. Stump, Stanford UP, 1996, pp. 101–17.

"*It's Always Sunny in Philadelphia*: Season 8 Ep. 10: Mac Evolution Highlight." *YouTube*, uploaded by FX Networks, 18 Aug. 2020, www.youtube.com/watch?v=GiJXALBX3KM.

Kuhn, Thomas S. *The Structure of Scientific Revolutions*. U of Chicago P, 1962.

Lewes, George Henry. *Seaside Studies at Ilfracombe, Tenby, the Scilly Isles, and Jersey*. William Blackwood and Sons, 1858.

Lightman, Bernard. *Victorian Popularizers of Science: Designing Nature for New Audiences*. U of Chicago P, 2007.

Love, Heather. "Close Reading and Thin Description." *Public Culture*, vol. 25, no. 3, 2013, pp. 401–34.

Pertwee, Ed, et al. "An Epidemic of Uncertainty: Rumors, Conspiracy Theories and Vaccine Hesitancy." *Nature Medicine*, vol. 28, 2022, pp. 456–59.

Porter, Theodore M. "Thin Description: Surface and Depth in Science and Science Studies." *OSIRIS*, vol. 27, 2012, pp. 209–26.

Putnam, Hilary. "What Is Realism?" 1976. *Scientific Realism*, edited by Jarrett Leplin, U of California P, 1984, pp. 140–53.

Rensberger, Boyce. "Science Journalism: Too Close for Comfort." *Nature*, vol. 459, no. 25, 2009, pp. 1055–56.

Shah, Meeta. "The Failure of Public Health Messaging about COVID-19." *Scientific American*, 3 Sept. 2020, www.scientificamerican.com/article/the-failure-of-public-health-messaging-about-covid-19/.

Stengers, Isabelle. "The Thousand and One Sexes of Science." 1991. *Power and Invention: Situating Science*, by Stengers, U of Minnesota P, 1997, pp. 133–51.

Wells, H. G. "Popularising Science." *Nature*, vol. 50, no. 1291, 1894, pp. 300–01.

Matthew Newcomb

Science Writing as a General Education Linchpin

This essay narrates and theorizes the planning and value of a first-year general education science writing course currently under development as part of an effort to further integrate the elements of the general education program and build connections between the English department and programs in the sciences at the university where I teach, with the goal of enhancing the coherence of and connections within the general education curriculum. In this essay science writing is understood as writing that takes scientific processes, methods, and results as central to its work but emphasizes the need to contextualize those processes, methods, and results and communicate them to a wide variety of audiences, considering the experiences, emotions, and identities of those audiences as relevant to science writing choices. Science writing also serves as a link between fields and as a way to think about general education as centered in mutuality. Just as the sciences can be used to reshape understandings of humans, the humanities can help us understand the workings of science and particularly science writing's role in public life.

At my state institution, we have ten required general education content areas: basic communication (where composition courses fit), math, natural science, social science, humanities, arts, diversity, US history and

138

civic engagement, world languages, and world history and global aware-ness ("SUNY General Education Framework"). For most content areas, there are a variety of courses that fulfill the requirement, held together in the content category by one or more common learning outcomes. No particular system is currently used to link courses across content areas other than an occasional pairing of courses, done on an ad hoc basis by instructor agreement. While the variety of content areas is encouraging to many instructors, particularly those wanting to encourage a broad liberal arts education, instructors and advisers face common struggles to mo-tivate students for general education classes that are not connected to a larger sense of purpose.

In advising students, one main difficulty is to help them find courses they might want to take that tick off all the necessary general education boxes and that also fit into their course, work, and extracurricular sched-ules. Time and day are often the determining factors for which general ed-ucation course to take in a particular category, which means that students are not signing up for courses based on content. Rather, they are signing up for courses based on work schedule, family responsibilities, and other pressures. Students may initially be motivated, but once a class begins, de-spite efforts by the university's General Education Board to train instruc-tors in sharing the purposes of general education, both broadly speaking and in their particular category, students may struggle to find connections between a writing course, an introduction to psychology course, a world history course, and an astronomy course for nonscience majors.

Science writing courses are not brand-new, but they are still not com-mon. In some of the limited research on science writing courses, Nathan-iel Rivers, Christopher Grabau, Kate Kavanaugh, and Katie Zabrowski emphasize media variety and articulation in science writing as a way to "address issues of authorship and the knowledge-making practices of sci-ence writing, the mechanical practices of new media writing, the peda-gogical practices and assumptions at work in teaching new media writing, and the evolution of science literacy into science electracy." David Brauer argues against a scientism that simply accepts scientific knowledge as fact, particularly when students may embrace competing epistemologies and value systems: "With an incomplete grasp of scientific discourse, inexperi-enced teaching assistants and even seasoned instructors risk oversimplify-ing matters for their students by positing that science is a publicly accepted discourse that trumps any private discourses positioned agonistically in relation to science" (73). Brauer suggests creating a conversation between scientific issues and student expectations and beliefs. This approach of treating scientific information as publicly negotiable and related to other elements of students' beliefs meshes with the idea of making it a connecting point for general education.

Multifaceted science-oriented texts like Robin Wall Kimmerer's *Braiding Sweetgrass* fit well for the kind of course and connections proposed here. *Braiding Sweetgrass* integrates different cultural knowledges while also providing information about sweetgrass, thereby keeping the experiential and biological together. For additional (global) Indigenous science readings, the ecological work of Ian Saem Majnep and Ralph Bulmer, the astronomy of Karlie Alinta Noon and Krystal De Napoli, and the soil science of Lydia Jennings all provide possibilities. Along with brief descriptions of class activities and texts like Kimmerer's that have persuaded me to promote the value of a general education science writing course, this essay addresses—from my perspective as a rhetoric and composition instructor and decade-long writing program administrator—the process of selling the science writing course to multiple university audiences. It also reflects briefly on what might be gained, what might be missed, and what barriers might arise with the described approach to developing general education connections through science writing.

Experiments with Rhetoric and Science Writing

The idea of shifting to a first-year science writing course emerged initially from conversations about upper-division science writing in combination with general education changes. Faculty members in the biology and engineering programs spoke about a desire for students to work on writing with numerical data. Issues like overt organizational structures for writing that emphasize evidence and separate the conclusions from the presentation of evidence came up too. In earlier discussions during a minor revision of the general education program, faculty members in multiple fields raised concerns about how to better integrate courses within the general education curriculum. Ideas included pairing courses, creating themed tracks, team teaching, and others. None were ultimately adopted, but there was a brief increased emphasis on using early days of general education courses to educate students about the importance of the particular category that course was in and, ideally, how it might connect to other categories. Advising efforts were made to help incoming students think about general education courses as a form of exploration and as a means of discovering different worldviews, but scheduling concerns continued to dominate most course decisions. In some advising sessions I worked, we provided an example of a nearby object (such as a tree) or something people like (such as chocolate) and talked about how it could be approached or analyzed from many perspectives—including historical, biological, sociological, and even poetic. The practical difficulties of instituting a large system to connect or integrate courses, along with funding limitations around interdisciplinary and team-taught courses, motivated me to consider stand-alone course options as a way of making connections within the general education curriculum. Writing courses immediately came to mind as the courses that the highest percentage of students tend to take.

As a first step, I started including science writing elements in some of my English courses, which was particularly manageable when teaching environmental themes. Journalistic examples in courses I have taught provided concrete moments for class activities where students worked at bringing concepts or information from every course they were taking that semester to the same issue—already linking different parts of the curriculum, even though this was not necessarily a general education course. For example, writing about the causes of late-summer forest fires let students include concepts from introductory psychology (individual reactions focused on blame and denial of causes), biology (the impact of fires on particular species and ecosystems), US history (land use in California), and art (visual depictions of forest fires) all in the same analysis activity. We then worked to try brief writing experiments that emphasized different angles (individual psychology, climate issues, land use) one at a time without losing the connections to the other fields. While difficult for students at times, this kind of integration and then specialization led to moments of more contextualized and nuanced writing for many students.

For another project I created a list of a half dozen books for students to choose from, and we created reading and writing groups for each book based on whoever chose it. One text was Elizabeth Kolbert's *Field Notes from a Catastrophe*—a kind of science-oriented climate journalism for broad consumption. Students read about forty pages of the book per week for half the term, responding to prompts and to one another once per week on a discussion board. Each book group had their own discussion board for considering writing strategies for conveying scientific information or motivating audiences and other topics relevant to their books. After the initial responses about how they did not know some of the information in Kolbert's book and that everyone should know and do something, we could move to a few key questions: How does Kolbert depict scientists as both characters and interviewees? How does she integrate the scientific information she learns from them? What background knowledge does she need to have to do this work? What roles do the location and story-based chapters play in creating reader experiences? The combination of direct data, such as samples from glaciers, and human stories leads to conversations about interdisciplinarity, about the value of combining skills and knowledge from different areas, and about the kind of education the author must have and provide to readers to be effective.

We approached *Braiding Sweetgrass* differently, as a kind of foundational book for a class. Students generally latched onto the legends, such as the legend of Skywoman, that Kimmerer includes and moments of her personal story. From there we began to look for connections between those legends and personal moments and botanical information, for example, often by focusing on the chapter titles, which frequently refer to a plant of some sort. The mix of personal narrative, cultural history related to plants, and scientific botany presents a triad that Kimmerer interweaves throughout, not unlike one of the baskets she references in *Braiding Sweetgrass* (5).

Students followed up discussions of Kimmerer's writing style with considerations of their own areas of technical knowledge (how an archery bow works, snowboarding, crocheting, mushroom identification) and written explanations of some aspect of that knowledge intended for nonexpert audiences. Students later wrote a paper that involved combining personal narrative with historical and scientific information (the latter usually involving minor research) in a manner that was distantly modeled on some of Kimmerer's chapters. This paper overtly integrated multiple disciplines and, in a science writing context, contextualized botanical research with the roles plants have played in the author's life.

The section of *Braiding Sweetgrass* titled "The Three Sisters" was useful in discussing how Kimmerer, drawing on her own experiences as a teacher, positions her readers as curious students (134–37). Students could then consider different options for what kind of audience to address and invoke (Ede and Lunsford) in the tricky business of making hermeneutical guesses (Dobrin) about the knowledge level and types of interests their audience might have and how to establish familiar relationships (like a student-teacher relationship) in order to clarify the role of the science reader—whether expert or nonexpert.

These efforts to include science writing in my English courses led to a plan for general education science writing as a version of my institution's standard Writing and Rhetoric course, ideally with a science writing focus advertised to students on the schedule of classes. I provided the rhetorical concepts and concrete writing strategies throughout the course, we planned to explore one chapter of Christopher Thaiss's *Writing Science in the Twenty-First Century* each week, and *Braiding Sweetgrass* was spread out into many short readings to allow for a different concept to be applied or connected to it in various weeks. Other, smaller examples of public or, occasionally, more specialized science writing were brought in as desired as supplements. While *Braiding Sweetgrass* has helped spur connections between fields when I've taught it, letting the writing course focus on science and culture and values and rhetorical situations all together, the brief journalistic examples showed the pervasiveness of combining science and culture and politics to some extent in nearly all public topics.

Not only have faculty members in the natural sciences appreciated some of the more scientifically oriented reading selections; they have also suggested that classes that incorporate scientific writing help round out their own students' education. The focus from my perspective has been on selling scientific writing courses as courses that are fundamentally about writing, not on stepping into fields where I am not fully trained, and on communicating the idea that these humanities-centric classes can be useful for science majors in very practical ways. Students might even be able to directly apply principles learned in these classes to their science classes. Simply asking science professors what they want their majors to learn in these classes can help with buy-in across campus and give practical ideas for science writing content for writing instructors. (Writing with data was a big one.) These beginning efforts at science writing could be used in developing a general education science writing course or in interdisciplinary programs, projects, and course pairings between writing-focused and science-focused parts of the institution.

Science Writing, General Education, and Interdisciplinarity

The next effort involved developing a pilot general education science writing course. All students at my institution take one or two first-year sequential writing courses based on placement. Both courses are credit-bearing, and the second one fulfills the official general education requirements.

The second course in particular is where there is opportunity to reach nearly all students, and there has been a history of debate about how to thematize or organize that course, mostly in keeping with the history of debates about the content of composition courses in US colleges and universities (see, e.g., Berlin; Smit; Elbow; Bartholomae; Crowley). While my college has historically used various approaches, including courses focused on life writing, literature, research and argument, an instructor-chosen theme, or wicked questions—all grounded to some degree or another in a rhetorical approach—none of these approaches had a significant effect in helping unify or create connections between various elements of the general education curriculum. The most recent approach, using "wicked problems" (Marback) as complex, interdisciplinary global issues to bring multiple disciplines to a course, was perhaps the most successful.

In my state university system, general education categories have been established for all schools. Some categories are fairly standard, such as natural sciences and written and oral communication. Additional traits like critical thinking are embedded across the curriculum, but none engage directly with attempts to integrate the general education curriculum. Something like critical thinking, which is supposed to work across areas, tends to be treated as something one does either in general or in specific ways in different fields. Making connections between general education categories and skills is left to chance and individual instructors. Some institutions use cross-cutting themes as a way to link general education courses. A topical or content-based connection (like health or environment) serves as a way for at least some students to experience a more integrated general education curriculum. Portland State University, for example, has broad cluster areas like "American Identity," "Understanding Communities," and "Design Thinking," to name a few ("Sophomore Inquiry"). These clusters are broad but attempt to establish some connection between general education courses and across the years of college. Focusing on first-year writing courses does not work at the scale of a full general education program but emphasizes in-class activities and thinking that overtly make the connections between courses. Such a focus also utilizes a liberal education philosophy in trying to create habits of identifying humanities-oriented, scientific (social and natural), artistic, and other elements of an issue or topic. For cases where this level of integration is not feasible, science writing courses can be a valuable way of making these cross-disciplinary connections.

An early structural question for my new general education science writing course was whether it should simply be a version of the standard first-year writing course or whether it should have a separate identity through a course number and name. To get the word out about it to students and to differentiate it from the fifty other sections of first-year writing, especially when so many students are, out of necessity, signing up for courses based on the days and time of the course, it seemed necessary for the course to have a separate identity. On the other hand, getting a new general education course approved would be a long and arduous process and could lead to confusion for advisers who were used to the main writing course. The solution we tried was to work with our records and registration office to create a subcategory for the existing writing course. On the schedule, the standard version of the Writing and Rhetoric general education course would still be ENG 170, while the science writing version would be ENG 170–Science, allowing for clear marking on the course schedule but maintaining the same course number. It took some significant persuasion to get the assistance to make it work in terms of the software used to create the course schedule, but ultimately the notion of connecting sciences and humanities and the idea that we would have other ENG 170 categories listed to help students differentiate between sections was compelling.

To help solidify the notion of the science writing course as a general education linchpin, following any exercises intended to link content across courses, students would be asked to reflect in writing on ways that principles of science writing might influence, or might have already influenced, their work in other courses taken concurrently. At one level, this is a basic writing transfer task (Haskell; Wardle; Yancey et al.). However, in this kind of activity sequence, it also furthers the sense of multidirectional influence and interaction between courses and disciplines. Sometimes a focus on developing skills like global awareness or critical thinking, which works for a range of topics, helps link courses, but it is difficult to integrate areas and establish connections between specific areas. These connections can happen in specific courses with specific instructors, of course, but they are not built in. A general education science writing course has the potential to make some of those connections part of its structure: instructors can develop activities that help students identify those connections and select texts that not only take science seriously but also show it as contested and intertwined with other ways of knowing.

This approach to using science writing as a means to help tie together a general education program while effectively teaching writing skills can be enacted on a variety of scales. It could happen at the program level: for instance, all writing classes or a significant subset of general education writing classes might take a science writing approach. It could also happen at the level of an individual course or a unit or assignment within a course. Of course, a semester-long course is much more likely to reinforce connections throughout a general education program. Composition and writing studies instructors are asked to do many things in first-year courses. Using these courses as a linchpin for integrating general education programs runs the risk of creating yet another obligation that instructors simply do not have time for. However, the innate multidisciplinarity of public science writing; the importance of visuals, statistics, technologies, and audience knowledge levels in science writing; the variety of oral and written genres in science writing; and the potential for engaging students across disciplines all suggest significant potential for science writing as a useful communication starting point rather than an add-on.

Pressures and Realities

Of course, ideas do not always go entirely according to plan. Despite significant support across campus, I have not yet taught the general education science writing course. I was in the process of developing the course before I began working on this essay and was supposed to have taught it at least twice before finishing this essay. Additional sections of the course, with additional instructors, had also been part of the plan. Instead, departmental needs at the upper division in the major have pulled me out of the science writing course multiple times, so I have been able to utilize only some aspects of it and not all in one focused course. Efforts to meet a high-speed timeline for slightly adjusted general education curriculum requirements from our state meant that energy also had to go into making those changes, and extensive and thoughtful course revision was not feasible.

One of the other big struggles was working with the course scheduling software program to find a way to designate different versions of the main writing course. Ultimately, we hope to model the plan on our first-year interest group courses: two courses might be paired, and students would be encouraged to take them both, giving a larger sense of common experience and cohort of colleagues for students in those courses. While the timeline has slowed down, discussions in the writing and rhetoric program have focused more on integrating the general education curriculum than they otherwise would have, allowing some trickle of elements like writing with data into our standard curriculum.

Works Cited

Bartholomae, David. "Writing with Teachers: A Conversation with Peter Elbow." *College Composition and Communication*, vol. 46, no. 1, 1995, pp. 62–71.

Berlin, James A. *Rhetoric and Reality: Writing Instruction in American Colleges, 1900–1985.* Southern Illinois UP, 1987.

Brauer, David. "Writing between Two Worlds: Science and Discourses of Commitment in the Composition Classroom." *Composition Studies*, vol. 34, no. 1, 2006, pp. 71–93.

Crowley, Sharon. *Composition in the University: Historical and Polemical Essays.* U of Pittsburgh P, 1998.

Dobrin, Sidney I. "Paralogic Hermeneutic Theories, Power, and the Possibility for Liberating Pedagogies." *Postprocess Theory: Beyond the Writing Process Paradigm*, edited by Thomas Kent, Southern Illinois UP, 1999, pp. 132–48.

Ede, Lisa, and Andrea Lunsford. "Audience Addressed / Audience Invoked: The Role of Audience in Composition Theory and Pedagogy." *College Composition and Communication*, vol. 35, no. 2, 1984, pp. 155–71.

Elbow, Peter. "Being a Writer vs. Being an Academic: A Conflict in Goals." *College Composition and Communication*, vol. 46, no. 1, 1995, pp. 72–83.

Haskell, Robert E. *Transfer of Learning: Cognition, Instruction, and Reasoning.* Academic Press, 2001.

Jennings, Lydia. "Indigenous Food Knowledges Network Shows Connections between the Southwest and the Arctic." *Indigenous Foods Knowledges Network*, 2025, ifkn.org/food-story/indigenous-food-knowledges-network-shows-connections-between-southwest-and-arctic.

Kimmerer, Robin Wall. *Braiding Sweetgrass: Indigenous Wisdom, Scientific Knowledge, and the Teaching of Plants.* Milkweed Editions, 2013.

Kolbert, Elizabeth. *Field Notes from a Catastrophe: Man, Nature, and Climate Change.* Bloomsbury Publishing, 2006.

Majnep, Ian Saem, and Ralph Bulmer. *Birds of My Kalam Country.* Oxford UP, 1977.

Marback, Richard. "Embracing Wicked Problems: The Turn to Design in Composition Studies." *College Composition and Communication*, vol. 61, no. 2, 2009, pp. W397–W419, https://doi.org/10.58680/ccc20099494.

Noon, Karlie, and Krystal De Napoli. *Sky Country.* Thames and Hudson Publishing, 2022.

Rivers, Nathaniel A., et al. "The Mechanics of New Media (Science) Writing: Articulation, Design, Hospitality, and Electracy." *Kairos: A Journal of Rhetoric, Technology, and Pedagogy*, vol. 19, no. 2, 2015, kairos.technorhetoric.net/19.2/praxis/rivers-et-al/.

Smit, David W. *The End of Composition Studies*. Southern Illinois UP, 2007.

"Sophomore Inquiry (SINQ) and Junior Cluster Courses, 2023–2024." Portland State University, Aug. 2023, docs.google.com/document/d/1_yk_BMEcZk5 wr9wIH5A8TziLSvp3MhbFI23el-gu82U/edit.

"SUNY General Education Framework." State University of New York, 8 Jan. 2025, system.suny.edu/academic-affairs/acaproplan/general-education/ suny-ge/.

Thaiss, Christopher. *Writing Science in the Twenty-First Century*. Broadview Press, 2019.

Wardle, Elizabeth. "Creative Repurposing for Expansive Learning: Considering 'Problem-Exploring' and 'Answer-Getting' Dispositions in Individuals and Fields." *Composition Forum*, vol. 26, 2012, compositionforum.com/issue/ 26/creative-repurposing.php.

Yancey, Kathleen Blake, et al. *Writing across Contexts: Transfer, Composition, and Sites of Writing*. Utah State UP, 2014.

Part III

Science Writing for Change

Davy Knittle, Aneesha Manocha, and Arielle Rivera

Anti-Racist Science Writing: Environmental Justice and Energy Futures in the Interdisciplinary Humanities Classroom

In her essay on the Flint water crisis, the geographer Laura Pulido argues that "the situation in Flint is of concern to all of us, not only because of its tragic nature, but because as a racially devalued, surplus place, it is a testing ground for new forms of neoliberal practice that will become increasingly common" (2). Pulido demonstrates that the ongoing crisis disproportionately affects Black women and children. She argues that the conditions of crisis require new ways of thinking about how power unevenly affects daily life in cities.

The Flint water crisis has been narrated largely as a social problem—an environmental form of systemic anti-Blackness. Pulido describes the crisis not only as a social problem but also as a governance problem, resulting from the willful neglect of city, county, state, and national officials who turned away from a toxic water supply affecting a community racialized as Black. Beyond the social and governance perspectives, the Flint water crisis is also a problem of applied science, resulting from the insufficient maintenance of both the Flint River and the treatment and pipe system carrying water from the river to city residents. Thinking about how to represent the water crisis as an applied science problem raises questions about how science writing addresses the way that applied science is used as a tool of state power. How, in the case of the Flint water crisis, did engineering projects produce inequitable resource access along lines of race, class, and gender? As we address this problem in this essay, we consider an anti-racist approach to science writing. We ask, for instance, How have engineers working on distributing toxic water to city residents understood their role in perpetuating the crisis? How was the specialized training of infrastructure managers, civil engineers, and water scientists operationalized by the city's decision to save money rather than to protect residents from toxic water? How are engineers and other applied science practitioners trained to think about questions of race and power?

We use the terms "science writing" and "climate science writing" in this essay to refer to writing that describes scientific research for a public audience in order to improve public literacy about scientific concepts. We also ask how scientists learn to talk about the way their work intersects with material histories of racial inequality. We are interested in how anti-racist science writing might address both concerns in relation to each other. Using the frame of science writing to discuss descriptions of applied science and its role in environmental justice presents several interesting challenges. It requires us to think about histories of inequitable urban planning and their impact on climate futures as topics relevant to science writing. It also requires reflecting on how inequitable water access compels scientists and non-scientists to describe a complex problem against the grain of disciplinary divisions of expertise. Describing a situation such as the Flint water crisis requires putting concepts from water science in dialogue with principles from civil engineering and urban planning and policy. It also requires explaining how forms of expertise that are often rendered as objective are conditioned by and also participate in the inequitable distribution of racialized power.

In this essay we consider the humanities classroom as a context for helping STEM students think about how collaborations between disciplines in the humanities and the sciences can contribute to environmental justice in the United States. We ask what counts as science writing. We bring to an analysis of climate precarity in disinvested cities what Stacy Alaimo asks of scholarship in the blue humanities: "how can scholarship in decolonial science studies, Traditional Ecological Knowledge (TEK), indigenous sciences, and activist and citizen science become central?" (431). We are particularly interested in thinking about how STEM students develop vocabulary for locating environmental justice advocacy within longer histories of racialized power and inequality. How can the tools of science writing in the humanities classroom help us understand how scientists and engineers are asked to use their expertise to perpetuate anti-Black infrastructures and resource distribution? How can the humanities classroom invite STEM students to think about the social and political implications of their training in new ways?

We reflect on the spring 2022 Princeton University undergraduate American studies seminar Race, Gender, and the Urban Environment. We have composed this essay by reflecting on each of our contributions to the course and the impact of our academic specialization on our relationship to the seminar. Davy Knittle, the instructor of the course, has doctoral training in English and was a postdoc with the Mellon Forum on Architecture, Urbanism, and the Humanities when he taught the course, and Aneesha Manocha and Arielle Rivera, two students in the course, were undergraduate electrical and computer engineering majors at the time of their enrollment in the seminar.

Our goal in this essay is to reflect on our experiences in the course in order to draw broader conclusions about what makes discussions of anti-racist climate science writing in the humanities classroom most useful to STEM students, especially those interested in using their training to contribute to environmental justice in their professional work. We reflect on what the course was designed to accomplish and on how engineering students in the course combined the humanistic methods modeled in the course to interrogate how histories of racialized inequality condition the work they are being trained to undertake as electrical engineers. These questions were of particular interest to Arielle and Aneesha, who plan to use their training in their professional lives to work toward a just energy transition.

Davy's Reflections on Race, Gender, and the Urban Environment

Race, Gender, and the Urban Environment was housed in American studies and cross-listed in women's, gender, and sexuality studies; urban studies; and environmental studies. Because the course was cross-listed in environmental studies, it attracted many engineering juniors and seniors who were completing a certificate in environmental studies. The goal of Race, Gender, and the Urban Environment was to address the intersection of environmental, racial, and gender justice by focusing on how inequitable urban infrastructures perpetuate social inequality. The final weeks of the course focused specifically on how inequitable spatial histories shape debates about climate futures. Addressing questions of urban and environmental crisis in the course required us to articulate how norms of race and gender shape the conditions of crisis and to advocate for new ways of thinking about racial and gendered power to call for the equitable distribution of urban and environmental resources.

In the final weeks of the course, we theorized about how an anti-racist approach to climate futures differs from approaches that do not think explicitly about race and sociopolitical power, even as they use the language of environmental justice. One affordance of the humanities classroom was the opportunity to explore how many scholars across disciplines who work on questions of environment, power, and climate change use the same language to produce complex meanings. While students were familiar with concepts like "environmental justice," many students had previously taken for granted that everyone using this term agreed on what it means. Revisiting how scholars in different fields use the term *environmental justice*, students compared usages of the term that never mention race with other usages that situate the term as a tool for explaining how histories of racialized inequality produce uneven access to environmental resources and exposure to environmental harm.

As students considered how the same terms are used to reflect a wide range of connotations and meanings, they also identified contexts in which key terms were used to articulate opposing interpretations of a topic. For example, we began the course with the introduction to Julie Sze's *Environmental Justice in a Moment of Danger*, in which Sze articulates a genealogy of environmental justice activism in the United States. She traces how decades of anti-racist and decolonial activism have centered environmental issues and have identified how environmental racism has been amplified by decades of neoliberal governance. Sze is focused on community activism as the locus of meaningful change, and she is skeptical of the capacity of state policy or major private corporations to produce political or market-based solutions that address environmental racism. For engineering students who have learned the concept of environmental justice as an approach to mitigating harm as they design technical solutions within a market-based system, Sze's reading introduced a fundamental problem: How can *environmental justice* circulate as a term that refers at once to market-based approaches and to the impossibility of eradicating environmental racism within a racial capitalist system?

We also read Eve Tuck's "Suspending Damage: A Letter to Communities," which introduced for students the distinction between "damage-centered" research, which often equates communities with the harm caused to them, and "desire-based" research, which frames social and environmental harm as a negotiation between marginalization and resistance (409, 416–17). I assigned these readings to introduce students to the idea that discussions of environmental justice are inextricable from long histories of racialized dispossession of land in the United States. I also wanted students to begin to think about the range of disciplinary approaches to telling the history of resource and land access in United States and to understand that negotiating between these approaches can help reframe work that applies ideas of environmental justice to questions of climate equity and energy futures.

The final assessment for the course asked students to write a research essay of eight to ten pages, choosing one of three approaches: an interdisciplinary analysis of a topic in urban environmental justice, an urban environmental justice history, or an analysis of a cultural or literary text as it relates to an urban environmental justice issue. Many students chose the first option and selected a case study that allowed them to describe how two fields or interdisciplinary conversations (electrical engineering and the environmental humanities, for example) discussed a shared core concept. Many students also considered how applying two different disciplinary or interdisciplinary approaches to their case study nuanced the way they were thinking at the intersection of technical knowledge and critiques of racialized power. The following sections describe Arielle's and Aneesha's approaches to this final assignment and include their reflections on how they combined the methods of the course with their disciplinary training as electrical engineering majors.

Arielle's Reflections on Anti-Racist Climate Research

My final paper in this course was titled "Full Electricity Restoration in Puerto Rico: Decolonizing Electrical Infrastructure as an Engineer." I came to Princeton knowing that I wanted to major in electrical engineering because of my interest in strengthening electrical infrastructure in Puerto Rico, where my family originates. My coursework in electrical and computer engineering and Latin American studies had previously stayed separate, but this final project gave me the chance to merge my interests in sustainability, energy justice, and community resilience within the context of Puerto Rico's energy transition.

Our first reading from the course was an excerpt from Sze's *Environmental Justice in a Moment of Danger*, in which Sze writes that "[t]he status quo is too deeply invested in the institutional forces and ideological structures that exacerbate already existing conditions of environmental and social injustice" (7). I was driven to reexamine how built infrastructure is a result of a "political-economic system based on racialized extraction of land and labor, including from Indigenous peoples" (7), which inspired me to connect what I understand about Puerto Rico's history as a colonized land and how displacement of power from Indigenous people has influenced access to essential services like electricity.

My course project became an examination of how Puerto Rico's electric grid, from power plants to transmission lines, was built on racial capitalism; how disaster has exposed systemic inequities on the island; and how we can incorporate disaster planning strategies in engineering training to ensure that future engineers proactively seek ways to decentralize electricity in order to give more power to communities. The urban planning scholar Fayola Jacobs's "Black Feminism and Radical Planning: New Directions for Disaster Planning Research" gave critical insight into how dialogue between planners and communities can inform disaster management planning (even using Hurricane Katrina as an example), so I extended Jacobs's thinking to electric grid planning. Rethinking ideas of vulnerability versus resilience in disaster planning could be the key to enabling engineers to make decisions that will strengthen rural and Black communities, which have historically experienced the longest power outage times.

I also looked into Puerto Rican scholars who have engaged with environmental justice in energy activism. In *Energy Islands: Metaphors of Power, Extractivism, and Justice in Puerto Rico*, Catalina M. de Onís provides perspectives on a sudden interest in technological innovation for Puerto Rico's electric grid, linking this project to the colonial practice of regarding islands as exploitable experimental spaces. From these readings, I conclude with some broad recommendations for engineers to engage more critically with systemic inequities by enforcing training that specifically includes strategies to identify systems of racial capitalism in power grid planning. I also highlight how engineers in Puerto Rico should commit to sharing knowledge through outreach to local talent in order to promote growth in the workforce that could be more considerate of community needs.

Major Takeaways

I have identified a few key takeaways from my work on this project: First, I found that language plays a key role in disaster planning because it determines how engineers set goals and make decisions regarding grid planning. Highlighting community resilience over vulnerability, for example, motivates engineers to find ways to empower communities and learn from their perspectives rather than build on top of infrastructure that is not strong at the foundation.

Second, engineers can learn from community solutions. While advanced technology was deployed to communities in Puerto Rico after Hurricane Maria, communities were ultimately unable to maintain those systems just a few years after they were installed. Sustainable infrastructure is infrastructure that can be sustainably managed by communities, and engineers must make efforts to understand community dynamics in order to design environmentally conscious infrastructure. Sharing knowledge and promoting energy literacy, including through science writing and other modes of public communication, is critical to ensuring that Puerto Ricans can continue to take charge of their energy future.

Concluding Remarks and Post-Course Plans

After completing the course project, I began my senior thesis project, which involves modeling alternative plans for Puerto Rico's power system so that Puerto Rico can meet its renewable energy goals for 2030. While many models optimize systems for least cost without extreme weather considerations, I will be testing potential system reliability by simulating hurricane conditions. This project gave me insight into how energy systems modeling can incorporate community interests and made me recognize the limitations of my research in providing clear plans for achieving a reliable system on a community level without direct contributions from communities. My goal is to expand my project in the future to consider increased community-owned and -operated distributed energy generation in regions that have historically seen the longest power recovery times. After graduation I will be working in electric grid planning and learning more about how to bring community perspectives to decision-makers.

Aneesha's Reflections on Anti-Racist Climate Research

As an electrical and computer engineering student interested in working on clean energy pathways, I entered the course with a background in analyzing how various technology portfolios could decarbonize energy systems. Having limited understanding of how we define environmental justice but recognizing that this issue is critical in climate discourse, I aimed to finish the semester with a clear answer of what a clean, just energy transition means and how engineers could utilize this definition to pave the way for low-carbon futures.

However, similar to Arielle's class takeaways and from our first course reading, the introduction to Sze's *Environmental Justice in a Moment of Danger*, I learned that our approaches to environmental justice in a market-based context reinforce rather than mitigate harm within a capitalist society. Sze's work highlights the precarious nature of the status quo, which is characterized by neoliberal ideas and privatization of markets, societal mistrust, and the interwoven inequities of the climate crisis (2–4). I realized, first, that the language used to describe environmental injustices in engineering classrooms differs drastically from the discourse of scholars in the humanities and social sciences and, second, that there is not a clear consensus on what environmental justice means.

Thus, the goal of my final project was to understand how a range of research communities interpret environmental justice. I aimed to analyze the various usages of environmental justice in engineering, science, and modeling research communities and to juxtapose these usages with coursework on anti-capitalist frameworks described in some environmental justice literature. Another aim was to determine how engineers and scientists who are not trained to think about our racialized energy systems unknowingly perpetuate invisible and reinforcing systems of harm. I concluded my final project with key recommendations to engineering research communities focused on the energy transition who aim to think more critically about environmental justice in their work. While my final project did not extensively cover the available literature on environmental justice, I note five major takeaways on how scholars have described environmental injustices that I hope to continue to learn about, discuss with engineering and science research groups, and expand upon in my future work.

Major Takeaways

My findings and takeaways are based upon readings and applications mainly in the contexts of the United States. First, the topic of environmental justice tends to exist in separate and limited contexts in academic fields. I conclude that this isolation of discourse promotes thinking in silos. Environmental justice issues need to be incorporated in all dialogue on energy technologies, policies, and regulation because this crisis is intertwined in all aspects of infrastructure.

Second, we need to reconcile the language used by scholars in the humanities and social sciences with the language used by scientists and engineers. Research that is "damage-centered," as elaborated upon by Tuck in "Suspending Damage: A Letter to Communities," often provides a single viewpoint of people living in marginalized communities as being "depleted, ruined, and hopeless" (409). In course discussions on this reading, I learned how simplified the language surrounding environmental justice can often be in other fields. The failure to recognize harmful descriptions and homogenize the discourse on communities disproportionately harmed by environmental inequality perpetuates these viewpoints and can cause further miscommunication of issue prioritization and separation in how inequities are quantified and evaluated.

Third, environmental justice depends on both ordinary people's and researchers' ability to understand the history and importance of colonial structures, which requires researchers to engage with how our existing energy infrastructure has been created. Max Liboiron's *Pollution Is Colonialism* presents the contexts of colonialism that have been foundational to numerous environmental injustices: "Colonialism is more than the intent, identities, heritages, and values of settlers and their ancestors. It's about genocide and access" (9). Indigenous lands have historically and consistently been used to produce and consume energy in urban and populated areas, showcasing the history of devaluing Indigenous populations' lands and lives. Dina Gilio-Whitaker's *As Long As Grass Grows: The Indigenous Fight for Environmental Justice, from Colonization to Standing Rock* makes a similar argument, emphasizing that the ways environmental justice is often discussed does not solve issues of how Indigenous people have been marginalized (23–24). Energy systems and infrastructures have been built through oppressing various groups of individuals with colonialist acts. Environmental justice requires confronting histories of different Indigenous communities and acknowledging how these past harms have affected anti-Indigenous infrastructure and development (see, e.g., Liboiron 1–38). As engineers continue to change and build on the existing energy infrastructure, it is critical to understand how the current systems perpetuate systemic harms.

Fourth, students and scholars planning to build and engineer climate solutions need to take anti-racist courses and training. Otherwise we will create a fleet of researchers who are knowledgeable on science and engineering topics but fail to recognize relationships within their work as inherently racialized.

Lastly, it is imperative to engage with and talk to communities in order to understand lived experiences in relation to environmental injustices. Students within the confines of academic institutions and bubbles are often physically removed from these injustices and read narratives from other scholars. These surroundings reinforce relations, echo chambers, and familiarized discourse that fail to acknowledge the perspectives of those who have grown up in communities disproportionately harmed by environmental inequality.

Concluding Remarks and Post-Course Plans

Upon reflection on the final project, I pivoted my academic direction to prioritize analyzing environmental justice frameworks in modeling and engineering research environments. While I came into the course hoping to achieve a holistic and objective understanding of environmental justice, I left the class realizing there is no clear consensus about what a clean, just energy future means. Scholars across various fields need to collaborate, work in and with communities, and elevate marginalized voices in order to begin to understand how we will achieve our climate goals while prioritizing environmental justice. In my graduate studies, where I plan to analyze energy systems and pave net-zero emission pathways, I aim to center environmental justice, not only in the contexts of models and engineered solutions but also outside academic research.

Science Writing, Humanities Instructors, and STEM Students

As we revisited the course for this essay, we identified elements of the course procedures that helped students grapple with dissonant ideas of environmental justice. Much of the course foregrounded the process of negotiating key terms that at once have multiple conflicting definitions and are important shared vocabularies across fields. We found it helpful to spend much of our class time brainstorming collectively, using the discursive affordances of the humanities classroom to negotiate the fact that "environmental justice," "race," and "gender" were all concepts that we each believed we could define but that we came to understand we each define differently. We used different definitions for the same keyword not as a point of contention but as an opportunity for discussion that drew not only on humanistic tools but also on the interdisciplinary expertise of the students in the room.

Another aspect of the course that made it successful was that the writing assignments got longer over the course of the semester. Students who were not accustomed to doing a lot of writing in their courses found it helpful to begin with a short keywords assignment (500 to 750 words), in which they negotiated competing definitions for a key term in the course, and gradually work up to the final eight-to-ten-page paper. It was also helpful for students to receive extensive instructor feedback and for the course to be cross-listed so that many students from across the university were able to find the course. Additionally, the course modeled interdisciplinary inquiry by bringing in two guest speakers: a geographer and a planning scholar, both of whom use participatory action research methods in their scholarship.

Our course sought to rethink both public understanding of scientific research and how scientists conceptualize the sociopolitical impact of their research. Whereas other work in science writing asks how nonscientist audiences understand scientific concepts, the materials in our course also asked students, many of whom would be future practitioners in the applied sciences, to rethink the relationship between their work and histories of racialized and settler colonial inequality. At the conclusion of the course, both the students and the instructor felt that we had developed a framework to begin a conversation. We experienced both the excitement and frustration of spending an entire semester on what felt like a beginning, but we each took that beginning with us to our work in our respective fields. In a future version of the course, it would be helpful to be able to continue the conversation through cross-departmental collaborations and discussions that become long-standing conversations, which was not possible in a course that enrolled juniors and seniors and that was taught by an instructor with a one-year postdoctoral fellowship. We each look forward to having more sustained versions of this conversation in our future work both within and beyond academic institutions.

Works Cited

Alaimo, Stacy. "Science Studies and the Blue Humanities." Introduction. *Configurations*, vol. 27, no. 4, fall 2019, pp. 429–32.

de Onís, Catalina M. *Energy Islands: Metaphors of Power, Extractivism, and Justice in Puerto Rico.* U of California P, 2021.

Gilio-Whitaker, Dina. *As Long As Grass Grows: The Indigenous Fight for Environmental Justice, from Colonization to Standing Rock.* Beacon Press, 2019.

Jacobs, Fayola. "Black Feminism and Radical Planning: New Directions for Disaster Planning Research." *Planning Theory*, vol. 18, no. 1, 2019, pp. 24–39.

Liboiron, Max. *Pollution Is Colonialism.* Duke UP, 2021.

Pulido, Laura. "Flint, Environmental Racism, and Racial Capitalism." *Capitalism Nature Socialism*, vol. 27, no. 3, 2016, pp. 1–16.

Sze, Julie. "Environmental Justice at the Crossroads of Danger and Freedom." Introduction. *Environmental Justice in a Moment of Danger*, by Sze, U of California P, 2020, pp. 1–24.

Tuck, Eve. "Suspending Damage: A Letter to Communities." *Harvard Educational Review*, vol. 79, no. 3, fall 2009, pp. 409–28.

Bridgitte Barclay

Women's Historical Ecomedia and Environmental Advocacy

As the field of feminist science studies has emphasized for decades, investigating science narratives is important to critiquing past work, to establishing the importance of science narratives in public policy, and to creating more just science going forward. Who scientists are, who writes about science, what questions scientists and science writers ask, and what ideological perspectives they have affect both what stories they read and what stories they tell. When I teach Environmental Research and Writing: Popular Science and Advocacy—an undergraduate course with environmental studies, English, and premed majors at Aurora University—I emphasize historically paradigm-shifting narratives, we critique marginalizing narratives, and students create better ways forward. Students read ecocritical theory and use that scholarship to write a critical analysis essay about the author and habitat diorama artist Delia Akeley's and the author and videographer Osa Johnson's early-twentieth-century expeditionary science writing and ecomedia[1] before creating final ecomedia projects focused on environmental justice. In their archival work, students address how these pioneering women, who made lasting contributions to early-twentieth-century environmental popular science that we still see today, also participated in patriarchal, anthropocentric, and racist expeditionary colonial science. This focus on the impact of science narratives helps students move through critical inquiry of historical science writing, engage with current questions of diversity in environmental justice, and think through their own ecomedia creation.

The Course: Environmental History and Theory, Archival Ecomedia, and Ecomedia Creation

Environmental Research and Writing focuses on science communication and environmental justice. We analyze US popular science narratives and advocacy writing, and students research environmental science communication in museum habitats, popular science writing, and wildlife films before writing, creating, and presenting their research. I ask in the assignments that students think through the animal, environmental, gender, race, and slow violence issues in their topics, and by the end of the semester, they generate their own ecomedia. My goal in creating the course was to tap into the media that drew students to environmental studies and the sciences and to have them think through those artifacts while also reading about environmental justice and how to make impactful media themselves. Thus, the course outcomes focus on awareness of audience, purpose, and authority; credible research; modes of retelling science for audience engagement; environmental justice and popular science narratives; and collaborative writing.

With these goals in mind, I begin the course with a history of popular science and ecomedia in US environmental movements, specifically the 1893 World's Columbian Exposition in Chicago and the habitat dioramas and expeditionary science media that grew from there. I cover the Bone Wars of the nineteenth century that resulted in the dinosaurs we see in museums now, the questions of evolution and extinction that those expeditions and museum displays brought into popular media, the ways museums function as a result of such displays and animal extinctions, and how all these narratives tell a story about the United States and humans. I remind students that many of us still encounter wildlife through museums, wildlife media, or zoos, all of which this early-twentieth-century era was pivotal in producing. As one student, Jorge Sanchez, wrote, such media is "easily digestible" and accessible "to the general public." Museums such as Chicago's Field Museum and the American Museum of Natural History are both products of the paleontology of the Bone Wars, the habitat diorama creation and exhibition at the Chicago exposition, and the expeditionary science of going abroad to find spaces to colonize and document in museum media (Alder; Bruni; Vetter). By the mid–twentieth century, US citizens were seeing extinct species in museums and contemplating human extinction after the end of World War II, and science narratives affected and were affected by sociopolitical narratives.[2] Even today, the Field Museum and American Museum of Natural History, as well as nature documentaries and edutainment, still play major roles in human understanding of the natural world.[3]

Ecocritical Theory and Public Engagement

Building on these historical ecomedia, students read ecocritical scholarship, and this offers more depth to the problems they see in some of the historical ecomedia. I start by noting that feminist science scholars such as Sandra Harding, Evelyn Fox Keller, and others illuminated how scientific data are culturally affected by who is doing the science, the questions the scientists ask, and what they observe. In other words, this understanding prompts students to recognize how research questions, fieldwork, interpretation of data, and scientific communication are shaped by worldviews and values (see, e.g., Mortimer-Sandilands and Erickson). Especially important are issues related to the roles of nonhuman research participants, willing or not.[4] As Myra J. Hird writes, "[N]on-human animals have for some time been overburdened with the task of making sense of human social relations" (35; see also Jue; Neimanis). Confronting these complexities affects students' later collaborative ecomedia by drawing attention to the importance of diverse voices communicating science, the priority of understanding one's audience, and care in approaching topics justly.

This need for us to build better narratives and a strong ecocritical understanding, and the idea that the material world tells stories that we interpret and retell, structures how I teach the course. Teaching environmental science writing means teaching the ways in which policy, politics, literature, ecomedia, science, anthropology, history, and more thread together in scientific data interpretation and communication. And audiences reading and watching scientific texts create further interpretation. As the American Association for the Advancement of Science (AAAS) addresses, the public brings their own narratives to science, stories influenced by their values, political leanings, culture, and more. Science is currently politicized and has been so historically. The world is material, but human scientists interpret that materiality, the human public interprets it further as idea, and those layers of interpretation equal real, substantive changes in the world through policy.[5]

Exemplifying that idea, the specific ecocritical texts we read in the first portion of Environmental Research and Writing are Donna Haraway's "Anthropocene, Capitalocene, Plantationocene, Chthulucene: Making Kin"; Rob Nixon's "Slow Violence"; Rebecca Solnit's "Grounds for Hope," the foreword to *Hope in the Dark: Untold Histories, Wild Possibilities*; the introduction to Leilani Nishime and Kim D. Hester Williams's *Racial Ecologies*; and "Geology, Race, and Matter" from Kathryn Yusoff's *A Billion Black Anthropocenes or None* (1–22). Students write one-page response essays to the texts before class, connecting them with the ecocritical and environmental justice ideas we have read and discussed. The common thread students discern in all these texts is that colonial science has historically marginalized human and nonhuman communities, ignoring local Indigenous knowledges; has made resources out of places, humans, and nonhumans; and has conflated science and capital. For example, Nixon's idea of "slow violence"—"a violence that is neither spectacular nor instantaneous but instead incremental, whose calamitous repercussions are postponed for years or decades or centuries"—is rooted in larger systems of oppression. Slow violence is a major theme in the course, and students are deeply affected by it. Yusoff demonstrates the concept, noting how geological expeditions for precious metals created human capital that enriched European nations and plundered others, writing, "The human and its subcategory, the inhuman, are historically relational to a discourse of settler-colonial rights and the material practices of extraction" (2). My students struggle with Yusoff's writing but find the ideas useful. Yusoff's points are also significant in my own understanding of the topics.

Students read others applying these concepts in current issues before they move into their archival and ecomedia research on Akeley and Johnson to apply the concepts to historical issues. We read Harriet A. Washington's "How Environmental Racism Is Fueling the Coronavirus Pandemic," the Green New Deal (United States), *The Open Notebook* e-book, and the AAAS web pages on public engagement and advocacy ("Public Engagement"; "Take Action Toolkit"); we also watch videos of some UN climate-focused Conference of the Parties (COP) speakers, such as India

Logan and Elizabeth Wathuti ("Indigenous Activist"; "Climate Activist"). Analyzing these artifacts in class together allows students to see contemporary justice-oriented science and ecomedia theories in action. It is important for students to see how scholars, organizations, politicians, and activists work to realize just science narratives in interdisciplinary ways. Students connect this to Logan's COP26 speech—with its call to restore lands to Indigenous communities—and the policy proposals in the Green New Deal, addressing how both apply entangled understandings of environmental science and justice.

Archival Ecomedia and Critical Analysis Essay

Further applying these concepts, in the next section of the course we cover the archival writing and ecomedia of Akeley and Johnson. Their work, which helped build the museum and ecomedia popular science that we cover in the first few weeks, serves as case studies in both women's ecomedia and in the racist and anthropocentric expeditionary colonial science. Students write an essay in which they analyze Akeley's and Johnson's ecomedia using the ecocritical frameworks we have covered. Akeley's and Johnson's ecomedia changed the ways in which Americans approached the natural world. Akeley contributed to popular science narratives in her museum habitat diorama work (some of the founding dioramas in the Field Museum collection), her museum expeditions, and her writing (*J. T., Jr.*). Visitors to Chicago's Field Museum can see her work in one of the oldest dioramas—the Four Seasons of the Deer diorama—and in the bigger of the two taxidermy elephants in the entry atrium's Fighting African Elephants display. She was also the first woman to lead a museum-funded expedition. Imagine the impact of her museum work alone, with the vast number of Field Museum visitors every year.

Johnson's work equally affected US narratives of nonhuman animals and other cultures: Johnson's writing and proto-creature-feature adventure science set a tone for both thoughtful consideration of and sensationalist style of nature documentary. Her book *I Married Adventure* was the nation's top-selling nonfiction in 1940 (Imperato and Imperato 209) and was made into a film (Johnson; *I Married Adventure*), and she and her husband, Martin, filmed fourteen documentaries together, often on the Akeley field camera, invented by Carl Akeley, Delia's husband before divorce (Horak). Johnson not only filmed, edited, and organized shoots (though not credited) but also was on-screen (*Congorilla; Simba*). After she survived a 1937 plane crash in which her husband died, she made three more films and one television production, more than he had made on his own before marrying her, yet his name alone is the one often associated with their ecomedia (Horak). In fact, Osa was billed as "Mrs. Johnson" for most of her career. The entertainment documentaries not only did a lot to bring animals to the attention of twentieth-century Americans but also feature horrific scenes of possibly staged "animal attacks" (Willis), real animal deaths, and exploitative colonial racism.

Together with archival research on Akeley and Johnson in the Field Museum's archives of Akeley's work (libguides.fieldmuseum.org/Akeley), Columbia University's *Women Film Pioneers Project* (wfpp.columbia.edu), and the Martin and Osa Johnson Safari Museum's website archives (safari museum.com), students prepare for the critical analysis essay through our class discussions and short response essays. For the critical analysis essay, I ask students to apply the theoretical readings to Akeley's and Johnson's work, addressing how the critical readings changed students' understanding of popular environmental science narratives, how they imagine better approaches to future popular environmental science narratives, and how new modes of writing with diverse audiences in mind can be instrumental in changing environmental science narratives.

The estrangement of historical texts helps students understand how sociopolitical perspectives can influence popular science narratives, and students note the eye-opening experience of realizing this phenomenon. For example, one student, Gwen Schretter, found Johnson's commentary on being a woman expeditioner fascinating and complicated, citing Johnson: "I can hardly wait to get back to the jungle. I prefer it out there. When I sling my rifle over my shoulder and go out into the forest, I feel as if everything belonged to me . . . no worry about what to wear and what other women are wearing. I am Queen of the Jungle" (qtd. in Imperato and Imperato 30). As a biology and environmental studies student, Schretter found the contradictions of Johnson's lasting contributions to ecomedia, the pressure to perform traditional femininity, and her disregard for Indigenous communities and now endangered animals a complicated legacy that requires attention. Other students echoed Schretter's analysis. Marisella Kidd argued that Akeley's and Johnson's ecomedia writing and videography "reveals the American/Eurocentric ideals that are rooted in the nationalistic and social Darwinism that was believed during the early twentieth century" despite Johnson being a "trailblazer for women in the film industry." Isabella Pryor wrote that Akeley's and Johnson's "colonialist and expedition imagery" negatively "shaped current science narratives by building a foundation of dehumanization . . . , turning Indigenous, Black, and Brown people into nothing more than props to be posed for postcards, and often beside them, like a grisly omen, the carcasses of now endangered species." Understanding the complications of creating ecomedia helped students think through their own projects.

As they applied the ecocritical theories we read and let me know which were most effective in their thinking, many students cited Nixon's concept of "slow violence" and Nishime and Williams's assertion that ecological justice requires that we shine a light on intersections of environmental and colonial violence: "We must at once preserve and rewrite the knowledge of our past, present, and future relations" (253). Many struggled with Yusoff's writing but noted Yusoff's ideas of colonial extraction in analyzing their historical ecomedia. The takeaway for most students was that groundbreaking and impactful ecomedia, if helpful in some ways, can nevertheless be complicit in perpetuating racist and anthropocentric narratives.

Ecomedia Projects

Building on the ecocritical theory and historical narratives of the first half of the semester, the culminating project for the second half of Environmental Research and Writing is the final writing and ecomedia project and presentation. The assignment calls for students to clearly and effectively advocate for an environmental topic of their choice to digital and in-person public audiences. The project is shaped by the environmental critical theoretical readings, rhetorical strategies, and communication tools we cover the first half of the semester and continue as students work in steps. I ask students to decide on their pairs or groups and consider what environmental topic they find engaging, what audience they need to inform or persuade, and the larger goals (i.e., why it is important to inform or persuade that audience). I also ask them what research and writing skills they want to build, what media skills they want to build, and what they want to emphasize in their required digital portfolios (professional websites they create) for graduate schools, job interviews, or both. The various steps throughout the second half of the semester as students build their ecomedia are to write a preliminary proposal that outlines their topic, audience, and purpose; to research thoroughly, building an annotated bibliography; to produce in the final project at least three types of writing, at least one of which should be audiovisual ecomedia; and to present the information to the public digitally and in person. Throughout the portion of the course devoted to projects, we meet as a full class about one-third of the time, and the rest of the time students either meet with me or, if it's not their designated class period to meet with me, work as a group interviewing, going to sites, recording podcasts, filming documentaries, or the like. The project requires students to think about audience, clarity, and argument, and the collaborative component allows students' diverse perspectives to inform the creation of the ecomedia.

The ecomedia projects impressed me, both in the first iteration of the course, where students worked individually, and in the second, where I required collaborative work. The first time I taught the course, I had students work individually (we were still remote), but I have since changed that setup in order to push students to communicate and present their portions of research to their groupmates and to enable various perspectives in one group. If the goal is to communicate to a public audience clearly and effectively, I want students to first practice that on a smaller scale in their own groups. In the first run of the course, though, several of the students and I wrote an article for the Association for the Study of Literature and Environment, in which we highlighted their ecomedia projects: a podcast about permafrost in which the student interviewed Siberian and Alaskan scientists, a documentary about mental health and creating a monarch habitat, a children's book, and a digital comic and short story, for instance (Barclay et al.).

In the most recent iteration of the course, I required that students worked collaboratively for the whole second half of the semester. Groups created a campus sustainability proposal that they presented to the president and a larger audience (we now have a campus community garden as a result of this beginning work that students have since built on); a community garden website about composting, rain barrels, soil analysis, and sustainable food practices (camposmaggy.wixsite.com/my-site); a website about mental health and campus green spaces; a documentary on the water quality of the Fox River, a few miles from campus ("Fox River"); and a women-run digital environmental journal, *Environmentalese* (initially created and edited by Dalin Johnson, Marisella Kidd, and Sarah Morrell and edited by Brooke Karas, Natasha Leclercq, and Kimberly Leslie from 2024 to present), that seeks to build on Akeley's and Johnson's legacies as women in the sciences while rectifying their racist and speciesist ecomedia (environmentalese.weebly.com). In the often daunting fields of environmental humanities and science writing, students' creative, publicly engaged ecomedia are inspiring and energizing.

Feedback and Changes

In teaching this class, I have learned that students generally love the social justice ecocritical texts, find Yusoff's *A Billion Black Anthropocenes or None* a little too inaccessible, find *The Open Notebook* and the AAAS public engagement resources helpful, and love looking at current environmental political and policy issues. In response to this feedback and my own evaluation of the course, I have added more technology lessons in class, not only discussing script writing, op-eds, rhetorical strategies, and the like but also asking the professors who run our podcast and video studios on campus to visit class to discuss the basics of audio and visual ecomedia and how-tos. We also discuss website design and making students' ecomedia and websites accessible with alt text ("Guide"; Hiltner), closed-captioning, and search engine optimization. These more technical aspects are helpful to students, so I have had to learn enough to teach some of it, and I ask for guest lecturers when necessary. And I've had to learn how to teach new modes of writing—website creation, podcast intros and outros, museum exhibit placards, and the like. And in the next iterations of the course, I am changing some of the readings and expanding some of the excerpts to the full texts in response to students' feedback. (They wanted the full versions of some books!)[6]

Perhaps unsurprisingly, environmental studies majors and English majors who choose to take this course care deeply about social justice issues and want to learn how to effectively communicate ecomedia to a public audience. Environmental humanities scholars talk frequently about how easy it is to lose hope when you study, teach, and write about environmental destruction for a living, and, as we know, teaching writing is taxing, and anything having to do with science and public engagement is especially difficulty in our current climate of science denial and misinformation. However, teaching students to analyze and create better science writing and ecomedia is a balm. Akeley's and Johnson's work highlights women's contributions to environmental sciences while also providing a means for critiquing the problematic expeditionary colonial science that they perpetuated in their ecomedia. Perhaps, then, analyzing Akeley's and Johnson's work enables students to analyze historical science writing in order to understand how science narratives affect public understanding before then applying the same concepts to current scientific writing, thereby changing future science writing and ecomedia. Narratives matter, and we can look back at science narratives to learn how to move forward in more just, publicly engaged ways.

While Akeley and Johnson were pioneering scientists, students critique their racist and speciesist shortcomings. Akeley and Johnson extracted resources by extracting humans and nonhumans as resources through the ecomedia objectification of people and animals. As Cajetan Iheka writes, "[R]ace [is] the elephant in the room of wildlife media" (154), and that is true of Akeley's and Johnson's ecomedia. Relatedly, a student in the course, Jorge Sanchez, wrote, "The principle of accessibility in past and present forms of media is crucial in shaping the environmental narrative in America by promoting ecological advocacy and inclusivity." Looking at the past enables better ways forward. Another student, Dalin Johnson, wrote, "[E]ffective advocacy requires we reimagine our perception of and discourse surrounding history in order to think about the environment more inclusively and, in turn, seek social equality." At the Hispanic-serving institution where I teach, which has a greater percentage of first-generation students compared with many universities and an energizing number of women in the sciences and environmental studies, the works of Akeley and Johnson hit home, both inspiring and inciting a need for better science writing and ecomedia. As Magdalena Campos, one of the students in the course, wrote, "Hope requires context and a story."

Notes

1. Generally defined as nonprint media such as documentaries, podcasts, films, websites, dioramas, exhibits, spoken word, theater, and the like. See, for example, Rust et al.; Iheka.

2. We discuss work by science fiction authors such as Judith Merril, Carol Emshwiller, and Leigh Brackett, among many others, who wrote about atomic apocalypse and mass extinction.

3. Museum dioramas still date back to these expeditions and thereby affect understanding of relations among humans and between humans and nonhumans. Additionally, the Akeley camera, invented by Carl Akeley, used in early films and expeditions and in Osa and Martin Johnson's work, made possible the overhead, running, and action shots still seen in ecomedia today.

4. Nate Otjen writes that "[e]ncounters with matter emerge from, and have reshaped, the conditions of daily existence" (306), asking "[h]ow . . . individuals from various social groups and identity categories experience differently the hail issued by things" (307). While Otjen writes of the ways in which humans make meaning out of objects, his point is also useful in relation to how humans interpret other human and nonhuman subjects as objects depending on their own sociopolitical biases.

5. Consider, for instance, historical "science" and public belief in narratives turned policy in eugenics and other racist policies ("scientific" data about races), reproductive rights and other sexist policies ("scientific" data about reproduction

and the female mind), and LGBTQIA rights and other heterosexist policies ("scientific" data and the AIDS crisis).

6. This semester students read the full text of Nishime and Williams's *Racial Ecologies*, and I replaced Yusoff's *A Billion Black Anthropocenes or None* with Stacy Alaimo's *Exposed: Environmental Politics and Pleasures in Posthuman Times*, which discusses more ecomedia. And students were absolutely delighted that Williams and Alaimo joined us on Zoom for a class session to answer student questions.

Works Cited

Akeley, Delia. *J. T., Jr.: The Biography of an African Monkey*. Macmillan, 1928.

Alaimo, Stacy. *Exposed: Environmental Politics and Pleasures in Posthuman Times*. U of Minnesota P, 2016.

Alder, Emily. "(Re)Encountering Monsters: Animals in Early-Twentieth-Century Weird Fiction." *Textual Practice*, vol. 31, no. 6, 2017, pp. 1083–100, https://doi.org/10.1080/0950236X.2017.1358686.

Barclay, Bridgitte, et al. "Hopeful Ecomedia in the Pandemic." *ASLE*, 2024, www.asle.org/features/hopeful-ecomedia-in-the-pandemic/.

Brackett, Leigh. *The Long Tomorrow*. Doubleday, 1955.

Bruni, John. *Scientific Americans: The Making of Popular Science and Evolution in Early-Twentieth-Century U.S. Literature and Culture*. U of Wales P, 2014.

"Climate Activist Elizabeth Wathuti Speech at World Leaders Summit of COP26 at Glasgow." *YouTube*, uploaded by KENYA News MEDIA, 1 Nov. 2021, youtu.be/OUR3HMRhHT4?si=xioyB-gr8WFkey2J.

Congorilla. Directed by Martin Johnson, performances by Osa Johnson, 1932.

Emshwiller, Carol. "Day at the Beach." *The Magazine of Fantasy and Science Fiction*, vol. 17, no. 2, Aug. 1959, pp. 35–43.

"The Fox River—Water Quality and Supporting Sustainability." *YouTube*, uploaded by Calvin Fritsch, 21 Apr. 2023, www.youtube.com/watch?v=kCQ5gmjPIFc.

"Guide to Creating Accessible Presentations." *Digital Library Federation*, www.diglib.org/dlf-events/2016forum/guide-to-creating-accessible-presentations/. Accessed 25 Mar. 2025.

Haraway, Donna J. "Anthropocene, Capitalocene, Plantationocene, Chthulucene: Making Kin." *Environmental Humanities*, vol. 6, no. 1, 2015, pp. 159–65.

Hiltner, Ken. "A Nearly Carbon-Neutral Conference Model." *Ken Hiltner*, hiltner.english.ucsb.edu/index.php/ncnc-guide/. Accessed 25 Mar. 2025.

Hird, Myra J. "Animal Transex." *Australian Feminist Studies*, vol. 21, no. 49, 2006, pp. 35–50, https://doi.org/10.1080/08164640500470636.

Horak, Laura. "Osa Johnson." *Women Film Pioneers Project*, wfpp.columbia.edu/pioneer/ccp-osa-johnson/. Accessed 25 May 2025.

Iheka, Cajetan. *African Ecomedia: Network Forms, Planetary Politics*. Duke UP, 2021.

I Married Adventure. Directed by Osa Johnson, 1940.

Imperato, Pascal James, and Eleanor M. Imperato. *They Married Adventure: The Wandering Lives of Martin and Osa Johnson*. Rutgers UP, 1992.

"Indigenous Activist India Logan-Riley's Full Speech at COP26." *YouTube*, uploaded by Doha Debates, 5 Nov. 2021, youtu.be/Qdxa1H4y-hw?si=Qkww WX15Rk3qTFGj.

Johnson, Osa. *I Married Adventure*. Stratford Press, 1940.

Jue, Melody. *Wild Blue Media: Thinking through Seawater*. Duke UP, 2020.

Merril, Judith. "That Only a Mother." *Astounding Science-Fiction*, June 1948, pp. 88–95.

Mortimer-Sandilands, Catriona, and Bruce Erickson, editors. *Queer Ecologies: Sex, Nature, Politics, Desire*. Indiana UP, 2010.

Neimanis, Astrida. *Bodies of Water: Posthuman Feminist Phenomenology*. Bloomsbury Academic, 2017.

Nishime, Leilani, and Kim D. Hester Williams. Introduction. *Racial Ecologies*, edited by Nishime and Williams, U of Washington P, 2018, pp. 3–15.

Nixon, Rob. "Slow Violence." *The Chronicle of Higher Education*, 26 June 2011, chronicle.com/article/slow-violence/.

The Open Notebook: The Story behind the Best Science Stories. American Association for the Advancement of Science, May 2012, aaas.org/sites/default/files/con tent_files/AAAS_Open_Notebook_eBook.pdf.

Otjen, Nate. "When Things Hail: The Material Encounter in Anthropocene Literature." *Configurations: A Journal of Literature, Technology, and Culture*, vol. 28, no. 3, 2020, pp. 285–307.

"Public Engagement." *American Association for the Advancement of Science*, 2025, www.aaas.org/focus-areas/public-engagement.

Rust, Stephen, et al., editors. *Ecomedia: Key Issues*. Routledge, 2015.

Simba: King of the Beasts. Directed by Martin Johnson, performances by Osa Johnson, 1928.

Solnit, Rebecca. "Grounds for Hope." Foreword. *Hope in the Dark: Untold Histories, Wild Possibilities*, by Solnit, 3rd ed., Duke UP, 2015, pp. xi–xxvi.

"Take Action Toolkit." *American Association for the Advancement of Science*, 2025, www.aaas.org/resources/take-action-toolkit.

United States, Congress, House. Recognizing the Duty of the Federal Government to Create a Green New Deal. *Congress.gov*, www.congress.gov/bill/ 117th-congress/house-resolution/332/text. 117th Congress, 1st session, House Resolution 332, introduced 20 Apr. 2021.

Vetter, Jeremy. "Cowboys, Scientists, and Fossils: The Field Site and Local Collaboration in the American West." *ISIS*, vol. 99, no. 2, 2008, pp. 273–303.

Washington, Harriet A. "How Environmental Racism Is Fueling the Coronavirus Pandemic." *Nature*, 19 May 2020, www.nature.com/articles/d41586 -020-01453-y.

Willis, Matthew. "How Two Kansans Invented the Safari Documentary." *JSTOR Daily*, 1 July 2021, daily.jstor.org/how-two-kansans-invented-the-safari -documentary/.

Yusoff, Kathryn. *A Billion Black Anthropocenes or None*. U of Minnesota P, 2018.

Nicole M. Merola

Jamaica Kincaid's Anti-Colonial, Black, Cross-Species, Embodied, Feminist Onto-Epistemologies

The Antiguan-born writer Jamaica Kincaid's *My Garden (Book):* comprises essays that portray and enact a form of intentionally discomfiting critical botanizing. Throughout the essays Kincaid names her participation in networks of desiring plants and unpacks the imbrication of her gardening practices with colonialist modes of "arranging a landscape" (134). *My Garden (Book):* iterates a project Kincaid pursues across fiction and nonfiction: to surface and particularize the histories of arrival and the conditions of ongoing survival of people (and nonhuman animals and plants) forcibly extracted for empire.[1] Kincaid's refusal to look away from these histories and conditions and the literary techniques through which she grounds and presses her anti-colonial critique make *My Garden (Book):* a provocative text.

In *My Garden (Book):* Kincaid narrativizes personal and historical events. She uses methodologies including close reading of written text, layered descriptions of landscape, and etymological investigation. And she employs literary tactics such as circumlocution, ellipsis, exposition, parenthesis, parataxis, and repetition. The phrase "what to do" peppers the essay "Wisteria" (11–28), echoing her persistent use of the question form throughout the book, its proliferating versions, and its multiple guises. The question form operates, variously, as refrain, as demand for self-reflection simultaneously addressed to herself and to the reader, as signal for analytic exposition to follow, and as comportment. This inquisitive comportment, an onto-epistemology (or relational being-doing-knowing), was the initial catalyst for including Kincaid's work in the class I discuss below: Theories of NatureCulture, which was a required first-semester course in the Nature-Culture-Sustainability Studies master's program at the Rhode Island School of Design.[2]

Required courses in the master's program, an interdisciplinary degree housed in the school's division of liberal arts, were taught by environmental humanities and environmental social sciences faculty members. The program enrolled domestic and international students with a wide range of academic training, including undergraduate degrees in art and design, business, English, interdisciplinary liberal arts, and philosophy. When there were open seats, master's-level students from other programs within the school could register for the class. To develop a shared lexicon within an interdisciplinary cohort, Theories of NatureCulture introduced concepts, onto-epistemologies, thinkers, and writing styles students might utilize in future coursework and research. To support this goal, the course was organized topically; for each week's seminar, students read pairs or groups of texts. Through facilitated discussion, we examined the arguments and forms of the assigned texts and identified interventions, methodologies, genres, and disciplines commensurate with students' individual interests.[3]

While each set of readings was scaffolded toward multiple learning objectives, the one I highlight here is the development of an "epistemic community" to inform the study of nature, culture, and sustainability. I taught this concept through *Getting Started on Research* (Boden et al.), an accessible text for an interdisciplinary master's cohort in their first semester.[4] In the book Rebecca Boden and colleagues define "epistemic community" as "a strong sense of belonging to a particular community of scholars" with whom one's research is "in conversation" (18) and as a way of situating one's research "in a particular area of literature" (19). Students considered the concept of intellectual networks communally, in seminar discussion, and independently during a semester-long inquiry that resulted in a final project titled "Question/Concept/Thinker Map." This project, which rendered epistemic community in visual form, asked students to pick their own focus and conduct independent research to constellate a focused set of authors, keywords, texts, or critical conversations. Students explained the networked relationships through graphics and writing. While students could include some texts or thinkers from the syllabus, they were not required to ground their investigation in those texts or thinkers. One opportunity the map afforded was for students to extend, challenge, or depart from the concerns represented by the texts and authors on the syllabus. The assignment also functioned as a culminating exercise in citation practice and an instance of communal archive building that recorded the interests of the cohort. To emphasize the importance of creating and fostering their own supportive research community, I explicitly framed the end-of-semester presentation of a draft of the map as a moment for peer-to-peer feedback prior to finalizing and submitting the assignment. For students who entered the program with a strong sense of direction regarding their master's thesis, the map directly seeded their prospectus; for students who were still exploring topics and research methodologies, the assignment provided preparatory skill building.

Students read Kincaid's essays "My Garden (Book):" (3–8), "Wisteria" (11–28), and "In History" (153–66) in a midsemester unit focused on cross-species entanglements between and across human animals, nonhuman animals, and plants. The inclusion of human-plant relationships in this textual grouping recognized both the longer histories of attention to encounters between human animals and nonhuman animals in the environmental humanities and social sciences and the more recent emergence of critical plant studies.[5] In the context of the course unit, Kincaid's writing dialogued with and pressured Matthew Fuller and Olga Goriunova's chapter "Plant" (93–119), excerpts from Jacques Derrida's *The Animal That Therefore I Am* (1–14, 23–35, 37–41, 47–51), and excerpts from Donna Haraway's *Staying with the Trouble: Making Kin in the Chthulucene* (1–29). For example, while both Kincaid and Fuller and Goriunova are interested in "the significant way in which plants make themselves felt" (Fuller and Goriunova 94), the "expanded aesthetics of plants" (94) that Fuller and Goriunova unfurl is grounded in cybernetics and discussion of plant behavior and physiology. The intellectual network they engage in "Plant" includes Mikhail Bakhtin, Gilles Deleuze and Félix Guattari, Friedrich Nietzsche, Francis Ponge, and Isabelle Stengers. As the discussion below details, Kincaid works different ground. And while the syllabus presented the four texts as two pairs—Kincaid and Fuller and Goriunova on plants, Derrida and Haraway on nonhuman animals—I chose these texts in part because of the way they encourage other crosscuts. For example, as my brief gloss of Fuller and Goriunova might signal, in class discussion we drew out the affinities of their intellectual networks with Derrida's. We considered Kincaid and Haraway together to discuss the accessibility of different writing styles for different audiences, techniques used to signal authorial standpoint, and affinities and differences of their intellectual networks.

In addition to how Kincaid's work sat within the unit, it also functioned as an interlocutor for writing by Robin Wall Kimmerer, Enrique Salmón, and Lauret Savoy, among others, highlighting the idea of a community of Indigenous and Black thinkers that served as a thread throughout the semester. For example, Kincaid and Savoy present different but related anti-colonial, anti-Eurocentric perspectives on socioecological frameworks canonical to mainstream twentieth- and early-twenty-first-century US environmentalisms. To briefly elaborate, in "Prologue: Thoughts on a Frozen Pond" (1–3), "The View from Point Sublime" (5–13), and "Provenance Notes" (15–30), Savoy critiques spectacular monumentalism, its relation to the theory of the sublime, its embeddedness in US national parks tourism, and its exclusions. The connections Savoy explores between memory, origin stories, experiences of land and landscape, and race echo some of Kincaid's interests. So, too, does Kincaid's engagement with scientific practice echo some of Savoy's interests; Savoy's training in geology is central to how *Trace* unfolds. Although I did not teach them in the same unit, the work of Kincaid, Kimmerer, and Salmón is connected through notions of critical botanizing and being-in-relation. Indigenous practices of being-in-relation also resonated in a lecture by endawnis Spears and Cassius Spears, Jr., on Narragansett ecological knowledges and cultural traditions and in texts from the climate change unit, including poetry by dg nanouk okpik and excerpts from Ellavut: *Our Yup'ik World and Weather: Continuity and Change on the Bering Sea Coast*, which aims "to document Yup'ik oral traditions, not as arcane facts but as knowledge systems with continuing relevance in our rapidly changing world" (Fienup-Riordan and Reardon viii). One goal with this set of texts was to expose students to commonalities and differences across multiple Indigenous ecological knowledge traditions.[6]

In what follows I examine the natureculture theorizing Kincaid performs in the essay "Wisteria" in order to highlight the value of her writing for an interdisciplinary environmental studies cohort. I focus here on "Wisteria" because it encapsulates so many of the key concerns and literary tactics that Kincaid utilizes across the three essays I assign. In particular, in "Wisteria" Kincaid foregrounds affect, attention, care, classification, dislocation, and embodiment as key thematics for simultaneously mapping empire's inheritances across multiscalar, more-than-human socioecologies and representing her layered critical botanizing practices. Her use of the question form, parenthesis, and recursion plays an especially central role in how this exploration unfurls in "Wisteria." Of these literary devices, the question form is the most pronounced and most readily discussed with an interdisciplinary cohort. In other words, the question form operates in class discussion as both a heuristic and a pedagogical lever, a way into discussion about how Kincaid's multiple interventions are composed.

Kincaid's question forms are lively, compounding, and reiterating devices. One role they play is pedagogical. In both the phrasing of the question and the response she provides, Kincaid foregrounds particularized concerns that emerge through intersubjective engagement with the denizens in her garden. More specifically, Kincaid's question forms fold and unfold her many, layered knowledges. As an example, Kincaid opens "Wisteria" with a question about why her *Wisteria floribunda* is blooming at the wrong time (11). The way she asks the question places this particular wisteria in relation to other wisteria cultivars and also to some of the other flora in her garden. It also enables Kincaid to showcase her precise observations about plant behavior. In other words, the *Wisteria floribunda* is not abstracted from its particular environs, her garden in Vermont, which includes other flora and fauna and which is subject to fluctuations in weather, temperature, rainfall, and soil life, all of which could be affecting the *Wisteria floribunda*'s irregular blooming. Kincaid packs all this activity into the two long, compound sentences that make up the first section of this paragraph-long question form. Through consideration of the state of the *Wisteria floribunda*, Kincaid muses on different types of botanically related inquiry: those that she can decisively address, like the existence of slugs (12), and those that require conversation with others, like the visible and invisible consequences of standardizing a vining plant into a tree form (12). This latter query opens onto a cross-species analogy about standardization that focuses on culturally constructed ideas about beauty: "does the whole process of holding it all together become so difficult that precise bloom time becomes a casualty, something like appearing at the proper time to have your hair examined by the headmistress: you show up but your hair is not the way it should be, it is not styled in a way that pleases her, it is not styled in a way that she understands" (12). The next sentence, which ends the paragraph, explicitly returns to the wisteria, but the trace of the prior sentence's focus on human beauty strongly reverberates. While Kincaid considers a wide range of topics as "Wisteria" proceeds, and while the particular configurations of her question forms change in relation to the topic at hand, the technique of multilayered questioning that moves across many registers of attachment, desire, perplexity, and curiosity—from scientific inquiry to affective inquiry to geopolitical inquiry to existential inquiry—is a hallmark of the writing. And as I hope this brief gloss of the opening of "Wisteria" indicates, I see Kincaid's question forms as relational propositions for purposefully interacting with her work.

If students do not address the topic on their own, I ask them to discuss how they might adapt Kincaid's mode of asking questions as a method for their own studies in nature, culture, and sustainability. To elaborate, we interweave conversation about the flourishing of the flora and fauna with whom Kincaid lives with examination of how, precisely, the questions position the reader. For instance, we track the ways Kincaid's question forms disarm and arm, sometimes in the same sentence, sometimes in the next sentence, and sometimes paragraphs or pages later. We also scrutinize how the question forms intersect with and produce temporalities that simultaneously move in multiple directions: retroactive, belated, deferred, reiterative, cumulative, recursive, speculative. One aim of considering these temporalities is to collaboratively work through the argument that Kincaid's question forms underline and perform the labor required for the continual remaking of multiscalar, cross-species relations. In other words, through unpacking the repetition and proliferation of questions that are never quite the same, even when the phrasing is verbatim, we practice textually grounded analysis in order to parse how Kincaid demonstrates that the labor of relational thinking and doing is ongoing.[7] The sort of ongoingness Kincaid values in "Wisteria" offers the following reminders: that thinking and doing are always provisional and grounded in bodies that are multiply located; that relationships with others (humans, nonhuman animals, and plants) cannot be fixed but must be, rather, continually reframed and reconsidered; that in relationships with others (humans, nonhuman animals, plants, and environments), desires for control are met by others' liveliness; and, finally, that while questions can be posed in a way that demonstrates the inquirer's multiple knowledges, the act of questioning inhabits a comportment that turns toward continuing curiosity and growth.[8]

Kincaid's vexation with scientific practices that emerge from and perpetuate Eurocentric colonialist frameworks is palpable throughout *My Garden (Book):*. For instance, from an anti-colonialist standpoint, Kincaid critiques binomial naming and taxonomic classification of flora for its rootedness in Eurocentric forms of knowledge and its blindness to other knowledges. She indicts the ongoing consequences of pseudosciences of racial classification. And she investigates how displaced plants do or do not flourish in their new environments while foregrounding her own complicity in planting non-native species. Against activities that abstract and decontextualize, Kincaid embodies a grounded, emplaced, observational comportment that exemplifies the fundamental activities of scientific investigation: study, hypothesize, experiment, examine results, repeat.

The questions at the intersections of scientific practice and racialization that concern Kincaid and the embodied, interested, feminist, critical method she employs to investigate these intersections situate Kincaid within an epistemic community of Black science writing that includes recent work by Alexis Pauline Gumbs, Katherine McKittrick, and Chanda Prescod-Weinstein, among others. While space prevents a fuller unfolding of the multiple lines of communication between and across the work of Kincaid, Gumbs, McKittrick, and Prescod-Weinstein, all four authors interrogate how knowledge is produced, by whom, for whom, and toward what ends. And by insisting that knowledge production should be participatory, they create room for new narratives about scientific inquiry, its accountability, and its representation.

Notes

1. Scholars who attend to the botanical in Kincaid's writing include Bergren; Didur; Feder (118–29); Fidecaro; Gersdorf and Sandilands (1–2); O'Brien; Spartacus; and Wong.

2. The term "natureculture" is borrowed from Donna Haraway, who uses it to challenge binary understandings of the world that separate nature and culture and to foreground multispecies stories focused on "co-constitutive relationships in which none of the partners pre-exist the relating, and the relating is never done once and for all" (*Companion Species Manifesto* 12).

3. Because this course changed each time it was taught, Kincaid's work was not always included. The version of the course discussed here, in other words, is just one iteration. Between the initial writing of this essay and its publication, the school paused the master's program and will instead offer a twelve-credit interdisciplinary graduate concentration that will include Theories of NatureCulture as a core course.

4. I have also successfully used Boden et al. in liberal arts–based research courses for undergraduate art and design students.

5. Lawrence provides an overview of critical plant studies. Texts often cited in environmental humanities critical plant studies include Aloi, Gagliano et al.; Kimmerer; Kohn; Marder; Meeker and Szabari; Ryan et al.; and Tsing. The publishers Brill, Lexington Books, and Peter Lang have each launched book series focused on plant studies.

6. Writing from different homes and disciplines, Gregory Cajete, Raymond Pierotti and Daniel Wildcat, Kate Harriden, and Kyle Powys Whyte, Joseph P. Brewer, and Jay T. Johnson each emphasize that traditional ecological knowledges share similar values that are expressed differently because these bodies of knowledge are emplaced. Harriden offers one iteration of these common values: "centring the other-than-human, incorporating relationality and reciprocity, relying on long-term, place-based multi-sensory observation to produce complex evidential and expert understandings of the natural world" (201). Emplaced does not mean static; see, for example, Kolopenuk; Roué and Nakashima; Simpson, "Land"; and Whyte. Additional modes of being-in-relation from other traditions that might also productively dialogue with Kincaid's work include the writing of Natalie Diaz, Layli Long Soldier, Simpson (*Islands*), and Kim TallBear.

7. The difference between how Kincaid makes visible the labor of thinking, doing, and writing through the question form and the way published academic prose often obscures this labor is a potential topic for seminar discussion.

8. Although we do not read Gayatri Chakravorty Spivak in Theories of Nature-Culture, I see close alignment between many elements in Kincaid's *My Garden (Book):* and Spivak's theorizations of ethics. By mentioning this connection in class, I gesture to another pathway in postcolonial theory that students might investigate.

Works Cited

Aloi, Giovanni, editor. *Why Look at Plants? The Botanical Emergence in Contemporary Art.* Brill, 2019.

Bergren, Katherine. "Localism Unrooted: Gardening in the Prose of Jamaica Kincaid and William Wordsworth." *Interdisciplinary Studies in Literature and Environment*, vol. 22, no. 2, 2015, pp. 303–25.

Boden, Rebecca, et al. *Getting Started on Research.* Sage Publications, 2005.

Cajete, Gregory A. *Native Science: Natural Laws of Interdependence.* Clear Light Publishers, 2000.

Derrida, Jacques. *The Animal That Therefore I Am.* Translated by David Wills, edited by Marie-Luise Mallet, Fordham UP, 2008.

Diaz, Natalie. *Postcolonial Love Poem.* Graywolf Press, 2020.

Didur, Jill. "Strange Joy: Plant-Hunting and Responsibility in Jamaica Kincaid's (Post)Colonial Travel Writing." *Interventions*, vol. 13, no. 2, 2011, pp. 236–55.

Feder, Helena. *Ecocriticism and the Idea of Culture: Biology and the Bildungsroman.* Ashgate, 2014.

Fidecaro, Agnese. "Jamaica Kincaid's Practical Politics of the Intimate in *My Garden (Book):.*" *The Global and the Intimate*, special issue of *Women's Studies Quarterly*, edited by Geraldine Pratt and Victoria Rosner, vol. 34, nos. 1–2, pp. 250–70.

Fienup-Riordan, Ann, and Alice Reardon. Ellavut: *Our Yup'ik World and Weather: Continuity and Change on the Bering Sea Coast.* U of Washington P, 2012.

Fuller, Matthew, and Olga Goriunova. *Bleak Joys: Aesthetics of Ecology and Impossibility*. U of Minnesota P, 2019.

Gagliano, Monica, et al., editors. *The Language of Plants: Science, Philosophy, Literature*. U of Minnesota P, 2017.

Gersdorf, Catrin, and Catriona Sandilands. "Gardening (against) the Anthropocene: An Introduction." *Ecozona*, vol. 14. no. 1, 2023, pp. 1–7.

Gumbs, Alexis Pauline. *Undrowned: Black Feminist Lessons from Marine Mammals*. AK Press, 2020.

Haraway, Donna J. *The Companion Species Manifesto: Dogs, People, and Significant Otherness*. Prickly Paradigm Press, 2003.

———. *Staying with the Trouble: Making Kin in the Chthulucene*. Duke UP, 2016.

Harriden, Kate. "Working with Indigenous Science(s) Frameworks and Methods: Challenging the Ontological Hegemony of 'Western' Science and the Axiological Biases of Its Practitioners." *Methodological Innovations*, vol. 16, no. 2, 2023, pp. 201–14.

Kimmerer, Robin Wall. *Braiding Sweetgrass: Indigenous Wisdom, Scientific Knowledge, and the Teachings of Plants*. Milkweed Editions, 2015.

Kincaid, Jamaica. *My Garden (Book):*. Farrar, Straus and Giroux, 2001.

Kohn, Eduardo. *How Forests Think: Toward an Anthropology beyond the Human*. U of California P, 2013.

Kolopenuk, Jessica. "*Miskâsowin*: Indigenous Science, Technology, and Society." *Genealogy*, vol. 4, no. 1, 2020, https://doi.org/10.3390/genealogy4010021.

Lawrence, Anna M. "Listening to Plants: Conversations between Critical Plant Studies and Vegetal Geography." *Progress in Human Geography*, vol. 46, no. 2, 2022, pp. 629–51.

Long Soldier, Layli. *Whereas*. Graywolf Press, 2017.

Marder, Michael. *Plant-Thinking: A Philosophy of Vegetal Life*. Columbia UP, 2013.

McKittrick, Katherine. *"Dear Science" and Other Stories*. Duke UP, 2021.

Meeker, Natania, and Antónia Szabari. *Radical Botany: Plants and Speculative Fiction*. Fordham UP, 2019.

O'Brien, Susie. "The Garden and the World: Jamaica Kincaid and the Cultural Borders of Ecocriticism." *Mosaic*, vol. 35, no. 2, 2002, pp. 167–84.

okpik, dg nanouk. *Corpse Whale*. U of Arizona P, 2012.

Pierotti, Raymond, and Daniel Wildcat. "Traditional Ecological Knowledge: The Third Alternative (Commentary)." *Ecological Applications*, vol. 10, no. 5, 2000, pp. 1333–40.

Prescod-Weinstein, Chanda. *The Disordered Cosmos: A Journey into Dark Matter, Spacetime, and Dreams Deferred*. Bold Type Books, 2021.

Roué, Marie, and Douglas Nakashima. "Co-production between Indigenous Knowledge and Science: Introducing a Decolonized Approach." *Resilience through Knowledge Co-production: Indigenous Knowledge, Science and Global Environmental Change*, edited by Roué et al., Cambridge UP / UNESCO, 2022, pp. 3–23.

Ryan, John C., et al., editors. *The Mind of Plants: Narratives of Vegetal Intelligence*. Synergetic Press, 2021.

Salmón, Enrique. "Sharing Breath: Some Links between Land, Plants, and People." *Colors of Nature: Culture, Identity, and the Natural World*, edited by Alison H. Deming and Lauret E. Savoy, Milkweed Editions, 2011, pp. 196–210.

Savoy, Lauret. *Trace: Memory, History, Race, and the American Landscape.* Counterpoint Press, 2015.

Simpson, Leanne Betasamosake. *Islands of Decolonial Love: Stories and Songs.* ARP Books, 2013.

———. "Land as Pedagogy: Nishnaabeg Intelligence and Rebellious Transformation." *Decolonization: Indigeneity, Education and Society*, vol. 3, no. 3, 2014, pp. 1–25.

Spartacus, Josette. "Graphing and Grafting in Jamaica Kincaid's Garden Memoirs." *Jamaica Kincaid as Crafter and Grafter: Agency, Practice, Interventions*, special issue of *Wagadu: A Journal of Transnational Women's and Gender Studies*, edited by Corinne Bigot et al., vol. 19, 2018, pp. 65–75.

Spears, endawnis, and Cassius Spears, Jr. "Indigenous Landscapes: Narragansett Homeland and History." 10 Mar. 2021, Rhode Island School of Design, liberalartsmasters.risd.edu/ncss/events/endawnis-spears-cassius-spears-jr/. Virtual lecture.

TallBear, Kim. "Caretaking Relations, Not American Dreaming." *Kalfou*, vol. 6, no. 1, 2019, pp. 24–41.

Tsing, Anna Lowenhaupt. *The Mushroom at the End of the World: On the Possibility of Life in Capitalist Ruins.* Princeton UP, 2015.

Whyte, Kyle. "Critical Investigations of Resilience: A Brief Introduction to Indigenous Environmental Studies and Sciences." *Daedalus*, vol. 147, no. 2, 2018, pp. 136–47.

Whyte, Kyle Powys, et al. "Weaving Indigenous Science, Protocols and Sustainability Science." *Sustainability Science*, vol. 11, no. 1, 2016, pp. 25–32.

Wong, Shirley Lau. "The World and the Garden: Ekphrasis and 'Overterritorialization' in Jamaica Kincaid's Garden Writing." *Cambridge Journal of Postcolonial Literary Inquiry*, vol. 5, no. 1, 2018, pp. 36–52.

Nathaniel Otjen

Multispecies Relationships: Nonhumans and Knowledge Production in Science Writing

As a college student majoring in botany, Robin Wall Kimmerer was taught to assume a hierarchical relationship to the plants she studied and the knowledge she coproduced. In *Braiding Sweetgrass: Indigenous Wisdom, Scientific Knowledge, and the Teachings of Plants*, the plant ecologist and author recounts learning a "reductionist, mechanistic, and strictly objective" science where plants were viewed as "objects" that yielded knowledge only when appropriate questions and techniques were applied (42). However, as a young Potawatomi woman who had been raised to appreciate "the embrace between plants and humans" (41), she could not reconcile her personal values with the mechanomorphism taught by her botany professors. "In moving from a childhood in the woods to the university," she writes, "I had unknowingly shifted between worldviews, from a natural history of experience, in which I knew plants as teachers and companions to whom I was linked with mutual responsibility, into the realm of science" (41–42). While her "natural inclination was to see relationships, to seek the threads that connect the world, to join instead of divide," science asked her to be "rigorous in separating the observer from the observed, and the observed from the observer" (42). Western science, she learned, could never answer her burning question of why asters and goldenrods appear so beautiful together.

When I read *Braiding Sweetgrass* with students in my environmental humanities classes, we concentrate on Kimmerer's experiences in the college classroom. As we unpack the above passages and consider them within Kimmerer's longer personal history, we discuss how Western science works to detach itself from the nonhumans who bring its knowledges and practices into existence. Many students, especially those belonging to historically disadvantaged groups, know firsthand the erasures enacted by dominant knowledge systems, including the systematic exclusion of those who do not look or behave like idealized knowledge producers (Schusler et al. 976). Others express surprise that science continues to be imagined as disconnected from the environments and beings responsible for creating different ways of knowing. Science writing like *Braiding Sweetgrass* gives students the opportunity to consider how scientific disciplines and practices vacate nonhumans from the knowledges and knowledge systems that these beings bring into existence. Even more crucially, science writing teaches students to question their assumptions about how science works and to think critically about how human-nonhuman relationships inform their own ways of knowing. By featuring science writing in humanities courses, college instructors can teach undergraduate and graduate students to consider how nonhuman beings participate in science—both willingly and unwillingly, along with all positions in between—and how multispecies relationships enable the production of knowledge.

With the genre's reflexive interest in the everyday operations, material conditions, and nonhuman research subjects that make modern science possible, science writing offers students from all disciplinary positions the chance to trace how particular knowledges and ways of knowing are produced and to contemplate the better and worse relations that emerge through scientific practice. When students attend to the beings and relations that constitute modern science and its knowledge systems, they learn that science develops through multispecies relationships with particular individuals, species, and environments and amid specific cultural moments and historical periods (Birke et al. 176). Regardless of students' disciplinary orientation, critical engagement with science writing can shape students' research methodologies and help them conceptualize better modes of relating and being with others. In my own teaching, for instance, the larger goal is to move students away from thinking of knowledge as being *about* the world to instead thinking of knowledge as being *of* the world. In this epistemological shift lies the beginnings of more equitable orientations to living with nonhuman beings and environments.

This essay offers reading units, assignments, activities, and strategies for teaching multispecies relationships and knowledges in late-twentieth- and early-twenty-first-century science writing. Joining other contributors to this volume, I invite readers to rethink what counts as "science writing" and to expand the archive of material available to teachers and students to include genres such as fiction and authors who practice non-Western science. The approaches and ideas presented here have emerged from my experiences teaching all levels of undergraduates in a four-year public institution on the West Coast as a graduate student and a four-year private institution on the East Coast as a postdoctoral fellow. As such, I discuss two core topics that have emerged from my teaching and pedagogical commitments. The first prompts students to consider how science has functioned, and continues to function, as a colonial project of control and management. As postcolonial, Indigenous, and feminist authors have observed, dominant scientific procedures and narratives not only obscure the multispecies relationships central to the operations of science but also disrupt the ability of humans and nonhumans to develop meaningful relationships in everyday life. The second asks students to examine how science functions as an entangled practice. Popular science texts written by primatologists demonstrate the degree to which scientific knowledge is fashioned through multispecies relationships and, in the process, raise questions of ethics and justice.

Science as Colonialism

Throughout *Braiding Sweetgrass,* Kimmerer shows how botanical science uncouples itself from the plants that coproduce disciplinary knowledge and from the relationships that develop between plants and researchers. In doing so, she argues, Western science operates as a colonial project. More precisely, it denigrates and denies Indigenous knowledges, and it impedes the ability of Indigenous peoples to develop meaningful relationships with the beings who sustain their cultures (Harding). A key learning outcome for any class that takes up science writing and nonhumans, then, is for students to understand how science manages multispecies relationships and communities. In my environmental humanities classes, I assign writings by Indigenous and postcolonial authors who engage with the institutions of science and colonialism. Together with Kimmerer's *Braiding Sweetgrass*, I teach nonfiction life writing such as Wangari Maathai's *Unbowed* and Jamaica Kincaid's *My Garden (Book):*. However, as I discuss below, I also see a place for fiction in these conversations, particularly for postcolonial novels like Amitav Ghosh's *The Hungry Tide*. When read together, these texts expose some of the deep historical ties that bind science and colonialism, and they critique the ways that modern science, especially Western conservation, damages mutual relationships with nonhumans.

The reading unit presented below on the topic of science as colonialism has been developed for a mid- to upper-level humanities course that meets twice a week. Instructors would, of course, modify the readings and schedule to correspond with the academic level and goals of their class. The reading load in the first two weeks might be reduced for lower-level classes, and the instructor might choose to assign secondary materials such as excerpts from Londa Schiebinger's *Plants and Empire* or Mark Dowie's *Conservation Refugees*, for instance.

Week 1

Meeting 1   Kincaid, *My Garden (Book):* (part 1 [3–96])

Meeting 2   Kincaid, *My Garden (Book):* (parts 2 and 3 [99–229])

Week 2

Meeting 1   Ghosh, *The Hungry Tide* (part 1 [1–145])

Meeting 2   Ghosh, *The Hungry Tide* (part 2 [149–329])

Week 3

Meeting 1   Maathai, *Unbowed* ("Beginnings" [3–28], "Cultivation" [29–52], "Foresters without Diplomas" [119–38])

Meeting 2   Kimmerer, *Braiding Sweetgrass* ("Asters and Goldenrod" [39–47], "Learning the Grammar of Animacy" [48–62])

Each reading takes up a different aspect of colonialism as it has been enacted through science. *My Garden (Book):* asks students to unravel some of the connections between British imperialism and botany, including the transatlantic movement of plants and enslaved humans. Kincaid's gardening memoir offers an opportunity to think about how science has historically developed through colonial activities and how narratives of imperial science are told. *The Hungry Tide* asks students to consider how international organizations implement conservation programs to protect charismatic species and, in the process, displace local inhabitants and sever multispecies relationships. Ghosh's novel considers what happens when fortress conservation, in its quest to make "the whole world . . . a place of animals," forgets that humans have always lived "from the water and the soil" (217). Finally, *Unbowed* and *Braiding Sweetgrass* discuss efforts to decolonize science by prioritizing the authors' positionalities and epistemologies over Western ways of knowing. Maathai's memoir describes the Green Belt Movement, a grassroots tree-planting effort in Kenya, as an alternative to Western conservation—a way to produce knowledge and intervene in the world that accounts for the needs of arboreal and women-led communities. Kimmerer's collection argues for the role of Indigenous knowledges and belief systems in the botanical sciences.

The following questions are designed to guide classroom conversations on the readings. They are intended to prompt students to situate knowledge within historical contexts, read comparatively, and think across scales spanning from the microscopic to the structural.

How have scientific practices and knowledges emerged from colonial projects? How are nonhumans treated in these contexts, and how do scientific authorities engage with research subjects?

What counts as violence in each of these narratives? Who causes suffering, and who suffers?

What kinds of knowledge and knowledge-making activities does Western science prioritize? Which positions, knowledges, and experiences do these authors argue are missing from, or obscured by, Western science?

How is the state involved in colonial activities? What effects do state-sanctioned scientific policies have on multispecies communities and ecologies?

How does Western science compromise the ability of humans and nonhumans to live together? Which groups of humans and nonhumans matter the most under these frameworks?

How do plants and animals demonstrate agency in these narratives? What might this reveal about the scientific process?

I raise these questions in different ways across my humanities courses. In one version of an introductory environmental humanities class, for example, I asked students to post a reflection on Canvas. Rather than prompt the class to reply to a discussion topic, I requested that they share a link to a digital post that helped them better understand one aspect of the reading drawn from the above list of questions and to respond in five sentences. These reflections provided a way to begin most classes. Instructors might also select one of the questions to guide the conversation for a class meeting, assign individual questions to small groups, or use the questions to prompt freewriting that then becomes larger discussions. For a graduate seminar, instructors might ask students to develop a list of keywords and working definitions derived from their responses.

Near the end of the unit, instructors might evaluate student comprehension and build deeper connections by assigning a short writing project. The appendix features a writing assignment that asks students to compare two readings and to think about how they reveal continuities in and departures from the topics discussed in class. While I developed this for a mid-level environmental literature class with an enrollment of thirty students, the assignment can be adapted for different class sizes and levels. Two learning objectives guide the assignment. First, students will use comparative literary analysis to derive greater meaning from at least two texts. Second, students will examine how scientific knowledge and practices shape relations with nonhuman beings as they play out in the scientific process and the communities affected by scientific intervention. Reading comparatively requires students to pay attention to the ways that narratives are told and arguments are constructed. Comparative, or "lateral," reading, argues Aaron Rosenfeld, not only situates literature within wider conceptual and textual frames but also reinforces the lesson that "the work of reading is never done" (225).

Science as Entangled Practice

As Maathai, Kimmerer, Kincaid, and Ghosh illustrate, Western science excludes, separates, categorizes, and divides the world, even as it depends upon interconnectedness to produce knowledge. By reading their work, students come to understand that science—though perhaps well-intentioned—is a violent activity, particularly for marginalized communities that suffer from science-based policies and for the nonhuman beings who often unwillingly participate in research activities. Yet, having been trained in the sciences or having carefully studied them, these authors also recognize that science is needed to understand and make sense of the world. For them, science can become an entangled practice, one that arises from and takes place through interconnection and may produce more equitable modes of relating in the process. In teaching science as a project that involves diverse knowledge positions and beings and that works toward more just worlds, instructors can prompt students to consider how existing knowledge production systems and ways of living might be transformed. Science writers from Jane Goodall to Hope Jahren, Barbara McClintock, Suzanne Simard, and Irene Pepperberg have proposed alternative ways of doing science. In these models science is premised upon responsibility, trust, reciprocity, reflexivity, and care. What would science, and the world, look like if nonhumans were acknowledged as integral parts of knowledge production? How can research studies be designed with ethics and equity in mind? And how can science help humans and nonhumans coexist in mutually beneficial ways?

Primatology offers an especially useful site for thinking about less coercive modes of science that acknowledge the role of nonhumans and the importance of multispecies relationships in the production of knowledge. I like to teach field primatology of the 1960s and 1970s, when efforts were underway among female scientists to develop long-term research studies based on sustained relationships and mutual trust. It helps that students tend to be familiar, in some capacity, with Goodall. As a specific case study, primatology offers the chance to examine how knowledge is coproduced with animals and to consider the ethical implications of field research (Otjen). The proposed reading unit that follows is organized around the popular written and visual work of three primatologists:

Week 1

Meeting 1   Brian Noble, "Politics, Gender, and Worldly Primatology: The Goodall-Fossey Nexus"

Meeting 2   Goodall, "My Life among Wild Chimpanzees"; *Miss Goodall and the Wild Chimpanzees*

Week 2

Meeting 1   Goodall, *In the Shadow of Man* (1–100)

Meeting 2   Goodall, *In the Shadow of Man* (101–96); Shirley Strum, "Life with the Pumphouse Gang"

Week 3

Meeting 1   Robert Sapolsky, *A Primate's Memoir* (parts 1 and 2
             [13–166])

Meeting 2   Sapolsky, *A Primate's Memoir* (parts 3 and 4
             [168–304])

The unit begins with Noble's essay from the edited collection *Primate Encounters*, which provides historical context and positions Goodall's research within contemporary developments in field primatology. Noble discusses how Goodall's "social world" emerged through her sustained engagement with the chimpanzees of Gombe Stream "in a way not instanced or recorded before" (447). The unit then takes up two of Goodall's earliest and most popular pieces: "My Life among Wild Chimpanzees," a personal essay published in *National Geographic*, and *Miss Goodall and the Wild Chimpanzees*, a television special aired by the National Geographic Society. Together, the pieces give a sense of what Goodall's research was like on the ground in Tanzania, and they provide the chance for students to engage visual material ranging from photography to film. Next, the unit turns to *In the Shadow of Man*, which recounts how Goodall designed her research and her experiences with individual chimpanzees, including Flo and David Greybeard. Strum's personal essay reflects on the process of becoming part of a baboon troop in Kenya and the ethical obligations that follow. Finally, the remaining week takes up a humorous memoir by Sapolsky that recounts the ethical conundrums and personal investments he felt while studying stress in male baboons near Strum's research site. Instructors can determine which sections they would like to assign.

In addition to developing key questions about the readings, I design measurable, specific, and attainable learning outcomes. They help organize class discussions, establish continuity across readings, and develop questions for assessments and check-ins. Weekly learning outcomes for the above reading unit might look like this:

By the end of week 1, students will be able to discuss how science is communicated with broader publics. Example: Goodall taught people in the United States and Britain new ways of engaging animals that went beyond dominant attitudes that regarded them as pets, food, or instruments for human use.

By the end of week 2, students will be able to describe how non-human primates are implicated in knowledge production. Example: Baboons and chimpanzees have taught us, as humans, about ourselves and have been used to reinforce norms around gender, sexuality, and race.

By the end of week 3, students will be able to articulate the relationships and power differentials that structure field research. Example: Sapolsky views himself as a member of the troop even as he tranquilizes baboons and draws their blood for his studies.

To help ensure learning outcomes are met, I devise classroom activities that prompt students to make connections between the readings and outside material. Our environmental literature class, for example, visited a photography exhibition at the University of Oregon's Museum of Natural and Cultural History, where we considered the exhibit as a mode of visual storytelling. The appendix presents a modified activity that draws upon the photographs featured in the exhibit. The objective is for students to think about how a visual medium communicates, or does not communicate, scientific knowledge. It also asks students to consider how representations of primates, in this case through the visual medium of photography, obscure relationships.

Science beyond the Classroom

Science writing illustrates how scientific knowledge and practices emerge through particular relationships with nonhuman beings and human communities. In doing so, science writing challenges dominant positions that present knowledge and the scientific process as anthropocentric, detached, objective, ahistorical, and universal. By taking up science writing, students grapple with the larger question of how to live well with others. "To equip our students to be participatory citizens in a world facing an extinction crisis," writes Jonathan Steinwand, "I urge us to infuse . . . media of multispecies entanglement into our courses and programs wherever possible" (184). For young natural scientists, identifying and examining the multispecies relationships that make science possible may compel them to design their research projects differently. For young social scientists and humanists, it may compel them to confront and challenge the philosophical tradition of liberal humanism that undergirds their disciplinary training. When knowledge becomes of the world, there is a good chance that we can too.

Works Cited

Birke, Lynda, et al. "Animal Performances: An Exploration of Intersections between Feminist Science Studies and Studies of Human/Animal Relationships." *Feminist Theory*, vol. 5, no. 2, 2004, pp. 167–83.

Dowie, Mark. *Conservation Refugees: The Hundred-Year Conflict between Global Conservation and Native Peoples.* MIT Press, 2011.

Ghosh, Amitav. *The Hungry Tide.* Houghton Mifflin, 2005.

Goodall, Jane. *In the Shadow of Man.* Houghton Mifflin, 1971.

———. "My Life among Wild Chimpanzees." *National Geographic*, Aug. 1963, pp. 272–308.

Harding, Sandra. *The Postcolonial Science and Technology Studies Reader.* Duke UP, 2011.

Kimmerer, Robin Wall. *Braiding Sweetgrass: Indigenous Wisdom, Scientific Knowledge, and the Teachings of Plants.* Milkweed Editions, 2013.

Kincaid, Jamaica. *My Garden (Book):.* Farrar, Straus and Giroux, 2001.

Maathai, Wangari. *Unbowed.* Anchor Books, 2007.

Miss Goodall and the Wild Chimpanzees. Directed by Marshall Flaum, National Geographic Society, 1965.

Noble, Brian. "Politics, Gender, and Worldly Primatology: The Goodall-Fossey Nexus." *Primate Encounters: Models of Science, Gender, and Society*, edited by Shirley C. Strum and Linda Marie Fedigan, U of Chicago P, 2000, pp. 436–62.

Otjen, Nathaniel. "Habituated Knowledges: The Entanglements of Science, Species, and Selfhood." *A/B: Auto/Biography Studies*, vol. 38, no. 1, 2023, pp. 355–83.

Rosenfeld, Aaron. "Wine, Poems, and Song: Lateral Reading and the Pedagogy of Appreciation." *Pedagogy*, vol. 17, no. 2, 2017, pp. 203–34.

Sapolsky, Robert M. *A Primate's Memoir: A Neuroscientist's Unconventional Life among the Baboons.* Touchstone, 2002.

Schiebinger, Londa. *Plants and Empire: Colonial Bioprospecting in the Atlantic World.* Harvard UP, 2007.

Schusler, Tania, et al. "Students of Colour Views on Racial Equity in Environmental Sustainability." *Nature Sustainability*, vol. 4, 2021, pp. 975–82.

Steinwand, Jonathan. "Teaching Multispecies Entanglement." *Teaching Postcolonial Environmental Literature and Media*, edited by Cajetan Iheka, Modern Language Association of America, 2021, pp. 181–97.

Strum, Shirley. "Life with the Pumphouse Gang: New Insights into Baboon Behavior." *National Geographic*, May 1975, pp. 672–91.

Appendix: Assignments and Activities

Comparative Reading Assignment

Class discussions have grappled with the inseparability of Western science and colonialism. Our conversations have attended to the process of science as it plays out on the ground and to the impacts that scientific knowledge has on particular communities and ecologies. We have studied how science operates on behalf of colonial systems and the ways that science, as a colonial project of management and control, excludes nonhumans from knowledge systems and creates boundaries that separate humans from other beings.

Compare two passages from separate readings that discuss either the scientific process operating through colonial logics and mechanisms or the impacts that scientific knowledge has on specific communities and ecologies as an ongoing form of colonialism. Passages should be no longer than one paragraph in length.

Once you've selected two passages from different readings and know what you'll be arguing, develop an essay that presents your findings. Your essay should feature the two passages, and it should draw upon supporting evidence gathered from the texts. Your comparative reading must have a central thesis or argument that guides the discussion. The goal of the assignment is to place two texts in conversation and to draw deeper meaning through this comparison.

Photo Ark Activity

Budget thirty minutes for this activity.

1. Visit the following website: www.joelsartore.com/photo-ark/. [Provide students with context about the project: Joel Sartore, a photographer for *National Geographic*, is photographing members of species living in captivity in order to draw attention to their beauty and vulnerability. The portraits in the Photo Ark feature black-and-white backgrounds and close-up shots of individual animals.]

2. Type "primate" in the search bar. Scroll through the photographs and identify one that speaks to you.

3. Take a few minutes to study the photograph. Imagine you are a primatologist.

4. Jot down responses to the following questions:

    How would you describe the subject or subjects? How are they presented?

    What do you think they might be feeling or thinking in this moment?

    Are they presented as an individual, as a representative of their wider species, or as both?

    What do you feel when you view this photograph?

    What is absent from the photograph? What isn't the photograph showing?

    Where is science in this photograph?

5. Pair up with a partner and discuss the photograph you selected and your responses.

6. Come back together for a whole-group discussion.

Part IV

Courses and Assignments

John MacNeill Miller

The Critic Afield: Field Guides as Tools for Interdisciplinary Close Reading

The Literature and the Environment course I teach always begins with this advice to writers, drawn from Henry James's essay "The Art of Fiction": "Try to be one of the people on whom nothing is lost!" (390). James is a notoriously dense stylist, and it might seem odd to begin such a course with him: James's essay isn't about nature at all, and most of my students would probably find it a frustrating read. At our small liberal arts college, Literature and the Environment can serve both as an introductory course in the English department and as an elective in the Environmental Science and Sustainability program, so every year it enrolls an unpredictable crop of students. Some have just arrived on campus with no idea what they want to do with their lives. But most are planning to focus on the sciences, and some have already declared their majors. For many of them, the course is simply a way to satisfy humanistic distribution requirements as scientifically as possible; a few have a long-standing passion for writing. Regardless, almost all of them would experience a deep dive into James as an unpleasant start to the semester.

Still, I begin with this quotation because it focuses on perception. It insists that a writer's most fundamental tool is the art of noticing—noticing the world around them just as much as they notice how words work on a page. And because noticing is an art anyone can appreciate, the quotation establishes some common ground for the variety of students drawn to the course's unusual curricular niche. To function as an Environmental Science and Sustainability elective, the course needs to include some ecological knowledge; when I teach it, we focus on the diverse ways nature has been represented in writing as well as the history of environmentalist concerns. But to act as an entry-level course in the English program, it must also teach the fundamental skills of literary study, introducing students to basic rhetorical terms as well as to the practice of close reading. In short, the course needs to center assignments and foster discussions that somehow link these apparently divergent disciplinary aims. Close reading becomes indispensable to forging such links. While English departments often frame close reading as a special tool wielded by literary critics, its innate power and potential become clear to a broader audience when it is introduced as a cross-disciplinary strategy for noticing what others overlook.

Before students can fully appreciate the art of noticing, however, they must realize how little they themselves notice. In much of higher education the art of noticing is only haphazardly taught, even in courses on the environment that are explicitly devoted to the world around us. This neglect of noticing hit home for me the very first time I taught Literature and the Environment. One day that semester, a graduating environmental science major excitedly described seeing a mysterious, beautiful bird that was utterly new to her. After a minute or two, it became clear that the bird in question was a female northern cardinal (*Cardinalis cardinalis*), one of the most abundant and approachable birds in our ecoregion. She had seen one many times before—she must have—but she had never actually noticed that she had seen one. It wasn't her fault: nothing in either our broader culture or her extensive coursework in environmental science and policy had encouraged the kind of noticing necessary to perceive such creatures. She saw them now because our course was structured around a series of assignments designed to foster close reading as the backbone of a larger interdisciplinary art of noticing. Her account of the cardinal was freely offered to the class as part of those assignments, which have both formal written elements and more informal oral components.

This essay provides a brief outline of such assignments, with the hope that others find them as helpful as I do to teaching at the margins of science and writing. I call the assignments "nature journal entries," but they are much more than unstructured musings about the natural world. They have a specific format designed to help students build a bridge between the humanities classroom and the assorted environments they navigate on a daily basis—environments that include the natural, the cultural, and the textual. When students learn to link these environments through the art of noticing, their perceptions change—not just their perceptions of their surroundings but also their perceptions of literature and writing as somehow distinct from (and generally secondary to) the work of scientific observation. To build these links, I rely on a type of literature that is not considered literature at all but that nevertheless serves as a frequent inter-mediary between humanity and the natural world: the humble field guide.

Noticing What Field Guides Can Show Us

At least once a week, our Literature and the Environment class opens with "nature encounters," a kind of group share, a dedicated time for students to talk in an unstructured way about anything they may have recently noticed about the nonhuman world around them. I try to model this form of low-stakes contribution by bringing my own observations to the table, then inviting others to join in. Some weeks no one has much to say. Other weeks almost everyone wants to talk and build on one another's contributions until I'm forced to cut the conversation short to get to our assigned texts. The class typically grows more confident in these sharing exercises as the semester marches on because they are linked to the nature journal entries, which provide students with a growing sense of skill and expertise—a sense they develop through regular consultation of field guides.

Each nature journal entry has three components. The first component bears a strong resemblance to what many students already imagine when they hear the words "nature journal." Part 1 asks students to narrate and describe some recent encounter with the natural world. But there's a catch: their encounter must involve some nonhuman living thing whose name they do not know. They can include as many subjective experiences as they want in the entry, and I encourage them to run wild with it. The only stipulation is that they must describe the animal, plant, or fungus they encounter in as much detail as possible: Where was it? What time of day did they notice it? What was it in particular about the species that grabbed their attention? As they inspected it more closely, what features struck them, and why? These sensory perceptions make up part 1 of each nature journal entry, and they also make up the bulk of the "nature encounters" shared orally in class. Typically students excel at this portion of the assignment from the beginning, and they welcome the personal freedom it gives them to ramble both physically and verbally. I impose no strict length requirements on any portion of the assignment, but I do explain that the level of noticing I am asking for in part 1 would be hard to accomplish and explain in less than a page. They are welcome to write much more.

On the face of it, the second component of each nature journal entry appears very different: it requires students to hit the books. Part 2 asks them to try to identify the unknown species they encountered, using one or more field guides to do so. Our library has a smattering of field guides in its collection, and some students also have one or more of their own. In theory those might be enough, but a diverse array can be very helpful as the semester goes on—so I draw on my own personal collection, placing a curated set of guides on reserve at the library for student use.[1] (See the appendix for an annotated list of some of the more useful guides I place on reserve.) In both the written version of this assignment and our classroom discussions of it, though, I emphasize that the real goal of this second stage of each nature journal entry is not identification. Accurate species identification is great, but the real aim is much more in line with the prior section of the entry: students should try describing their experience of navigating the field guide or guides in just as much detail, and with just as much subjectivity and curiosity, as they use in their nature encounter with an unknown species. Part 2 thus asks for the same thing as part 1 asks for, but on a different subject. After the personal narration of their nature encounter, students should be primed to draw up a personal narration of their field guide encounter.

Almost no one succeeds at this portion of the assignment in the first go-round. The temptation to land on "the right answer" is strong. Plus, students have virtually no experience noticing the details of a text and then subjectively narrating the sensation of reading it. Field guides also inhibit this subjective treatment; they focus on supposedly objective scientific descriptions of species and use passive voice to downplay the subjectivity involved in every relationship with the nonhuman world. At the start of the semester, then, students will quite confidently use a field guide to pin a name to their species—sometimes an unlikely or even impossible name. They will say little to nothing about how they arrived at their conclusion, and often they won't even mention the name of the guide or guides they consulted. But these shortcomings pale in comparison to the problems most early assignments show in part 3, the reflection.

The third and final component of each nature journal entry is the shortest and most shapeless. It consists of a reflection on the experience of the entry as a whole. In this section I prod students to ask questions about their species that remain unanswered. As it turns out, they rarely have any. Instead, reflections are invariably dashed off, and they take the bubbliest and most predictable of forms. Students express happiness and relief at having identified their species (or thinking they have identified it), spout off some admiration for the field guide, then say how much they learned and how surprised they were that they enjoyed the assignment as much as they did.

That enjoyment would come to a screeching halt when they received their grades—if I graded these assignments in the standard manner. But this is an iterative assignment. Each natural journal entry is graded on a pass/fail basis, and the goal is growth. What I'm looking for is a sharpening of perception, which includes perception of the natural world, perception of the field guide as a genre, and perception of the expectations of the assignment itself. I assess each entry based on how closely it matches the assignment's instructions—typically not too closely, in the forgiving first weeks of the semester—as well as how earnestly students have incorporated my feedback on previous entries. On a student's first entry, a nice narrative of the initial encounter (part 1 of the assignment) followed by an unhelpful description of the identification process (part 2) and a hasty reflection (part 3) would result in a pointed comment on the entry, but the entry would still pass. However, a second entry that neglected that feedback and showed no improvement in those sections would not pass. (Final grades are determined based on the total number of passing and failing assignments in the class.)

In most cases students write three to five entries per semester, showing an arc of gradual improvement as they learn not only how to pay attention to the natural world but also how to pay attention to the field guides that structure their experience. As time passes their identification skills grow, as does their willingness to admit and explain a failure to reach a decisive identification. And just as their attention to their living environment brings to the fore all sorts of nonhuman creatures they never noticed before, their attention to the field guides brings to the fore all sorts of textual features they never noticed before. The result is close reading with an increasingly critical edge—an edge that prepares them for their more creative and research-oriented final projects.

Noticing What Field Guides Don't Show Us

As students become more adept at navigating field guides, two aspects of our course complicate their journey. The first is the diversity of writing we discuss in the classroom. The second is the diversity of guides available to them. While the opening portion of the semester focuses on a chronological and canonical tradition of nature writing—one dominated by white male voices—the later portions pivot toward the voices and experiences that such writings tend to marginalize or overlook. After students come to appreciate how canonical nature writing helped define what nature is and how we should approach it, they must reckon with the way the same canon has sidelined those experiences of the nonhuman world that do not fit within its conventions. And that makes it possible to think more critically about other conventions, too, including the conventions structuring field guides. Although students rarely appreciate them at first, the conventions of field guides are on full display in the range of texts I place on reserve for my students (see the appendix). The reserves include relatively standard guides published by a range of well-known names and institutions. Even those standard guides diverge in ways worthy of analysis. But my list also includes outliers of the field guide genre, such as guides that focus on urban nature or guides that skimp on identification in favor of belletristic essays on individual species.

The third portion of each natural journal entry, the reflection component, gives students a space to meditate over these differences and their impact—but only after they have started to see the field guides as malleable, subjective cultural texts produced by human beings. The reflection portion tends to grow as the semester advances, with students learning to ask questions about their species that extend beyond what a particular guide tells them. In early entries, students who come up with questions tend to confine them to the scientific domain encouraged by the guides themselves (What does this species eat? What eats it? How large is its population?). Later, nudged by our shared reading, by the diversity of approaches across our guides, and by my targeted feedback, their questions tend to branch out. They may be linguistic (What does this Greco-Latin scientific name mean?), historical (When was this species first recorded, and why?), cultural (What meanings have different groups of people assigned to this species?), or economic (What uses and impacts have humans found for this species?), to take just a few examples.

What I try to show students is that these questions are also fundamentally literary. They are questions about the structuring conventions of a text, about what the seemingly cut-and-dried genre of the field guide does and does not say. They represent potential starting points for an investigation into why those inclusions and omissions might matter socially, politically, and ethically. Once students have developed the ability to ask questions beyond the information guides readily provide—that is, once they have developed the crucial close reading skill of seeing not just what a text says but also what a text pointedly does not say—they are prepared for their final project, which gives them a chance to reimagine the field guide genre.

Recomposing Natural History

At the end of the semester, students in Literature and the Environment move from noticing and analyzing to creating and producing. Their final project has two components: a brief report on the cultural history of nature and their own field guide entry. Both elements center on a single species, ideally a local species that the student has learned about through their nature journal entries. They begin by doing research on their species in books and databases available through our library, with the goal of turning up answers to the questions they have gradually learned to ask. I give them a brief tutorial on accessing and searching those resources that tend to be especially rich in overlooked and forgotten information, including digital newspaper archives and online book repositories. Once they have found three to five sources that provide some sense of the cultural, historical, or economic values assigned to their species, they draft a three-page report on the cultural history of nature that cites those sources and sketches out the shifting significance of their species.

Here, too, close reading matters, because the information gleaned from this research often requires some analysis of the sources students find. A student researching the American red squirrel (*Tamiasciurus hudsonicus*), for example, might find it mentioned in a nineteenth-century poem, an early-twentieth-century children's story, an advertisement for fur-trimmed hats, and a late-twentieth-century newspaper article about the changing distribution of the species. Synthesizing those sources into a coherent story about attitudes toward the animal requires thinking through how each text is characterizing it and valuing (or failing to value) its unique traits. This report, combined with a semester's worth of experience using different field guides, provides the foundation for the creative portion of their final project: composing a new field guide entry for their species.

In the space of a single 8.5″ × 11″ page, I challenge students to create their own field guide entry using the media and technology of their choice. Their goal is to educate readers in how to identify the species and to explain why someone should care to identify the species in the first place. This second element is something that conventional field guides rarely include, since they prioritize scientific descriptions over subjective interest and values. The entry is accompanied by a brief written reflection that gives students a chance to explain the decisions they made in their entry, with reference to both the historical sources they have read and the field guides they consulted.

The days students get to share their field guide entries with the class are a highlight of the semester, both for them and for me. Students take on the role of environmental educators, introducing their peers to species they might not know. They also get to show off their creative work in writing, drawing, and arranging their entries. But from where I sit, the most rewarding part of their presentations is the way they showcase a new batch of science-minded students who have really begun to notice, to close-read, and to attend to the relationship between forms of life and forms of literature. Having learned to see scientific conventions, they have also learned to see through them and to make their own decisions about how nature ought to be represented to human beings struggling to come to terms with our entangled and increasingly imperiled world.

Note

1. Typically I ban use of the internet or identification apps—at least until students have consulted at least one guide. For instructors who don't have adequate campus resources or guides of their own, it is possible to modify this assignment using freely available identification tools on the web. I used that strategy myself during the remote instruction stage of the COVID-19 pandemic, and it still worked well.

Work Cited

James, Henry. "The Art of Fiction." *Partial Portraits*, by James, Macmillan, 1888, pp. 375–408.

Appendix: Select Annotated Bibliography of Field Guides for the Northeastern United States

Alden, Peter, et al. *National Audubon Society Field Guide to the Mid-Atlantic States*. Alfred A. Knopf, 1999.
Each entry in this field guide from a conservation organization features basic information about the species's appearance and distribution as well as a

thumbnail-sized photograph to aid in identification. The guide covers a wide range of plants and animals (and a few fungi) from a huge region, but it only loosely arranges them by taxonomy and alphabetical ordering, and it leaves little room for expansion on any given entry.

Del Tredici, Peter. *Wild Urban Plants of the Northeast: A Field Guide.* Cornell UP, 2010.

Del Tredici focuses on those species overlooked by guides preoccupied with the ideal of pristine, undisturbed nature, dedicating each spread to a species (native or not) commonly found in urban and other disturbed environments. Every spread includes multiple photographs to demonstrate different growth habits as well as sections devoted to outlining the species's cultural and ecological significance.

Feinstein, Julie. *Field Guide to Urban Wildlife.* Stackpole Books, 2011.

Devoted exclusively to urban and suburban animals often overlooked in other guides, Feinstein's text includes a photograph or two of each species for identification purposes as well as a micro essay that provides some cultural history and explains how the animal survives in human-modified environments.

Kaufman, Kenn, and Kimberly Kaufman. *Field Guide to Nature of New England.* Houghton Mifflin Harcourt, 2012.

This book in the popular Kaufman series follows older institutional examples by covering a wide range of species in a large geographic area, but it makes room for larger photographs, includes helpful indicators of scale, and arranges species in clusters that are related or similar-looking for ease of navigation.

Peattie, Donald Culross. *A Natural History of North American Trees.* Trinity UP, 2007.

Peattie's lyrical volume from the early twentieth century worries less about helping readers identify species than about helping them build a philosophical and spiritual relationship with trees. It takes each species as a jumping-off point for personal memories, reflections, and lessons captured in essays that ramble over several pages, interspersed with Paul Landacre's evocative black-and-white etchings that try to capture each tree's unique beauty and majesty.

Sibley, David Allen. *The Sibley Guide to Trees.* Alfred A. Knopf, 2009.

Sibley's monumental achievement uses sketches and paintings to highlight identifying features and common varieties of each tree, providing details that are rarely discernible in photographic field guides. Species are arranged taxonomically, with more common and more prominent species receiving more space and attention.

Xan Sarah Chacko

Teaching the Invisible:
Science, Labor, and Pedagogy

How do you uncover the invisible? Technologies of visualization have developed myriad means by which things that cannot be readily seen—far-off galaxies, tiny particles, the insides of bodies—can be revealed (Lynch and Woolgar; Coopmans et al.). Each of these techniques comes with challenges and affordances. For instance, X-rays have the almost magical quality of being able to expose skeletal structures that are impossible to see without cutting open the body. At the same time, X-rays do little to show injuries to soft tissues like tendons or ligaments, for which a more detailed tool, the computed tomography, or CT, scan, is preferred. It is therefore important to know for what one is searching before a suitable visualization technique is chosen. Learning about the past is no different. A historical study needs to understand the kinds of evidence available and adjudicate which ones will best serve our attempts to understand how life was lived and decisions made in the past. Writing stories from the history of science has affordances and difficulties, and in this essay, I focus on one filter through which we can tell those stories: invisible labor.

By "invisible labor" I mean the diverse and specialized occupations and practices that are crucial to the production of scientific knowledge but are concealed or eclipsed by the standardized way by which credit is distributed in science. The most obvious of these roles is that of the technician. These are people who contribute important labor to the maintenance of laboratory spaces but are not understood to have made the most salient intellectual contributions. Historians and anthropologists of science have dedicated hours of research and reams of paper to expose these players as critically underrepresented, not only in the literature—they are often unnamed—but also in crediting mechanisms such as prizes and authorship (Traweek; Shapin).

From translators to curators, citizen scientists to test subjects, there are several other forms that this invisibility takes, which I explored with my two coeditors, Jenny Bangham and Judith Kaplan, in an anthology titled *Invisible Labour in Modern Science* (Bangham et al.). The book features twenty-five short case studies of invisible labor organized into four domains—people, power, process, and practices—each with a synthetic commentary. The featured authors represent a broad variety of geographies, areas in science, and methods. We designed the book to be a teachable text that showcases the diversity of approaches in creating a better understanding of how science is made and who is left out of the story. After the book was published, I used it as a starting point to design a course I taught in spring 2023 in the Science, Technology, and Society program at Brown University. What follows is a reflection on my experience designing and teaching Invisible Labor in the Making of Science, the topics that gained most traction with students, and my use of assessment to instill a mixed-methods approach when studying science from a humanistic perspective.

Course Design

I pitched Invisible Labor in the Making of Science as a lower-division course that would introduce students to the skills of close reading, conducting interviews, archival research and analysis, and critical thinking. Invisible Labor was designated as qualifying for the writing requirement, which students at Brown fulfill with a minimum of two courses. The key concepts I wanted to engage during the course were that of authorial credit (Who gets it? Who decides?), gendered labor (When do we recognize it? When is it rendered invisible?), embodied and tacit knowledge (How do we notice these ways of making knowledge, especially in science?), and incommensurability (the idea that studying the past is different from understanding it because on some experiential level, you had to have been there to fully grasp the meaning). The course focused on content from the twentieth and twenty-first centuries, and I divided the course into modules that invited comparisons across geographic, temporal, and disciplinary boundaries in order to show how invisible labor in science manifests as well as the approaches taken by science and technology studies scholars in uncovering it. The modules also facilitated different forms of self-reflexive practice, which opened the possibilities of research avenues for students and encouraged them to consider how we should approach research and narrative method and how contemporary interest in invisible labor relates to the history of science and science and technology studies.[1] The course objectives were as follows:

> To sharpen our ability to read sources for laboring people and practices that are obscured based on differences including gender, sexual orientation, class, religion, ability, citizenship status, and geography.
>
> To ask critical questions regarding how invisibility structures the ways different forms of power and privilege produce knowledge about racial and identity formations.
>
> To examine the practices and ethics of care that are foundational to scientific, technological, and medical practices but have been thus far dislocated because of the power of historical formations such as racism, sexism, and colonialism.

Still reeling from the constrained in-person teaching protocols of the COVID-19 pandemic, by spring 2023, the classroom atmosphere was approaching a sense of intimacy without fear. Our designated room was on the second floor of the John D. Rockefeller, Jr. Library (lovingly referred to as "the Rock") and seemed to be in a state of climatic extremism compared with the rest of the library. When the library was warm, Rock 201 was sweltering. When the stacks and reading rooms were cool, our little classroom was frigid. However we were dressed for the outside world was inadequate, and the feeling of shared discomfort did a great deal to engender a sense of togetherness. As a class with no prerequisites being taught by a relatively unknown professor for whom this was only their second semester at Brown, Invisible Labor gathered a real mixed bag of enrollees. The class was evenly split between first-years and seniors, with a sprinkling of sophomores and juniors. This meant that some had experienced the pandemic from home as high schoolers, and the others were already at Brown when their studies were interrupted. The class was also evenly split between students who had already chosen to concentrate (the Brown

University version of a major) in a STEM discipline and others who were coming from the humanities or social sciences. They met in the middle, in my classroom, wanting to understand more about how science is made because they either were already thinking of themselves as scientists or were curious about science as self-ascribed outsiders.

Assessing the Invisible

If I wanted students to take away one concept from the class, it was the idea that there is more than meets the eye in the production of knowledge in science and that therein lies the politics. Who makes decisions about what counts as work worthy of credit changes depending on the discipline and period. I wanted students to become attuned to the way that power, or an imbalance of power, lies hidden in the decision-making practice. Alongside readings selected from a range of scientific disciplines,[2] the assessments of the course were intended to show that uncovering the hidden stories is always partial. Influenced by the feminist scholar Donna Haraway, my aim for the class assignments was to start in the creation of "a successor science project that offers a more adequate, richer, better account of a world, in order to live in it well and in critical, reflexive relation to our own as well as others' practices of domination and the unequal parts of privilege and oppression that make up all positions" (Haraway, "Situated Knowledges" 579). The first step—the midterm ethnography project, called "Making Science Visible"—was to contact a scientist. The midterm invited students to conduct a thirty-minute interview with a person who identifies as a professional scientist and a thirty-minute follow-up observation of them doing their work, whether in their laboratory or at their desk.

In having to solicit participation in the project, students learned how to write explanatory emails inviting scientists to collaborate with them. Getting email consent to participate in the study was the first hurdle because many faculty members were busy and did not at first understand why they, not the products of their labor, were the subject of the inquiry. Being able to explain why paying attention to the laboring body is salient to understanding the science was something that students gained familiarity with while reading the assigned course content. With examples ranging from technical labor in the production of chemistry glassware to the role of Indigenous hospitality in studies of human diversity, students used their interviews to showcase their growing expertise gained from their readings in the course—for example, Kapil Raj's chapter "Surgeons, Fakirs, Merchants, and Craftsmen" (*Relocating Modern Science* 27–59)—and to ask questions around invisible forms of labor that the contemporary scientist may notice. I specifically instructed them to pay attention to how gender, class, and racial inequities create systems of power and privilege in the making of science. The follow-up observation was also an opportunity for students to see how forms of labor and power are made in practice. The output of the midterm was a blog post (no longer than one thousand words) whose goal was to make a thing, person, or place visible and to reflect on the politics of that revelation. Students were invited to share drafts of their posts with their interviewees and to incorporate any changes they suggested. This recursive practice instilled in students a responsibility toward their interlocutors that also conformed to the feminist ethic that I tried to cultivate.

For the final project of the course, I solicited the guidance of Leo Lovemore, the subject area librarian for science and technology studies, in facilitating the use of the Brown University special collections. The assignment was to create a mini history of a hitherto understudied or overlooked topic or person that was represented in the vast but underutilized John Hay Library at Brown University. Students were required to use the theoretical tools offered in the course readings—Haraway's "modest witness," Steven Shapin's "invisible technician," Jill Lepore's "microhistory," and Saidiya Hartman's "critical fabulation"—to think through their own research findings in the archives. Broken into small parts, the final project was assessed with several interim checkpoints, including a proposal, a peer evaluation, an in-class presentation of early findings, and a final paper. To introduce students to the special collections, Leo curated a class visit to the Hay Library so that students could interact with a variety of sources. From books of herbal remedies from the eighteenth century to a series of letters written by incarcerated individuals to their loved ones, the tangible connection to the historical material drew students in. Providing guidance on the appropriate ways to handle these delicate materials and on how to navigate the library's website to find sources and request them for viewing, Leo captivated and empowered students to start their own projects. I was impressed by the range of topics that students addressed. One student studied the lists used by the quartermasters responsible for stocking ships for long voyages that came from the Carlton D. Morse whaling collection.[3] Another used the Snell mycology collection, which focuses on the work of Professor Walter Snell, to investigate the role that his wife and collaborator, Esther Snell, played in the research, even though she is rarely credited as an author.

The project that stunned me for its novelty focused on the work of an amateur magician, H. Adrian Smith. The student uncovered that this collection had not only the usual components of a personal archive, such as letters and journals, but also a massive collection of magic props, tools, and instruction books. In addition to presenting a study of the life of Smith, the student also tried to re-create some of the magic tricks by following the detailed instructions laid out by her historical subject. She performed these tricks in class and, as an appendix to her paper, made a video of herself performing more tricks. What struck me about the project was not only how well researched and written it was but also that it required her to embody or live through the instructions that she uncovered in the archives. Even though the student had no prior training or expertise in magic, the magic tricks worked. While the connection between magic tricks and scientific labor is tenuous at best, what I appreciated about the project was her commitment to the historical project and that she tried her best to understand the meaning of the instructions she found in the archive.

Witnessing History

Early in the semester students read about the concept of a "modest witness" in the history of science (Haraway, "Modest_Witness" 223), one who was able to efface his (and it was always a man) personal identity, biases, and opinions in favor of revealing the "truths in nature" as evidenced in scientific experimentation (Shapin 556). We discussed how this concept of the scientist has been seen as foundational to claims that present science as universal and objective. We also read Haraway's critiques of objectivity: Haraway points out that in practice, the "view from nowhere," or "god's eye trick," always turns out to have a bodily starting point and therefore a particular situatedness; as she puts it, "Vision is *always* a question of the power to see—and perhaps of the violence implicit in our visualizing practices. With whose blood were my eyes crafted?" ("Situated Knowledges" 585). Students started, albeit reluctantly, to appreciate that if science is a human enterprise, then the human attributes of choice, power, and prejudice are a part of science too. The hardest part of the course for many of the students, whether they were coming from STEM or humanistic fields, was to let go of their own expectations in order to learn completely, understand comprehensively, or fully capture the nuances of what life was like for their historical subjects. The partiality and subjectivity troubled them because they yearned to be able to say things definitively: a thing happened, or this person was a woman, and that is why things turned out the way they did for them. As it turns out, the historical archive is loath to give us smoking guns that putatively impute causation. Learning to read between the lines, with and against the grain, and to stay with the parts that troubled them, was painful and slow.[4]

A reading that at first confounded students but ultimately provided the most fruitful results in its application was Hartman's article "Venus in Two Acts." Hartman explains why, because of their identity nexus, some historical actors—in this case, enslaved women—did not leave traces in the archives themselves but only exist in the voices of others. Students latched on to Hartman's suggestion of a "failed witness," one who speaks from a position of privilege and ignorance and thus skews the archival traces toward "violence" and "excess" (2). One student was moved by the silences in the archives, writing in a reading response assignment, "If there are no archives, how can we tell stories? If we don't tell the stories of these women, how can we offer a more complete and complex view of the world?" Another student powerfully summarized the tricky and thorny politics of representation that comes from archival work: "This silence in the archive and the resultant quantitative bias of the historiography repro-duces the harm of slavery. . . . If you rely only on the historical record, you tell stories through what those in power wrote and thought."

While I don't rely solely on course evaluations to reflect on the suc-cess or limitations of a new course, a question I enjoy the responses to is one that asks students what they would like to say about the course to a student considering taking it in the future. Here are some of the answers offered by students in Invisible Labor:

> "If you are even slightly interested in this course, TAKE IT."
> "This course will change how you view the world."
> "This was a very interesting and innovative course, and I wish there were more courses like this!"
> "I loved it. I would go back and take it again even with my stressful semester."

To me the course was a success because it brought together a wide range of students with different levels of humanistic training and created the conditions of possibility for a shared space of thought in which they could struggle together to understand the complexities of trying to represent the past. Watching them figure out and hone their interests, strengths, and passions for contributing to a justice-oriented project of historical storytelling through the practice of doing research was edifying to me as an educator. I will be teaching the course going forward and am looking forward to learning from the new stories that will be told in each successive iteration.[5]

Notes

1. For more on this final point, see Roberts et al.

2. For a full list of readings, see Anthony et al.

3. I have chosen not to name any of the students in this essay in accordance with the 1974 Family Educational Rights and Privacy Act.

4. On the idea of reading with and against the grain in historical research, see Stoler; Scott. On the concept of "staying with" difficulty, see Haraway, *Staying*.

5. For an example syllabus on the topic of invisible labor intended for circulation and adaptation, see Anthony et al.

Works Cited

Anthony, Patrick, et al. "(Un)Making Labor Invisible: A Syllabus." *History of Science*, vol. 61, no. 4, Dec. 2023, pp. 608–24, https://doi.org/10.1177/00732753231180954.

Bangham, Jenny, et al., editors. *Invisible Labour in Modern Science*. Rowman and Littlefield, 2022.

Coopmans, Catelijne, et al. *Representation in Scientific Practice Revisited*. MIT Press, 2014.

Haraway, Donna J. "Modest_Witness@Second_Millennium." *The Haraway Reader*, Routledge, 2004, pp. 223–50.

———. "Situated Knowledges: The Science Question in Feminism and the Privilege of Partial Perspective." *Feminist Studies*, vol. 14, no. 3, fall 1988, pp. 575–99.

———. *Staying with the Trouble: Making Kin in the Chthulucene*. Duke UP, 2016.

Hartman, Saidiya. "Venus in Two Acts." *Small Axe: A Caribbean Journal of Criticism*, vol. 12, no. 2, 2008, pp. 1–14.

Lepore, Jill. "Historians Who Love Too Much: Reflections on Microhistory and Biography." *The Journal of American History*, vol. 88, no. 1, 2001, pp. 129–44.

Lynch, Michael, and Steve Woolgar. *Representation in Scientific Practice*. MIT Press, 1990.

Raj, Kapil. *Relocating Modern Science: Circulation and the Construction of Knowledge in South Asia and Europe, 1650–1900.* Palgrave Macmillan, 2007.

Roberts, Lissa, et al. "Historiographies of Science and Labor: From Past Perspectives to Future Possibilities." *History of Science*, vol. 61, no. 4, Dec. 2023, pp. 448–74, https://doi.org/10.1177/00732753231209023.

Scott, James C. *Against the Grain: A Deep History of the Earliest States.* Yale UP, 2017.

Shapin, Steven. "The Invisible Technician." *American Scientist*, vol. 77, no. 6, 1989, pp. 554–63.

Stoler, Ann Laura. *Along the Archival Grain: Epistemic Anxieties and Colonial Common Sense.* Princeton UP, 2010.

Traweek, Sharon. *Beamtimes and Lifetimes: The World of High Energy Physicists.* Harvard UP, 1988.

James Barilla

Teaching with the Hive: Beekeeping as a Scientific and Creative Practice

Imagine a group of students gathered with their professor in an unmown field. Everyone is zipped up in stiff white canvas, including a mesh face guard, elbow-length gloves, and a thick white canvas jacket cinched tight below the waist. The students are passing around a wooden frame that appears to be alive, since it's coated with a simmering cluster of honeybees. Undulations of honeycomb fill the rectangular space inside the frame like tripe in a butcher's case or the tonsils of an alien. Meanwhile, an expert beekeeper bends over the hive to point out the different structures hidden inside, the capped and uncapped brood, nibbles of wax moth, the mottled cells filled with pollen. Bees come and go from the entrance. They hover and spiral through the air, prospect along arms and backs, wander across the mesh of the face guards. The air thrums with the sound of many wings, surrounding us, immersing us, inspiring us.

Conceptualization

Planning for this course began a year in advance, when I was contacted by the service learning coordinator for the Honors College at the University of South Carolina. She pitched the idea of a beekeeping class that would allow students to fulfill the college's "Beyond the Classroom" requirement for graduation. Honors College students can fulfill the requirement by taking one course that offers meaningful service outside the traditional university setting. These courses are usually offered in a seminar format that is capped at fifteen students and malleable in content and approach. Students in the university beekeeping club had long advocated for such a course. A course in beekeeping seemed like an exciting prospect, not only because it would offer students a rich learning experience outside the classroom but also because the decline in health and number of honeybees, and of pollinators more broadly, offered a chance to perform meaningful service. The course would not be restricted by major, discipline, or pedagogy, so it could take an unconventional approach to its subject matter. Creative writing seemed to be a useful practice for pursuing an unconventional science writing, one that could bring together an immersion in the discourse of basic and applied science with the kinds of questions and insights that arise from a humanistic perspective. Science writing, as creative writing, suggested a range of experimental possibilities in genre and form that were consistent with the flexible expectations of the course.

The challenge, however, had always been finding the right faculty member, someone who had the flexibility in their teaching schedule to offer a new course and the knowledge and interest to develop the curriculum. While I had written about bees previously and had observed beekeepers in action as part of my nonfiction book research, I am a creative writing professor, not a trained beekeeper, and I had never kept bees myself. Thus, it was apparent from the start that in order for the course to involve hands-on experience with bees, we needed to develop a team-based model for teaching the course, dividing the pedagogical tasks so that a certified beekeeper could handle beekeeping practice in the field while I met with students in the classroom and handled discussion and the grading of their written work. Early on, through the student-run beekeeping club, we connected with David MacFawn, who had written the textbook *Applied Beekeeping in the United States* and served as president of the South Carolina Master Beekeeping Program, which offers training and certification courses to the general public. MacFawn had the time, teaching experience, and zeal for promoting apiculture, and he agreed to join the planning process, which initially included students from the beekeeping club as well.

In the beginning we had two goals in mind: to offer a service learning component and to include field-based learning through hands-on experience with beekeeping. However, as we learned that the university's beekeeping club attracted students from a variety of majors, we also began to see the art and science of beekeeping as an opportunity for a transdisciplinary approach. Ideally, a transdisciplinary course in beekeeping might bring together expertise in social insect research, beekeeping practice, and creative writing, but the time constraints of the semester and the availability of faculty expertise meant we would need to focus on the applied science of beekeeping practice. We would ground the explanation of beekeeping techniques in the biology, behavior, and ecology of honeybees, but we would forgo the pursuit of basic science research and the development of our own questions and experimental designs. We envisioned students witnessing and participating in the life cycle of the bees through their service learning, which would involve checking on the welfare of local hives during several important junctures in their life cycle. We would visit once in early spring to evaluate the health of the hive when it was conserving energy and preparing for the spring foraging season, once as the tree pollen season began to evaluate whether any hives might need to be divided in order to prevent swarming, and once in the prime nectar-gathering season when the number of workers in the hives would be near their peak and we could anticipate honey production for the season. This experience would then serve as inspiration for creative work that engaged imaginatively with the cultural and ecological implications of beekeeping practice and the natural history of honeybees. Thus, our discussions increasingly focused on the degree to which we could develop a curriculum that engaged with the biology and behavior of social insects through readings in the sciences while also examining apiarist practices in a literary context, through the extensive literature of beekeeping available in multiple genres. The field-based experiences would also serve as inspiration for students' own creative work. We envisioned a course that would involve semiweekly meetings in the classroom punctuated by a series of weekend visits to the hives.

Planning, Goals, and Challenges

Any service learning course—let alone one involving nonhuman creatures—requires careful planning and input from both internal and external partners. Some considerations—such as the accessibility of course materials or the possibility that a student may not be able to participate in particular activities—can be addressed through existing university structures, such as a disability services office or a center for teaching and learning. Others may be more difficult to predict, so a word of advice to readers interested in service learning: consult well ahead of time with university administration and, if possible, with other instructors who have already developed service or experiential learning courses at your institution. Any off-site course may involve safety, accessibility, transportation, or other nonacademic considerations.

Beekeeping poses some distinctive logistical challenges that must be addressed in the planning stage. The first is finding consistent access to the hives. Honeybees are highly adaptable, and urban hives occupy rooftops and other seemingly unlikely locations. However, the typical site is often intentionally out of the way to avoid conflicts with the public, which in turn means that the hives are not easily accessible, particularly for a large group that may want to visit frequently. In our case, we soon turned from trying to find an appropriate corner for a hive on campus to working with the beekeeping club and its contacts in the local community in order to find a set of hives we could visit. We ultimately settled on a location that was not too far from campus, on property owned by a local beekeeper who had situated a number of hives there. This location was a half-hour drive from campus, however, with no reasonable access by public transportation. In practice, we could address the transportation issue through carpooling, but we also included language in the course description, notifying potential students that off-campus travel on weekends was a requirement, and transportation would not be provided.

The second challenge involves the risk of bee stings and, related to this, the possible existence of bee sting allergies among class participants. We addressed this concern during advising for the course, recommending that those with a known allergy not enroll. We also developed a plan for potential allergic reactions that included two EpiPens as emergency treatment. These injectors were to be kept in an accessible location by the instructor during any field visit. As the instructor, I was responsible for completing the online Red Cross certification and training process, which included learning how to recognize the signs of an allergic reaction and how to use the injector in an emergency situation. The injectors added to what was already a hefty equipment budget, since each participant would need to be outfitted with standard protective gear. Because the cost might have stopped students from enrolling, the Honors College covered the equipment costs with course development funds. With the exception of the EpiPens, the equipment could be reused, meaning that the cost per class would decline each time the class was offered. In the end, no students were stung during the field sessions, and the EpiPens were never used.

A third challenge arose when we tried to establish a course calendar that would reconcile the hard-and-fast dates of the academic semester with the far less rigid time frame of spring activity in a beehive while also anticipating the potential for adverse weather to scramble our plans. At our institution the spring semester begins in early January and ends in late April, but the bees don't care about our dates. They care about temperature patterns, which tend to vary wildly in the spring in South Carolina, and how the local flora responds. If the temperature is below fifty-five degrees, they tend to huddle together inside the hive for warmth, and a responsible beekeeper will leave them alone until things warm up outside. A stretch of warm weather, however, will coax many plants into bloom and encourage the bees to head out and forage. There's no way of knowing in advance when cold snaps and warm spells will occur, so the schedule itself felt provisional at the outset, far more contingent than the teaching schedule for a conventional class. We planned three site visits, the first of which would involve checking on the health status of the hives and feeding at the end of January. The second would be a status update at the beginning of March, when the nectar season begins, and the third would occur at the end of March, when the honey-making season is fully underway. But we didn't know if the weather would cooperate. As a backup plan, I set up an alternative service opportunity with the Rosewood Community Orchard, which, as the name suggests, is a community-based orchard and garden located not too far from campus, with weekly volunteer workdays and long-standing relationships with university classes and volunteer groups. While the site does not include honeybee hives, it does feature a pollinator garden, meaning that it would still allow service opportunities, in keeping with the theme of the course.

Finally, composing the reading list for a transdisciplinary course raised several conceptual questions: How strictly focused on bees should the course reading be? How technical should the scientific reading be? How aesthetically ambitious should the stories and poems be? Teaching the class for the first time, I found it difficult to anticipate the background and majors of those students who might enroll. Consequently, I decided to broaden the thematic focus of the literary reading in order to pose broader questions of the human relationship to the natural world and to give students more flexible models for their own writing. We would read the novel *The History of Bees*, by the contemporary Norwegian author

Maja Lunde, and honeybee-focused poems by Sylvia Plath, Nick Flynn, and Jo Shapcott, for example, but we'd also consider the appeal of wilderness as individual testing ground in Jon Krakauer's nonfiction narrative "Death of an Innocent," the degree to which humans can imagine the subjectivity of nonhumans through excerpts from Charles Foster's *Being a Beast* (29–77), and even reflections on the nature of democracy, community, and conformity in texts such as Shirley Jackson's short story "The Lottery."

After reviewing a number of potential journal articles covering different aspects of apiology, and considering how much students could reasonably be expected to read and assimilate in a course with objectives in service learning, creative writing, and beekeeping practice, I decided instead to utilize excerpts from books intended for a general audience, such as Thomas Seeley's *Honeybee Democracy* (20–42) and *The Lives of Bees* (79–98). While this choice represented a sacrifice in that students would not be engaging directly with the primary literature, Seeley's texts describe the design and implementation of apiological experiments and provided the scientific context for what we'd experience in the field. For example, in chapter 4 of *Honeybee Democracy* (73–98), Seeley covers the history of research in swarm dynamics, poses a series of still unanswered questions, describes the experimental methods that might address those questions, and then narrates the resulting field research process.

Realization

As it turned out, most of the students who registered for the course were life science majors who were familiar with scientific literature and lab science practices. There were no English majors in the group, and most had never taken a creative writing course. Only two were members of the beekeeping club, so the majority had no experience with beekeeping and limited knowledge of the natural history of honeybees. Thus, while I had anticipated that the early portion of the class would involve introducing humanities students to the discourse of scientific research and technical writing, in practice, the focus of the first few weeks in the classroom shifted to familiarizing STEM students with the terms and practices of creative writing and literary analysis. Our early classes began with an in-class writing exercise, which we then shared in small groups to foster greater ease in sharing work in progress. I then covered several key concepts for literary analysis and creative writing, such as the difference between dramatic and situational irony and their relationship to point of view. We would then identify those terms in the reading for the day. For example, in an early session we considered how the situational irony unfolds in the plot dynamics of Roald Dahl's "Royal Jelly," a short story that also usefully models the assimilation of beekeeping terms and practices into a fictional context.

David MacFawn attended our first meeting so that he could introduce the beekeeping expectations for the course, but for the remainder of the course he led the Saturday sessions in the field, while I covered the semi-weekly meetings in the classroom. Prior to our first field session, and before each subsequent hive visit, MacFawn emailed several handouts, which he then covered in person. The handout for the first session, "Safety in the Beeyard," covered a number of not necessarily intuitive points. For example, while I was aware that dark fuzzy clothing was to be avoided because of its resemblance to potential threats like bears, I did not know that the honeybee alarm pheromone is said to smell like bananas. In fact, I completely forgot about this caution on our first early-morning hive visit, and I was about to peel and snack on a banana before we got started when someone in our group politely intervened.

Given their background in STEM, students were relatively comfortable drawing ideas and questions from the applied sciences of the fieldwork. However, students were understandably nervous about trying something new, and especially during the early stages of the course, we needed to spend our time defining what we were seeking in the readings, strategically and thematically. We needed to discuss the prose elements of plot, character, setting, and dialogue as well as the use of figuration in verse. We also needed time to become familiar with the goals and practices of a creative writing workshop, which initially meant sharing in-class exercises and modeling peer feedback in small groups. Over time the workshops gained momentum as students got more comfortable with this new approach, as they began to see the material of bee biology and the practice of beekeeping through the lens of a storyteller or poet, and as they began to take more risks in their creative work. They might, for example, see colony collapse disorder, a mysterious malady that causes hives to abruptly cease operation and disappear, as an extended metaphor or as a plotline, as it is in Lunde's novel *The History of Bees.* Or they might reflect on their visits to the hive, on the drama and mystery of lifting the lid on a super and extracting a frame, or on the vivid technical diction of such terms as *queen excluder*, *brood*, and *drone*, thereby locating the raw material for their work in verse. Or their work might be more loosely inspired by the beekeeping subject matter, exploring broader questions of nature and culture.

In their written evaluations, students often described the immediacy and novelty of their direct encounters with the hives as the highlight of the course. For example, reading about the social dynamics of bee colonies, the characteristics of a superorganism, and the way colonies come to collective decisions made more sense when we were involved in smoking the hives ourselves, directing puffs of burning pine duff smoke into the frames, and observing as the bees responded instinctively to protect the queen and the honey stores. We watched as undertaker bees worked to repair the damage our inspection had inadvertently caused, dragging dead and injured larvae out of the entrance and across the landing board and depositing the bodies unceremoniously in the grass. At the start of these visits, I helped students don their protective gear, and I carried the Epi-Pens with me in a backpack, but otherwise I allowed MacFawn to lead the class. MacFawn had extensive experience leading workshops and certification courses for novice beekeepers, which he frequently taught outdoors. Thus, the field-based learning component of the course could lean on established lecture topics and course materials, with minor adjustments for the student audience.

The service component of the course, however, was more difficult to realize because students' interactions with the hives offered limited opportunities for meaningful service. This was due in part to the relatively high level of technical skill that must be met before being able to work individually with the bees. We could learn about them, and we could interact with the hives under supervision, but we were not at a stage where we could perform much of the work that hive maintenance might require, and the timing of the course was such that it ended prior to the harvesting and processing of honey, the main labor-intensive activity of the year. It's also the case that a healthy hive doesn't require a great deal of human intervention, and it's often best to let the bees do their work without disturbance. In the end, these limitations led to some useful reflection on the nature of service: What were the needs we were seeking to address, and who were the intended beneficiaries of our work? Were we trying to help the bee colonies, or the beekeepers, or the plants that needed pollination, or the ecosystem more broadly?[1]

Reflection

In retrospect, there are two primary adjustments I will pursue when offering the course again. The first will be to integrate the service opportunities available through the community orchard more fully into the course, as a complement to the field-based learning with the hives. The maintenance of the pollinator garden allowed students the chance to perform meaningful work for the welfare of honeybees, other pollinators, and the plants they pollinate without requiring extensive training. The impact of the work was also readily observable over the course of a semester as plants came into bloom and pollinators visited the site, and because the site has an established volunteer program with frequent workdays, scheduling could be more flexible, and students had opportunities to participate individually.

The second change will involve finding ways to bring more elements of scientific inquiry into the curriculum, given that one of the transdisciplinary goals of the course is to discover and pursue the kinds of questions that arise when different epistemologies interact and intersect. As I mentioned earlier, one of the primary trade-offs in the course design involved focusing exclusively on applied science, and another involved relinquishing direct exposure to the scientific literature. However, I still believe the course could offer more engagement with the epistemologies of scientific inquiry, specifically by proposing models for our own potential experiments in bee behavior and biology. One way of doing so, without sacrificing other course modalities, would be to create a course assignment that involves the gathering and presentation of research in response to a question about the behavior, biology, or ecology of social insects as a preliminary step in the process of developing a final creative project. Another possibility would be to seek out opportunities for students to develop research questions and design experiments that they could choose to pursue in a subsequent independent study. An independent study would require additional faculty expertise as well as additional course and lab time, a hurdle that could be addressed by offering an additional semester-long course or through supervised individual research projects in the summer or participation in ongoing faculty research projects.

Note

1. To address these questions, we used Elizabeth Kolbert's essay "Stung" as well as the film *Queen of the Sun*. Both emphasize the impact of colony collapse disorder, a malady whose mysterious cause brought to light a number of problems responsible for declines in honeybee colony health. More recent attention has highlighted the decline in insect numbers more broadly, including those of pollinators. In the future I would include an extensive online report from *Reuters*, "The Collapse of Insects," which synthesizes scientific research on insect decline (Janicki et al.).

Works Cited

Dahl, Roald. "Royal Jelly." 1960. *Kiss Kiss*, by Dahl, Penguin Books, 2011, pp. 1–30.

Flynn, Nick. *Blind Huber*. Graywolf Press, 2002.

Foster, Charles. *Being a Beast: Adventures across the Species Divide*. Picador, 2016.

Jackson, Shirley. "The Lottery." 1948. *"The Lottery" and Other Stories*, by Jackson, Noonday Press, 1991, pp. 291–302.

Janicki, Julia, et al. "The Collapse of Insects." *Reuters*, 6 Dec. 2022, www.reuters.com/graphics/GLOBAL-ENVIRONMENT/INSECT-APOCALYPSE/egpbykdxjvq/.

Kolbert, Elizabeth. "Stung." *The New Yorker*, 30 July 2007, www.newyorker.com/magazine/2007/08/06/stung.

Krakauer, Jon. "Death of an Innocent." *Outside Magazine*, Jan. 1993, outsidemag.com/ magazine/0193/9301-ldea.html. Accessed 11 Jan. 2023.

Lunde, Maja. *The History of Bees*. Atria, 2018.

Plath, Sylvia. *Ariel*. Harper and Row, 1966.

Queen of the Sun. Directed by Taggart Siegel, Music Box Films, 2010.

Seeley, Thomas D. *Honeybee Democracy*. Princeton UP, 2010.

———. *The Lives of Bees: The Untold Story of the Honeybee in the Wild*. Princeton UP, 2019.

Shapcott. Jo. "Six Bee Poems." *The Poetry Society*, 2025, poetrysociety.org.uk/poems/six-bee-Poems.

Nancy Easterlin

Sex, Gender, and the Short Story

Today, most curricula in literary studies are still largely organized around a model that assumes historical coverage as the basis of knowledge. A glance at degree requirements at peer institutions and at hiring practices confirms this. Thus, in spite of the New Criticism, the reaction against it in the 1970s, and the many interdisciplinary areas and special topics courses that have emerged over the past six decades, the makeup of language and literature departments and the aligned education of students has not changed much since Gerald Graff identified their inconsistencies almost forty years ago. Now, although it's indisputable that many of us have benefited enormously from an education in historically defined periods, the question faculty members need to ask is this: Does the coverage model best serve present-day students? The majority of undergraduate English majors and MA candidates at my home institution and many others will not pursue doctoral degrees in literature or occupations that require a rudimentary background knowledge of English or American literature across the centuries.

Furthermore, today's students, living in an era of perceived ecological, political, and cultural crisis, increasingly demand curricula that conjoin nonliterary frameworks with literary studies. They are far more politically aware than were the students of twenty years ago, and many are spurred by a sense of social mission. And having grown up with the internet, social media, and prodigious, sophisticated, and aesthetically impressive television programming, they have had continuous access to a great deal of information and a range of ideas. Moreover, for students interested in women's and gender studies, an interdisciplinary perspective provides alternative paradigms for literary analysis and, ultimately, critiques of sex and gender inequality across world cultures. With the expansion of women's studies to include intersectional identities, the realignment of the social constructionist perspective in women's and gender studies with scientific theory and fact is timely.

A broad evolutionary perspective that integrates both robust and less demonstrated findings about sex and gender promises a fuller picture of what humans are than one that relies on the claim that all differences have social causes. Simultaneously, and just as importantly, critical attention to studies that apply evolutionary theory to the psychology of sex differences as well as their applications teaches students to discriminate between established findings and those that are more speculative. In so doing, this approach teaches today's students an open-minded yet discerning approach to findings and theory of all kinds and provides a critical consideration of social science's application to literature. Ultimately, in so doing, it helps them negotiate a complex world.

Course Design and Text Selection

The graduate course I describe in this essay, Sex, Gender, and the Short Story, evolved out of a somewhat different interdisciplinary upper-level undergraduate course, Sex, Power, and the Short Story, which I designed and first taught in 2007. This original course enrolled undergraduate English majors, women's and gender studies minors, and a few graduate students, and it introduced students to feminist theory (including Darwinian feminism), short story theory, and key modern and contemporary authors of short fiction. Taught twice, this course was redesigned as Sex, Power, and the Short Story II, which focused on an evolutionary approach and served as the basis for the current graduate course. The graduate course has been taught three times within a seven-year period.

The original course introduced students to a broad sweep of theories and offered experience in their application. Although this served students well, the English majors in the course already had some background in mainstream theories of sex and gender from a junior-level theory and research seminar but no such introduction to evolutionary psychology and related fields. Furthermore, in this first course, students were introduced to scientific psychology late in the semester, which gave them little time to thoughtfully consider or apply its concepts. For that reason, I redesigned the course with a focus solely on evolutionary psychology and related theories. This course, Sex, Power, and the Short Story II, established the plan that I then developed in the graduate course, Sex, Gender, and the Short Story.

Not a Chance Mutation: Sex, Gender, and the Short Story

Student learning outcomes for Sex, Gender, and the Short Story are basically divided between those applicable to all graduate-level courses and those pertaining to the course content. The first three outcomes require only brief comment:

- demonstrates ability to plan and execute a well-organized, well-written literary analysis
- exhibits proficiency in applying conceptual or theoretical knowledge to literature
- illustrates sensitivity and nuance in applying theory to literature

A course of this kind places extra demands on conceptual and writing ability. The significantly different intellectual load requires more guidance on writing assignments than traditional literature courses do. In particular, steering students away from overloading introductory paragraphs and toward providing preliminary background information on theory in a subsequent paragraph or two can help them structure a coherent argument.

The second three outcomes invite more extensive comment:

- displays knowledge of core concepts in evolutionary theory and evolutionary psychology, in both spoken and written discourse
- shows critical judgment in evaluating pros and cons of evolutionary psychology as a tool for literary analysis
- articulates issues of sex and gender and hypothesizes the varied and complex causes of those issues

Most students today have, at best, a passing sense of evolutionary theory but do not really understand how evolution works. Therefore, students need to grasp evolution by natural selection in the context of Charles

Darwin's place in post-Enlightenment intellectual culture as it shifted from static to dynamic understandings of natural processes and of the structure of reality. Unlike earlier evolutionists, Darwin and Alfred Russel Wallace recognized that adaptation is a matter of chance, that a change in the environment affecting one species often reverberates broadly, and that humans are part of the total process.

In contrast to the theory of natural selection, for which evidence has continued to mount and which nothing has disproven since the 1859 publication of Darwin's *On the Origin of Species*, evolutionary psychology is a far more recent application of a functionalist approach to the human mind. In its broad usage, evolutionary psychology embraces all the basic features of human cognitive functioning, including conscious and unconscious processes, emotions, and bonding, and it theorizes how these have contributed to human survival. Although the course's specific emphasis limits time available to study research on general cognition, especially cognitive flexibility, I provide grounding in this area in lectures and with Stephen Kaplan's essay on environmental preference and knowledge seeking.

The psychology of sex differences and of mating combines many disciplines and thus runs the gamut from well-demonstrated findings to those that are far more speculative. Whereas, for instance, demonstrable differences in hormonal levels throughout the lifespan correlate with variable levels of male and female aggression, hypothesizing the source of sexual behavior in human psychology is another matter (Campbell 64–100; Geary 103–05, 211–21, 317–25; Riggio 348–50, 374–88). The claim that men and women, on aggregate, pursue different mating strategies (also known as the Bateman-Trivers hypothesis) because of divergent reproductive demands is at once intuitively compelling and deeply deficient in its scientific foundation (Tang-Martinez and Ryder; Trivers). Likewise, although same-sex behavior has been demonstrated in over 450 animal species, and although a genetic link to male homosexuality has been identified, same-sex preference or choice, like heteronormative mating, may just as well be the outcome of social and developmental factors (Abrams; Sanders et al.; Bailey and Zuk; Roughgarden; LeVay).

Generally, a light touch is the best approach to considering how any of these theories applies or reaches a limit in analysis of literature. A relatively traditional approach to classroom discussion aids in the nuanced application of the concepts to course assignments. The design of the course around specific units of topically related texts directs students to possible application and criticism of the theories.

In designing and regularly revising the graduate course, my goal has been to match themes overtly displayed in the literature with relevant theories and to organize the course in units that speak to the primary themes of the course. Most recently, these units were Basic Concepts in Evolutionary Theory and Psychology; Same-Sex Behavior and Sexuality; Love, Sex, and Sociality; and Evolutionary Psychology: Critique and Revision. (A schedule of course units and readings can be found in the appendix.) Planning in accord with such units is, for me, indispensable, though its clarity is admittedly somewhat artificial. Thus, the third unit—Love, Sex, and Sociality—introduces psychological themes that are relevant to the stories taught in the first two units as well as a selection of works by lesbian authors and short stories by D. H. Lawrence. Casting a wider net than the first two units, this one encourages students to consider the sociocultural and affective dimensions that determine, or determine the viability of, sexual partnerships.

As with the first two undergraduate courses it grew out of, the graduate course divides course material and class time fairly equally between sex and gender theory and short fiction, with one caveat. The first two weeks of the course are devoted to an overview of evolutionary theory and psychology, and the third week pairs a sample of evolutionary scholarly criticism with the short story it interprets (Saunders; Anderson, "Untold Lie"). The first two weeks include texts that elucidate the theory of natural selection and evolutionary psychology as well as a short excerpt from Darwin's *On the Origin of Species*. Providing this background before turning to the fiction helps students grasp the complexity, interdependence, and accidental character of natural selection, and it guides them toward a nuanced understanding of evolutionary psychology.

Since I first taught this course, both the profession and students have become more receptive to evolutionary theory and no longer automatically equate it with so-called social Darwinism. The application of natural selection to the human social sphere to rationalize poverty and discrimination (social Darwinism) was the brainchild of Herbert Spencer, whose positivist spin on evolution and whose inhumane social theorizing were not endorsed by Darwin and other prominent naturalists of his day, nor are they endorsed by any of the major figures across the evolutionary sciences today (Hrdy 12–25; Spencer; Wright 329–32). In beginning the course with an overview of natural selection, including Darwin's chapter on that topic (145–79), students grasp that the foundational theory cannot be generalized to all individuals and depends on dynamic processes. By extension, they come to see that the psychological theories introduced later in the course also describe populations and aggregates, not individuals.

Until recently, selecting texts that explicate the theory has been difficult. I have always tried to include an overview text written for the layperson with selected essays and book chapters from psychology, using Robert Wright's *The Moral Animal* several times and Robin Dunbar, John Lycett, and Louise Barrett's *Evolutionary Psychology: A Beginner's Guide* on one occasion. Wright's book is now quite outdated, not generally in keeping with the emphasis on human cognitive flexibility that emerged in the 1990s, and its sometimes flippant tone, intended to attract the layperson, at times offends students. Perhaps most importantly, it does not give much attention to same-sex sexuality, and it gives none to gender. However, for years, I was not able to find anything that matched the quality of Wright's writing and his insights on the evolution of monogamy and some features of male psychology. Additionally, his interpolation of material from Darwin's own life and his suggestive insights about the application of evolutionary psychology to it offers the reader concrete application (a ground for disagreement or illumination, as may be).

With the publication of *Sex and Gender: A Biopsychological Approach*, Heidi Riggio helpfully eliminated my struggle to choose a primary theoretical text. Designed for an upper-level general education course at her home institution, the textbook foregrounds complexities of sex and gender. I reviewed this textbook on publication and used it as the primary text in the most recent offering of the course, and the student reviews were uniformly positive (Easterlin).

Along with Riggio's text, I post a number of articles and chapters on my university's online platform. These include essays on the evolution of patriarchy, on same-sex behavior (among nonhuman animals and among humans), and on problems of experimental design and definition in evolutionary psychology (Smuts; Bailey and Zuk; Kirkpatrick; Tang-Martinez and Ryder). I have also continued to assign chapters 5 and 6 from David Geary's *Male, Female*, because Geary's work offers nuance to the theory of mating strategies and because Geary is alone in emphasizing that the primary motivation of any organism is control over its own actions and decisions (121–57, 159–207). Defining the human mind as a control system, he foregrounds the centrality of self-agency, which helps explain interpersonal conflict, particularly between men and women who, on average, likely have different mating priorities. Furthermore, his discussion of preferences complicates the picture of mating strategies. In sum, Geary's comprehensive discussion of the research on these topics is crucial to Darwinian feminism.

Course Assignments

This section describes three assignments: an annotated bibliography, a research paper, and a take-home final exam.

Annotated Bibliography

Since ascertaining student comprehension of basic evolutionary psychological concepts and readings is critical to course success, I base the annotated bibliography assignment on the course readings in evolutionary and gender theory and require that these bibliography entries are turned in weekly. This certainly increases the instructor's workload, but it has multiple benefits. The weekly assignments not only provide feedback on student learning to the instructor but also offer continuous training for students in succinct written summary and evaluation of theoretical material. I specify a word limit for each entry (250 words for a chapter or article and 500 words for a book, for example) to help them organize and streamline their thinking and writing. In class, we discuss a sample entry on Wright or another author on evolutionary psychology whose work I no longer use so that students are not later writing an entry on the work used for the instructional sample.

Research Paper: Interdisciplinary Literary Analysis

I provide students with recommended topics for the research paper but give them the option of developing their own topic, subject to my approval. Because prompts on female mating dynamics are a good fit for this course's literary selections, I've offered this topic for stories including Edith Wharton's "The Other Two," "A Journey," and "Roman Fever"; Lawrence's "The Daughters of the Vicar," "The Thorn in the Flesh," "The White Stocking," and "Odour of Chrysanthemums"; and Alice Munro's "Save the Reaper," "Rich as Stink," and "The Children Stay" multiple times. Likewise, research on same-sex behavior and attachment serves to enlighten works including Colm Tóibín's "Three Friends," "A Long Winter," and "The Street"; Shani Mootoo's "Lemon Scent"; Elena

Georgiou's "Aphrodite's Vision"; and others, so this has become a repeated topic as well. I require a relatively short essay of twelve to fifteen
pages, emphasizing that argumentative development and organization are
more important than total number of pages, and I require only a few literary critical sources since students must already synthesize several sources
from psychology and other sciences in their work. I offer support for their
work by including a one-hour session with the humanities librarian at my
university, discussing organization in some detail several weeks before the
essay due date, and welcoming them to schedule conferences with me to
discuss their projects. I also provide specific guidance on how to organize
an interdisciplinary essay.

Take-Home Final Exam

A take-home exam of two relatively short essays (1,200–1,500 words each)
is the most beneficial format for the final exam. This offers another opportunity for students to practice what the course promotes, a nuanced
critical synthesis of theory with literary interpretation. Because the literary
component of the course represents about half of the reading assignments,
for the take-home exam I require that students write only on stories not
analyzed in the research paper. Even where our class discussions have not
much alluded to the theory considered in conjunction with the literature,
students are adept at seeing the connections and limitations of the scientific concepts.

These essay questions typically foreground one theorist but require
that students also draw on Riggio's discussions or the work of at least one
other theorist in their essays. Since students have access to their full annotated bibliography in addition to any notes they've taken, they are well
prepared to review and summarize the key concepts and to organize their
essays around them. In its current form, the final topics provide, first, a
choice between an essay on patriarchal dynamics or one on parental investment theory (i.e., the Bateman-Trivers hypothesis) and, second, a choice
of one of three topics: altruism, conflict between parents and children,
and same-sex behavior, including but not limited to same-sex preference.
Among the topics in the second set, students largely choose the final question, which receives significant attention in the course discussions, though
altruism and parent-child conflict are addressed in passing. The apparent
reasons for same-sex behavior in the short stories are complex, lending

themselves to a continuum of personal, social, and biological considerations, not least the exceptional human need for physical and emotional
bonds. This aligns with the scientific research across species; thus, both the
science and the stories encourage a nuanced understanding of same-sex
behavior and sexuality.

Student Responses

Below are some insights into student evaluations, based on a set of anon-
ymous, standard, university-administered questionnaire evaluations from
2018 and a nonanonymous questionnaire I sent to graduate students a
month after the submission of final grades at the end of the term in 2023.

In the recent (small) graduate class, taught on Zoom (our MA program
is completely online), all four students mentioned that reading the scientific articles was a challenge but that Riggio's textbook offered excellent
clarification and support for the more difficult readings. Additionally, all
four felt that evolutionary psychology evinced a generally new perspective
that led to insights and interpretations not offered by other theoretical approaches. Whereas one student said that spending the entire semester within
the framework of evolutionary psychology enabled her to interpret the literature in greater depth, another student maintained that since scientific
models and research come from outside the humanities, they result in a
generally passive interpretation. I still feel perplexed by this assessment, because we read, for instance, Zuleyma Tang-Martinez and T. Brandt Ryder's
essay on the design flaws in the Bateman-Trivers hypothesis and Monique
Borgerhoff Mulder's essay on how bias in terminological selection may in
fact predetermine results about mate selection strategies, clear indications
that science does not simply equate with truth or even validity.

Importantly, all four students, including those who had taken wom-
en's and gender studies courses as undergraduates, affirmed that the course
gave them a broader outlook on sex and gender, and they said they would
not have preferred to substitute this course with a traditional course. One
student indicated that they would have preferred a course that included
the evolutionary psychological perspective alongside canonical theories of
sex and gender; thus, they would have felt better served by the original
course, Sex, Power, and the Short Story. Notably, however, students in
the course seemed largely familiar with mainstream academic feminist
interpretations.

When the similar undergraduate-graduate course Sex, Power, and the Short Story II was offered in 2018, a handful of students (four undergraduates and two graduate students) answered the standard evaluation. (Unusually, numerical scores were higher on the undergraduate evaluation, but the graduate evaluations were skewed by the response of a single student.) Instructively, across these two small sets, at least four students commented on the heavy and difficult reading load. These students did not have Riggio's text available to them and, in fact, probably had a somewhat lighter overall reading load than that of the 2023 graduate students. I did assign Wright's *Moral Animal* in this class, which one student greatly disparaged.

Commenting on the positive aspects of the course, four of the six students were very enthusiastic about the connections between the literature and the theory. They commended my preparations, ability to make connections, and interpretations, and both the numbers and the comments acknowledged my availability and pointed to my interest in the success of my students. I don't know what numerical scores signify when a response level is this low, but these happened to be extremely high among the undergraduate respondents.

All in all, then, these evaluations of very similar courses suggest that students respond to the new perspective and the connections to the assigned fiction, in spite of the uniform acknowledgment that nonliterary readings present a steeper-than-usual learning curve.

For anyone who teaches a range of literary and scientific subject matter, staying up-to-date with theoretical developments as well as primary literature presents a challenge in reworking this course for each offering. For example, new findings in and theories of gender and sexual identity mean that future versions of this course must engage with a wider, more diverse range of LGBTQIA+ texts.

Overall, the course appears to validate judicious interdisciplinarity, providing literature and women's and gender studies students with an expanded view of sex and gender as they operate in realistic literature and as they manifest themselves in human experience. Rather than recommend that English majors restrict their learning to traditional courses designed to provide historical coverage, I believe that courses like these, with their many challenges, serve students' knowledge of literature and human beings, improve students' writing, and point toward meaningful futures.

Appendix: Schedule of Readings for Sex, Gender, and the Short Story

Unit A: Basic Concepts in Evolutionary Theory and Psychology

Week 1	Heidi Riggio, *Sex and Gender*, chapters 1–3 (1–58)
Week 2	Riggio, *Sex and Gender*, chapter 4 (59–81); Charles Darwin, *On the Origin of Species*, chapter 4 (144–62)
Week 3	Sherwood Anderson, "Nobody Knows" and "The Untold Lie"; Judith Saunders, "Male Reproductive Strategies in Sherwood Anderson's 'The Untold Lie'"
Week 4	David Geary, *Male, Female*, chapter 5 (121–57); Stephen Kaplan, "Environmental Preference in a Knowledge-Seeking, Knowledge-Using Organism"
Week 5	Geary, *Male, Female*, chapter 6 (159–207); Edith Wharton, "The Other Two" and "His Father's Son"
Week 6	Barbara Smuts, "The Evolutionary Origins of Patriarchy"; Riggio, *Sex and Gender*, chapter 5 (82–11); Wharton, "Roman Fever" and "A Journey"

Unit B: Same-Sex Behavior and Sexuality

Week 7	Nathan Bailey and Marlene Zuk, "Same-Sex Sexual Behavior and Evolution"; Riggio, *Sex and Gender*, chapter 6 (112–53); Colm Tóibín, "A Summer Job" and "Three Friends"
Week 8	R. C. Kirkpatrick, "The Evolution of Human Homosexual Behavior"; Riggio, *Sex and Gender*, chapter 7 (154–97); Tóibín, "A Long Winter"
Week 9	semester break

Unit C: Love, Sex, and Sociality

Week 10	Riggio, *Sex and Gender*, chapter 8 (198–250); Shani Mootoo, "Lemon Scent"; Elena Georgiou, "Aphrodite's Vision"; Gina Schein, "Minnie Gets Married"; Riggio, *Sex and Gender*, chapters 9–10 (251–343)
Week 11	Karen Williams, "They Came at Dawn"; Dale Gunthorp, "Gypsophilia"; Cynthia Price, "Lesbian Bedrooms"
Week 12	Riggio, *Sex and Gender*, chapters 11–12 (344–423); D. H. Lawrence, "The Daughters of the Vicar" and "Odour of Chrysanthemums"
Week 13	Riggio, *Sex and Gender*, chapter 13 (424–85); Lawrence, "The Thorn in the Flesh," "The White Stocking," and "The Prussian Officer"

Unit D: Evolutionary Psychology: Critique and Revision

Week 14   Monique Borgerhoff Mulder, "Serial Monogamy as Polygyny or
               Polyandry?"; Alice Munro, "The Love of a Good Woman"
Week 15   Zuleyma Tang-Martinez and T. Brandt Ryder, "The Problem
               with Paradigms"; Munro, "Save the Reaper," "The Children
               Stay," and "Rich as Stink"
Week 16   Tóibín, "The Street"

Works Cited

Abrams, Michael. "Born Gay?" *Discover*, vol. 28, June 2007, pp. 58–83.

Anderson, Sherwood. "Nobody Knows." Anderson, *Winesburg*, pp. 58–62.

———. "The Untold Lie." Anderson, *Winesburg*, pp. 202–09.

———. *Winesburg, Ohio*. 1919. Viking Compass, 1975.

Bailey, Nathan W., and Marlene Zuk. "Same-Sex Sexual Behavior and Evolu-
    tion." *Trends in Ecology and Evolution*, vol. 24, no. 8, 2009, https://doi
    .org/10.1016/j.tree.2009.03.014.

Borgerhoff Mulder, Monique. "Serial Monogamy as Polygyny or Polyandry?
    Marriage in the Tanzanian Pimbwe." *Human Nature*, vol. 20, 2009,
    pp. 130–50, https://doi.org/10.1007/s12110-009-9060-x.

Campbell, Anne. *A Mind of Her Own: The Evolutionary Psychology of Women*.
    Oxford UP, 2002.

Darwin, Charles. *On the Origin of Species by Means of Natural Selection*. 1859.
    Edited by Joseph Carroll, Broadview Press, 2003.

Dunbar, Robin, et al. *Evolutionary Psychology: A Beginner's Guide*. One World
    Books, 2005.

Easterlin, Nancy. Review of *Sex and Gender: A Biopsychological Approach*, by
    Heidi Riggio. *Evolutionary Studies in Imaginative Culture*, vol. 6, no. 1,
    2022, pp. 115–18, https://doi.org/10.26613/esic.6.1.283.

Geary, David C. *Male, Female: The Evolution of Human Sex Differences*. Amer-
    ican Psychological Association, 1998.

Georgiou, Elena. "Aphrodite's Vision." Holoch and Nestle, pp. 305–17.

Graff, Gerald. *Professing Literature: An Institutional History*. U of Chicago P,
    1987.

Gunthorp, Dale. "Gypsophilia." Holoch and Nestle, pp. 85–101.

Holoch, Naomi, and Joan Nestle, editors. *The Vintage Book of International
    Lesbian Fiction*. Vintage Books, 1999.

Hrdy, Sarah Blaffer. *Mother Nature: A History of Mothers, Infants, and Natural
    Selection*. Pantheon, 1999.

Kaplan, Stephen. "Environmental Preference in a Knowledge-Seeking, Knowledge-
    Using Organism." *The Adapted Mind: Evolutionary Psychology and the Gener-
    ation of Culture*, edited by Jerome H. Barkow et al., pp. 581–98.

Kirkpatrick, R. C. "The Evolution of Human Homosexual Behavior." *Current
    Anthropology*, vol. 41, no. 3, 2000, pp. 385–413.

Lawrence, D. H. "The Daughters of the Vicar." Lawrence, *"Prussian Officer,"* pp. 40–87.

———. "Odour of Chrysanthemums." Lawrence, *"Prussian Officer,"* pp. 181–99.

———. "The Prussian Officer." Lawrence, *"Prussian Officer,"* pp. 1–21.

———. *"The Prussian Officer" and Other Stories.* Edited by John Worthen, Penguin Books, 1995.

———. "The Thorn in the Flesh." Lawrence, *"Prussian Officer,"* pp. 22–37.

———. "The White Stocking." Lawrence, *"Prussian Officer,"* pp. 143–64.

LeVay, Simon. *Gay, Straight, and the Reason Why: The Science of Sexual Orientation.* Oxford UP, 2017.

Mootoo, Shani. "Lemon Scent." Holoch and Nestle, pp. 43–51.

Munro, Alice. "The Children Stay." Munro, *Love*, pp. 181–214.

———. "The Love of a Good Woman." Munro, *Love*, pp. 3–78.

———. *The Love of a Good Woman.* Vintage International, 1999.

———. "Rich as Stink." Munro, *Love*, pp. 215–53.

———. "Save the Reaper." Munro, *Love*, pp. 146–80.

Price, Cynthia. "Lesbian Bedrooms." Holoch and Nestle, pp. 107–08.

Riggio, Heidi R. *Sex and Gender: A Biopsychological Approach.* Routledge, 2021.

Roughgarden, Joan. *Evolution's Rainbow: Diversity, Gender, and Sexuality in Nature and People.* Reprint ed., U of California P, 2009.

Sanders, Alan R., et al. "Genome-Wide Linkage Study Meta-Analysis of Male Sexual Orientation." *Archives of Sexual Behavior*, vol. 50, 2021, pp. 3371–75.

Saunders, Judith P. "Male Reproductive Strategies in Sherwood Anderson's 'The Untold Lie.'" *Philosophy and Literature*, vol. 31, no. 2, 2007, pp. 311–22.

Schein, Gina. "Minnie Gets Married." Holoch and Nestle, pp. 328–35.

Smuts, Barbara. "The Evolutionary Origins of Patriarchy." *Human Nature*, vol. 6, no. 1, 1995, pp. 1–32.

Spencer, Herbert. *Principles of Biology.* William and Northgate, 1867. 2 vols.

Tang-Martinez, Zuleyma, and T. Brandt Ryder. "The Problem with Paradigms: Bateman's Worldview as a Case Study." *Integrative and Comparative Biology*, vol. 45, no. 5, 2005, pp. 821–30.

Tóibín, Colm. *The Empty Family.* Scribner, 2012.

———. "A Long Winter." Tóibín, *Mothers*, pp. 183–270.

———. *Mothers and Sons.* Scribner, 2008.

———. "The Street." Tóibín, *Empty Family*, pp. 205–75.

———. "A Summer Job." Tóibín, *Mothers*, pp. 183–96.

———. "Three Friends." Tóibín, *Mothers*, pp. 161–81.

Trivers, Robert. "Parental Investment and Sexual Selection." *Sexual Selection and the Descent of Man, 1871–1971*, edited by Bernard G. Campbell, Aldine, 1972, pp. 136–79.

Wharton, Edith. "His Father's Son." Wharton, *New York Stories*, pp. 248–62.

———. "A Journey." Wharton, *New York Stories*, pp. 88–99.

———. *The New York Stories of Edith Wharton.* New York Review Books, 2007.

———. "The Other Two." Wharton, *New York Stories*, pp. 118–39.

———. "Roman Fever." Wharton, *New York Stories*, pp. 438–52.

Williams, Karen. "They Came at Dawn." Holoch and Nestle, pp. 102–06.

Wright, Robert. *The Moral Animal: Why We Are the Way We Are: The New Science of Evolutionary Psychology.* Vintage Books, 1995.

Joshua DiCaglio

Science Writing and the Art of Interpretation

In *Annals of the Former World*, his creative nonfiction work about geology, John McPhee notes, in the midst of extensive poetic, yet also technical, descriptions of the geology of North America, that geologists have a way with words: "Geology was called a descriptive science, and with its pitted outwash plains and drowned rivers, its hanging tributaries and starved coastlines, it was nothing if not descriptive. It was a fountain of metaphor—of isostatic adjustments and degraded channels, of angular unconformities and shifting divides, of rootless mountains and bitter lakes" (31). A former English major, McPhee marvels at the colorful metaphors he encounters, images such as that of a "bitter lake," which any literature scholar would be tempted to analyze. He continues in this vein a few lines later when he notes that "[g]eologists communicated in English; and they could name things in a manner that sent shivers through the bones. They had roof pendants in their discordant batholiths, mosaic conglomerates in desert pavement. There was ultrabasic, deep-ocean, mottled green-and-black rock—or serpentine" (31). Here McPhee highlights more unexpected metaphors through unusual terminology—comparisons that seem to require specialized training to fully grasp. McPhee's playful, poetic experimentation with geology's jargon highlights the way it demands

241

interpretive practices. His remarks prompt readers to notice how science creates new questions about interpretation. These questions not only are difficult to bring into focus but also force one to reckon with the more or less implicit assumption that scientific practice is about eliminating the problem of interpretation and communication.

This problem of interpretation is, of course, not unique to geology: science's way of describing the world can present complex interpretative challenges. In this essay I explore a theoretical basis for why and how one can use writing about science—that is, both science itself and the many cultural productions generated around it—as a means to introduce, understand, and practice the key skills and tasks of the language arts. I also report on my own attempts to do so. At Texas A&M University I have taught on two occasions a course titled Bewildering Science, which introduces the English major using writing about science, and two capstone courses for the English major that focus on particular scientific and technological debates (one on geology and another on the Space Race). Rather than offering these courses as specifically rhetoric of science or science and literature courses, I taught them as program-wide introductions to, or capstones for, the English major. Doing so allowed me to frame our readings and assignments in relation to these particular tasks: first, to use writing and rhetoric arising from and about technoscience in order to prompt students to recognize the need for interpretative and communicative work outside literary studies and, second, to use this same material in order to practice reading, writing, interpretation, and analysis on scientific and science-related texts. I report here on the theoretical basis for doing so, how I converted this basis into a class structure, and how students reacted to this approach.

Science and the Assumptions about Interpretation

While science studies scholars have long deconstructed the model of science writing's neutrality, most students assume science is the discourse least amenable to the work of interpretation. For most students, at least in my context in the United States, if poetry is the most interpretive form of language, science is its opposite (perhaps beat out only by logic and mathematics). As English majors, students signed up for the course to read good literature (whatever they imagine that to be), practice their writing, and, in many cases, even escape the science or engineering degrees their parents or their own ideas of success pushed them to pursue. The idea that one could learn to read, write, and analyze (even Shakespeare, James Joyce, or Toni Morrison) better and more productively by playing with scientific writing seems absurd. In each of my courses, this reaction inevitably frames our first few days of discussion: a theoretical justification is needed, but such discussion also renders the exercise more meaningful. Ultimately, I aim to demonstrate to students that if we can discover the need for interpretation using the discourse that seems least amenable to interpretation, it will greatly improve our ability to perform similar work on other forms of communication. This approach allows us to see the extent to which the skills of the language arts are needed everywhere but in ways that are often unrecognized or misunderstood.

In teaching science writing to English majors, one ought to also emphasize that scientists often find themselves in need of such interpretive work—although they usually articulate this need primarily in relation to communication about science. For example, in *Getting to the Heart of Science Communication*,[1] Faith Kearns, who has a PhD in environmental science, describes how the need to communicate important research on topics such as climate change, the COVID-19 pandemic, or vaccines thrusts practitioners such as herself into public roles without training (3). As part of this discussion, she highlights examples in which scientists struggle to connect with nonscientist interlocutors for reasons ranging from simple misunderstandings to ideological dogma. If Kearns is searching for some communication training, we might note that such skills and training already do exist in the language arts, although perhaps not in a way that clearly bridges her position with humanistic expertise. What strikes me is Kearns's assumption that science communicators are first and foremost scientists, a strangely science-centered way of thinking about science communication. By extending humanities students' training in the art of interpretation to scientific writing, I aim to teach students to see that science's way of describing the world presents a radical transformation, redescribing the world in unusual yet powerful ways. This redescription of the cosmos operates both within scientific practice and within science communication. This mode of description is just as intense of a reinterpretation of reality as any of the best literary and poetic texts are. While scientists are primarily occupied with clarifying what can or should be said in relation to empirical data, following out the implications of these ways of describing the world requires extra work. Understanding this work highlights the importance of training in interpretive arts and reframes the task of processing the increasingly ubiquitous role of science in our understandings of reality.

Interpretation Rumbles under the Surface of Science

Communicative and interpretive questions proliferate as soon as one notes that science requires a significant change in perspective, language, and understanding of knowledge. This is often recognized by scientists talking about scientific practice. For example, when the geologist Andrew Knoll describes the key developments in geology that expanded the sense of time, he speaks of the "riddle" that "made clear that it was time to think about our planet in new ways" (44). It is a common trope in geology to suggest that "rocks tell our planet's story" (18). This is not just any metaphor but rather a metaphor about the discovery of a need for interpretation: that rocks record the passage of time in ways that can be interpreted. From the recognition that interpretation is possible, then, come practices for sorting out how to read the rocks and clarify what they say (record) about the history of the earth. This requires a shift in training: only "if you know how to look" can "the signature of life" be "written clearly" in the rocks (74). These questions about interpretation enter at each stage of producing and communicating about science because they require new ways of rendering the world.

Knoll's invocation of deep time at a planetary (geological) scale provides one way of clarifying this point. As I discuss extensively in *Scale Theory*, significant shifts in spatial or temporal scales clarify just how much science has transformed our reality and just how much there is to say (and interpret) in relation to what scientific knowledge asks of us (DiCaglio). When we follow through on these new objects (e.g., cells, viruses) and relations (e.g., climate effects, viral infections) that are introduced by science at new scales, we can see that scale puts us in relation to objects and relations that are literally outside unaided human experience. Our ability to perceive, define, and intervene in these other scales requires significant mediation. Scientists have essentially reinterpreted or rewritten the whole of reality according to these new levels of existence. If we go slowly on the science, we can notice that when we speak of cells or distant geological events, we do not have clear reference points in our experience to relate them to. If we are given a clear reference point at the scale of experience, cells and geological events either require us to redescribe given objects in new ways (your hand is made of cells) or are abstract (the diagram of a cell).[2] One can thus begin to interpret science by starting with the bewildering aspects of its redescriptions of our world: How do we handle a description of the cosmos as so old, so large, so intricately layered—and using such odd language that refers to objects and processes outside our usual scale of experience?

To my English majors, I describe science's reorientation as a deliberate periphrasis, a word that is usually used to describe unnecessarily elaborate wordings when simpler phrasing exists. I expand the meaning in a positive sense to describe how science develops new terminology and modes of description that expand our understanding of everyday phenomena. Rather than describe just "my body," science can describe a series of cells interacting in relation to DNA molecules developed by means of ribosomes in relation to environmental factors that include dynamic biological systems evolved over a billion years in relation to the geological history of the planet.

The key to getting going here is to follow the periphrasis, to analyze science's redescription, and to notice the possible effects (or lack thereof) and transformations it might bring. In drafts of papers, students often write statements such as "McPhee catches the reader's attention and makes them feel wonder." In response I comment, "Catches the reader's attention how? Why would this lead to wonder?" The student has noticed that there is a maneuver and a response, but this is only the first step in a longer process of digging into just how much a particular narrative or text is asking of its audience or what it is doing to them, how, and to what end. These questions are important for any text. Analyzing science writing in this way foregrounds this task in relation to our fundamental configuration toward reality: Why would McPhee's playing with the tropes of geology induce a particular flavor of wonder? What has science done to us? How does McPhee help us feel that?

The task is not always so easy, in part because of the current cultural climate. In the two examples Kearns cites, climate change and vaccines, the task of persuading others to accept the facts often takes on the character of survival. This is a useful context for teaching about the problems of interpretation since it clarifies just how much needs to be worked out and communicated in addition to the facts. As I have discussed in more detail in *Scale Theory*, the problem is that the scientific framework of objectivity appears to be threatened by the attempt to point to and practice the need for interpretation in relation to the production of science (DiCaglio 197–205). This problem plagued early scholarship in science and technology studies, which critiqued the idea of objectivity in part by demonstrating that social practices were involved in producing science and that science was not insulated from political priorities. Despite insistence that this scholarship would only strengthen science, this entangling of social and political practices with the epistemology of science appeared to threaten science. The problems with this approach began to be apparent when similar critiques came to be used to critique climate change or vaccines.[3] In teaching scientific writing, one must be aware of this risk just enough to see how it plays out in the assumptions students have about science and interpretation. The point is that scientists argue about facts—about what is appropriate to say in any given instance given certain constraints. But ideas like deep time or the size of galaxies or how life evolved involve so much more in terms of changes in conceptions of reality that to frame the conversation entirely as a matter of whether or not the science is "right" misses the additional work needed to reorient ourselves to the mode of description found in textbooks and scientific reports. When the results of what has been interpreted are communicated to other scientists, the whole challenge and transformation produced by scientific training and practice cannot be forgotten. There is more to be said to trace out this transformation in perspective and experiment with why or how anyone, not just a scientist, might get to and comprehend that way of understanding reality.

Interpreting the Tangle of (Scientific) Transformations

In my courses that use science writing in this way, I spend much of the semester continually pointing to the need for interpretation, performing it for students in class and having them practice it in class and in short papers. Framing this task requires a lot of time, effort, and repetition to get students to appreciate the need for interpretation themselves. As I like to remind students, just as geologists have to train and practice extensively to see how rocks serve as evidence for events that are long past and that occurred over large periods of time, we must be trained to find and communicate the meaning of texts and cultural productions. Ironically, flipping the script helps students understand this point. (Suddenly we're using a scientific example to remind ourselves that *language* requires training and interpretation.) But the comparison also strikes a chord in terms of just how much humanists have struggled to rearticulate the humanities in the face of technoscience.

In summary, we can say at this point that there are three things about science that invite interpretation. First, science itself produces a way of writing and thinking about reality that works from certain assumptions and introduces certain modes of argument, description, and narration. Second, science then asks people to do and be certain things in line with those assumptions (for instance, to interpret what it means to consider yourself part of a planet or made up of cells). Finally, we find that cultural productions (literature, movies, shows, video games, etc.) often play with and attempt to work out these additional aspects in relation to science. It can thus be useful to put them alongside the productions of science (from scientific articles to images to patents to climate reports), as places to examine how, why, and to what end we might examine the transformations produced by science.

Identifying avenues for interpretation can help instructors decide on texts to use and how to lead discussions; it also helps students see what kinds of questions to ask. What, then, do we mean by "interpretation"? To reiterate, the question is not entirely about the authority of science, even if it is partially about the epistemology of science. Rather, we also want to look at the following features.

How science conceptualizes, understands, and describes reality. One can do this with scientific texts themselves, such as actual scientific articles or reports. But one can also examine how someone like McPhee poetically plays with the language of geology, exploring in more detail how McPhee experiments with description and helps us see the strange way geology pushes us into specific ways of observing landscapes at new timescales.

How a given fact applies to a specific context. For instance, does a geological description of the Permian Basin apply to our everyday lives? Well, in certain ways, no; the scale is wrong. But in certain ways it does, in that it explains why oil exists there for us to extract and use in our cars. Similarly, climate change and the notion of the Anthropocene provide different frames for thinking about the spatial and temporal scales of geology that attempt to bring those scales into relation with our context.

How language and tropes travel beyond strictly scientific contexts. Here metaphor becomes of interest again not only because scientific language and arguments get used metaphorically but also because they get used in all kinds of ways that don't always have a clear connection to or reliance on what science can or cannot say about an object. This is particularly true for the cosmological statements of astronomy, or in the way quantum physics has generated its own set of tropes for fiction. While we could talk (and students often want to talk) about whether or not such uses are "scientific" or "accurate," I usually sidestep such discussions by directing students to notice why and how such tropes function at all. Why does quantum physics give us this narrative of mysterious entanglement?

Why do we love to rehearse it in fiction? What is the purpose of using language in this way in nonscientific contexts?

How scientific authority itself gets caught up in cultural imaginaries. We should also not neglect the ways that the scientist and science itself are articulated and imagined within cultural objects. Noticing these aspects (e.g., the trope of the "mad scientist," the insertion of a scientific fact at key points in a narrative) provides students with a place to reflect on our cultural assumptions about truth and interpretation.

How human concerns enter into science and how scientific knowledge proliferates into questions about value and understanding. Yes, it is useful to understand the more traditional science studies concern of how political and social issues enter into science. But in these moments, I always want to make sure we flip the script to also examine how science's way of describing and intervening in the world generates new ways of valuing and understanding our world. We can appreciate a leaf in the context of a billion years of biological evolution. We can consider each breath as a bizarre mixture of hydrogen, oxygen, carbon, and many other things churned out by exploding stars. We can understand digestion as the work of millions of microbes processing one set of molecules into another. From this view, we can start to see more clearly the misalignment between economic value and ecological values that is currently rocking our vast global economic system. In doing so we can also begin to understand that science's entanglements in social and political concerns are not primarily about critiquing objectivity but about rewriting the cosmos, making new relations, objects, processes, and values possible. Science often tries, for those reasons we call "objectivity," to keep those concerns out of its practice. That's fair: it is because scientists are occupied with this process of exclusion that others must learn the analytical habits I try to inculcate in my classes. Thus, "values" here indicates all the ways in which particular facts do not necessarily provide prescriptive or fully descriptive realities—how we should act is not always clear from what science says. Interpretation (or untangling) is required to bring the scientific description into a context in which it might make a difference. This is the same thing as reading, interpreting, and communicating. It is a basis for communicating.

Guiding Students through the Terrain of Periphrasis

I realize that all this risks sounding abstract. It is certainly difficult for many students. The reality is that it *is* abstract because we're attempting to look not at what is described (by science) but at how it is described (in science) and what that description can do out in the world. Is that not a basic assumption about the need for interpretation and close reading?

If you would like to use science to teach interpretation in this way, you can choose any scientific domain or set of texts you prefer and run it through the same set of questions: How has the text rewritten reality? To what end? I offer in closing three examples of how one might conceptualize proliferating questions of this sort.

How does science imagine the earth or cosmos differently? For examples, I've taught together Carl Sagan's *Cosmos*, Knoll's *A Brief History of Earth*, Olaf Stapledon's *Star Maker*, and Stanley Kubrick's *2001: A Space Odyssey*.

How does science put us into contact with and imagine microbes, evolution, ecology, or climate change? To help students begin to understand this question, I've often taught texts on Gaia theory (Lovelock) and Lynn Margulis and Dorion Sagan's work on microbes in relation to Ursula Le Guin and Octavia Butler.

How does science make it possible to imagine different pasts and futures? I have taught units on geology in relation to the Anthropocene alongside science fiction and climate fiction. I have also taught a unit on how nanotechnology produces seemingly inevitable futures, assigning K. Eric Drexler's *Engines of Creation* alongside Neil Stephenson's *Diamond Age*.

Notes

1. Thank you to my former student Andi for sending me this book as I was working on this essay.

2. When demonstrating this point to students, I often use the four descriptions of a cell found in DiCaglio 189–94.

3. The key moment in this conversation, Bruno Latour's "Why Has Critique Run Out of Steam?," deals with climate denialism to reflect on the legacy of science and technology studies.

Works Cited

Butler, Octavia E. *Dawn*. Grand Central Publishing, 2021.

DiCaglio, Joshua. *Scale Theory: A Nondisciplinary Inquiry*. U of Minnesota P, 2021.

Drexler, K. Eric. *Engines of Creation: The Coming Era of Nanotechnology*. Anchor Books, 1987.

Kearns, Faith. *Getting to the Heart of Science Communication: A Guide to Effective Engagement*. Island Press, 2021.

Knoll, Andrew H. *A Brief History of Earth: Four Billion Years in Eight Chapters*. Custom House, 2021.

Latour, Bruno. "Why Has Critique Run Out of Steam? From Matters of Fact to Matters of Concern." *Critical Inquiry*, vol. 30, no. 2, 2004, pp. 225–48. *JSTOR*, https://doi.org/10.1086/421123.

Le Guin, Ursula K. *The Word for World Is Forest*. 2nd ed., Tor Books, 2010.

Lovelock, James. *Gaia: A New Look at Life on Earth*. Oxford UP, 2000.

Margulis, Lynn, and Dorion Sagan. *Microcosmos: Four Billion Years of Evolution from Our Microbial Ancestors*. U of California P, 1986.

McPhee, John. *Annals of the Former World*. Farrar, Straus and Giroux, 2000.

Sagan, Carl. *Cosmos*. Random House, 1980.

Stapledon, Olaf. *Star Maker*. Methuen, 1937.

Stephenson, Neil. *Diamond Age; or, A Young Lady's Illustrated Primer*. Spectra, 2000.

2001: A Space Odyssey. Directed by Stanley Kubrick, Metro-Goldwyn-Mayer, 1968.

Bryan Shawn Wang and Sandy Feinstein

Taming a Two-Headed Beast: Integrating Science, Literature, and the Living World

The pesky little insects seem to do it all. Flies—*dipterans*, in scientific terms—pollinate, parasitize, and host parasites themselves, among many other ecological roles. Their anatomy and physiology (they fly, for goodness' sake) and incredible diversity (124,000 described species and counting) have made them objects of study and the subject of writing for centuries—and in our classroom today, where they transport us and our students among seemingly disparate academic fields.

Our interdomain course, From Beast Books to Resurrecting Dinosaurs, explores how Western thinkers, from classical philosophers to modern biologists, have described, explained, and expanded biological diversity. We—a molecular biologist (Bryan) and a medievalist (Sandy)—developed and teach this honors course together as one of the integrative studies courses in our university's general education curriculum. These cross-disciplinary kinds of courses, of which students are required to take two, are intended "to advance the student's ability to comprehend things from multiple perspectives, to see connections, and to . . . employ different modes of thinking, different epistemologies to understand more adequately the nature of things" ("Learning Objectives"). In Beasts, the study of flies, and many other creatures, has led us and our students to discover relationships not only among animals that fly, creep, slither, and swim but also among the sciences and the humanities. Although both disciplinary areas involve the interplay of seeing and ideating, their approaches are markedly different. To integrate the two,[1] we have turned to science writing, which we define as writing, including multimedia, about science—both the knowledge derived from science and scientific processes—for a nonspecialist audience.

We begin small, with flies, first by introducing students to Robert Hooke's seventeenth-century *Micrographia*, perhaps the world's first scientific bestseller (Falkowski 27) and a text that popularized microscopy. In his illustrations and descriptions of the compound eye of a grey drone-fly (obs. 39, scheme 24), Hooke exemplifies the careful technique, detailed documentation, and reasoning and conjecture that are integral to the scientific process. At the same time, his speculations led Margaret Cavendish, in *Observations upon Experimental Philosophy* (7–13, 23–26 [obs. 3 and 9]), to question not only his conclusions about insect eye structure but also microscopy itself and its consequent distortions. After reading both texts, students see and judge the legitimacy of the arguments for themselves in a lab exercise where they examine flies under the compound microscope. They then are assigned a contemporary scientific article that claims "mathematics is biology's next microscope" (Cohen) and write about how tools may mediate or change how one sees, whether those tools are literal lenses for observing dipteran ommatidia (eyes) or algorithms for identifying and representing correlations among large datasets.

In 1666 Cavendish was already complaining about the "hardest words and expressions which none but Scholars are able to understand," and through the subsequent centuries, the problem has grown only more pronounced. The technical language used by scientists often seems unnecessarily obfuscatory and can frustrate students seeking to understand current scientific thought. Popular science writing can help students navigate the complex concepts and complicated methods made more challenging by this language. Martin Brookes, in *Fly: An Experimental Life* (30), introduces the fruit fly as a model system, a genetically tractable organism—they breed quickly, with visible (under a microscope) inherited traits, and their molecular and cellular physiology parallels ours in crucial ways, making them ideal study subjects for potentially yielding insight into our own lives. This twenty-first-century work of popular science is complemented by William Blake's poem "The Fly," which in its series of rhetorical questions seems to anticipate what we have in common with flies without knowing about our shared genetics: "Am not I / A fly like thee? / Or art not thou / A man like me?" The deceptively simple twenty-line rhyming poem contrasts with Brookes's prose description of how the fruit fly helped the geneticist Thomas Hunt Morgan elucidate the mechanism of genetic inheritance in dipterans, humans, and all organisms in between (30–42).

The fruit fly commonly used for genetic analysis is *Drosophila melanogaster*—a name that's not undescriptive, even if it's a mouthful. By popular accounts, *Drosophila* apparently derives from the Greek for "dew-loving"; the insects reproduce on fermenting organic matter that stays consistently moist. *Melanogaster* is from the Greek for "black-bellied"; the tip of the abdomen is black ("*Drosophila melanogaster*"). In Beasts, the what, how, and why of scientifically naming species like *Drosophila melanogaster* is introduced by Michael Ohl in *The Art of Naming* (42–55). After learning about binomial nomenclature from Ohl (45), students look through the original tables of scientific names assembled in the tenth edition of *Systema Naturae*, by Carl Linnaeus, who established this simple, revolutionary system of naming. They compare this system and the names themselves with what Isidore of Seville had described in his seventh-century *Etymologiae* (book 12, part 8, presents the derivation of the monikers for various "tiny flying animals" [Barney et al. 269]) and then view pages from the Aberdeen Bestiary that represent, in words and pictures, the biblical creation story, Adam naming the animals (folio 5r) and creatures large and small. At the same time, the hierarchy of animals in the bestiaries is contrasted with Aristotle's description of land, air, and sea creatures distinguished by morphology and behavior and Linnaeus's ordering of organisms through a hierarchical scheme of nested categories.

Thus, we use Ohl's *Art of Naming* to link the processes of naming and classifying while connecting current scientific work to its foundations in centuries-old literature. Ohl's text also sets the stage for a series of related class activities—students creating etymologies for their own names; observing mutant fruit flies, identifying the abnormalities, and naming the mutants; devising nomenclature and classification systems for a collection of screws, bolts, nails, and other metal fasteners. The combination of assignments involving invention, observation, and distinct organizational systems crosses and recrosses the boundaries of multiple domains: language, taxonomy, literature, and genetics.

The exercise of naming and classifying fasteners, which leads to a consideration of shared traits and hypothesized relationships, also helps us reinterpret Linnaean classification through the evolutionary perspective that informs all modern biology. The excerpt from Brookes's *Fly: An Experimental Life* places the chromosomal theory of inheritance within the Darwinian revolution, and the concept of biological evolution is reinforced through additional science writing and texts by and about Charles Darwin that are both scientific and literary. The short film *The Making of a Theory: Darwin, Wallace, and Natural Selection* dramatizes how Darwin and Alfred Russel Wallace separately marshaled evidence that refuted the principle of special creation in favor of evolutionary theory and explains how the two naturalists ultimately came to copublish a communication to the Linnean Society of London, a portion of which students read next. In it, Darwin used examples from animal husbandry and selective breeding to point out how populations of organisms like sheep and cattle, familiar to his audience, may change over time (Darwin and Wallace 45–53). The examples have been made real for our audience too; in class one year, a guest speaker, a former student and peer mentor in Beasts, described his experiences breeding sheep while students saw and felt differences in the diameter, crimp, and color of wool fibers from various breeds. Analyzing these inherited traits both anticipates a future class discussion of Gregor Mendel and his pea plant genetics and revisits the idea of classification, now based on evolutionary kinship.

Elaborating on evolutionary theory, a contemporary article on biogeographical evidence—that the observed distributions of some species can most easily be explained as resulting from evolutionary and geological forces—prepares students for juxtapositions of scientific and literary texts. In "The Seeds That Sowed a Revolution," Henry Nicholls describes what Darwin found on the Galápagos in addition to finches: endemic plants, unique to their respective islands but that nevertheless resembled one another and those on the nearby South American continent—suggesting the plants had radiated, evolutionarily and geographically, from common ancestral species. Hypothesizing that ocean currents might have carried plant life from a single mainland source to the islands, Darwin tested the viability of garden seeds soaked for days in seawater, referred to measurements of ocean current movement from "Johnston's Physical Atlas," and concluded that many different types of seeds could travel over a thousand miles and remain able to germinate (357). Thus, Nicholls's essay, paired with Darwin's article, guides students to understanding not only biogeography and evolution but also the fundamental nature of scientific inquiry. Furthermore, these experiments themselves are alluded to in "Salting the

Seeds" by Ruth Padel, Darwin's great-great-granddaughter, who studied his notebooks and correspondence in writing her collection *Darwin: A Life in Poems*. She imagines that "the heart dances" as the naturalist continues to gather specimens and observations to formulate his argument for natural selection, all while haunted by a ghost, perhaps that of his eldest daughter, who died young. Thus, in studying the poem, students examine authority, sources, and evidence as considered in literature as well as science.

Padel's poem uses metaphors to link the personal and the professional—for instance, Darwin's companion dog is curled up as a primitive ammonite—and thereby provides a point of comparison for the way science uses representational images and models. Metaphor as a device for conceiving, communicating, and interrogating relationships among objects and ideas in both literature and science is more fully explored when we place May Swenson's poem "The DNA Molecule" alongside James Watson and Francis Crick's original report of the structure of the DNA double helix. In the scientific model, "the two chains are held together by the purine and pyrimidine bases," where "the planes of the bases are perpendicular to the fiber axis . . . joined together in pairs, a single base from one chain being hydrogen-bonded to a single base from the other chain, so that the two lie side by side with identical z-coordinates" (Watson and Crick 737)—an arrangement Swenson describes as "nature's pairs," made "with units / whose structures permit an interplay of forces / between the partners" (177). To guide students through the scientific and literary implications of the models and metaphors contained within these works—and to help them understand the relationship between models and metaphors—we also ask them to watch the short film *The Double Helix* and read an excerpt from Theodore Brown's *Making Truth: Metaphor in Science* (14–26). In class, as they view the atomic structure of the double helix on their computers and consider the biological data the structure takes into account, students examine how scientific models are hypotheses, tentative explanations of something observed. They then turn to Swenson's poem and identify its metaphors among the paired lines, allusions, and imagery that offer an alternative to the digital rendering, returning DNA to nature—the body, birth, and life. In short, they engage with the philosopher Monroe Beardsley's idea that "a metaphor is a miniature poem, and the explication of a metaphor is a model for all explication" (144). Journals and projects assigned in the course reinforce the contrasting uses of metaphor as well as other concepts that bridge science and literature.

Although DNA is central to a biological understanding of life, it is only one element that may be mixed and remixed to form new creatures, as seen in modern and historical texts. Ed Yong's article "The Unique Merger That Made You (and Ewe, and Yew)" provides both graphics and an account of how the branches of early evolutionary trees, as traced by DNA sequences, became tangled as organisms were engulfed and genes co-opted, resulting in the formation of new organelles that made complex life possible. Students are then ready to think about other kinds of hybridization. They read patents—for example, a patent of Stanley Cohen and Herbert Boyer that describes a unique laboratory method for recombining genes or otherwise altering them to generate "molecular chimeras." They also read about classical and medieval chimeras (the kind assembled from parts of goats, lions, and snakes), other mythological hybrids, and *paradoxa* in Pliny's *Natural History*, the Aberdeen Bestiary, and Linnaeus's first edition of *Systema Naturae* (29).

While current science writing guides students explicitly through the latest scientific breakthroughs, seventeenth-century writers demonstrate the conflicts between ideas of progress and presumption that continue to inform reception of such work. In the fictional *New Atlantis*, Francis Bacon depicts experiments of all kinds that anticipate modern ones. His characters seem eerily like genetic engineers who "make [beasts] greater or taller . . . and differ in colour, shape, activity." His admiring description of the "resuscitating of [beasts and birds] that seem dead" resonates when we read Ross Andersen's article "Welcome to Pleistocene Park," about de-extinction biology and efforts to resurrect the woolly mammoth. Similarly, Bacon's descriptions of the "means to make commixtures and copulations of different kinds; which have produced many new kinds" anticipate Carl Zimmer's account of scientists who seek to "create life as we don't know it." Cavendish, by contrast, warns against this kind of playing God in *The Blazing World*, her fictional response to Bacon and Hooke. In these invented worlds, students thus see fiction's critical ability to examine and question the developing sciences of an era and the sciences of the future.

In our course, then, science writing across the centuries provides access not only to scientific concepts, processes, and literature but also to a range of literary texts, viewpoints, and frameworks traditionally associated with the humanities. Examining science writing across the centuries also helps students integrate these different views of the living world, as can be seen in their responses to assignments, which demonstrate how they have synthesized what they have learned throughout the course while expressing the unique perspectives each has gained.

To hone observational skills and methodological approaches that are identified with science and how it is written, whether in patents or popular articles, students are presented with the following prompt: "Study a creature in the wild using only your senses. Then study it using one or more tools. Then name it. Present your observations, methods, purposes, and deductions." They were expected to use words, images, or any combination of both. Viktoriia, an accounting major, studied a fly she encountered, submitting drawings[2] and accompanying text that recall those of Hooke, as she carefully documented her observations, tools, and the processes by which she studied, named, and classified the animal. The name itself, maple-winged grey-fly, reflects the descriptive impulse, minus the Latin, seen in the name *Drosophila melanogaster* and Linnaeus's binomial system, and, in using the name of a tree, suggests a potential literary metaphor.

To measure their developing understanding of historical classification systems, students compiled and created zoological portfolios (nicknamed "zoo views") three times throughout the semester. The portfolio could involve creative interpretations of what we identified as an assembly of images of creatures, which students were to curate by naming, describing, or organizing according to different schemes and approaches used throughout history. In his final zoo view, Ryan, a biology major, took both inspiration and content from the Aberdeen Bestiary, combining its descriptions of eight different snakes with reports from the herpetological literature to identify the snakes by their modern common and scientific names and presenting his findings in a data table. Ryan placed the table alongside an image, illustrated in the style of the Aberdeen Bestiary, that portrayed him in place of Edenic Adam with the snakes arrayed around him, the most venomous (and therefore, as Ryan writes, "susceptible to temptation") positioned at the bottom of the hierarchy.[3]

For zoo views, students could create discrete representations of the readings or build on a single organizing conceit to create a composite, as Garrett, a biology major, did in three physical sculptures representing the Aristotelian system that organizes creatures by their habitat—land, sea, and air: first, a tree depicting evolutionary relationships among various organisms discussed in the course, along with descriptions and the works in which they appeared; second, seeds in seawater, one for each species Darwin tested in his experiments, labeled with scientific and common names and classified according to viability in saline solution; and, third, a cage with suspended birds portraying the steps to be taken in resurrecting the extinct passenger pigeon—namely, comparing and editing genomes followed by cloning and breeding the new generation of hybrid birds.[4]

To develop their understanding of scientific models, an integral apparatus in science and science writing, students also created models that represented the course's major themes and methodologies. A biochemistry major, Xuan, chose to "retell the 'story' of this Beasts class" through a microscope set up to study cells from a mythical creature, the chimera ant.[5] In her explanation, built into the cardboard model, Xuan incorporated and connected concepts and readings from throughout the course using key words—*etymology, evolution, experiment, hierarchy, hybrid, mutation, naming, observation, origin, technology.* Her account describes the ant's "voracious appetite" and ability to "impart the characteristics of ingested creatures onto the next generation of chimera ants," as seen in the hybrid organelles visible in the magnified specimen slide.

Finally, while Xuan put her chimera ant under a (metaphoric) microscope to study it, another student reimagined a dragon. Jacob, a business major, depicted his dragon, which he named "Interdisciplinator," as a charismatic creature whose two heads strain in different directions: scientific and literary.[6] Jacob explained that the "left head" has "incredible eyesight . . . able to see even the most microscopic of details," while the right "enjoys speaking in riddles or poetic form." The Interdisciplinator "open[s] up portals that pass to different times throughout the ages." While "both sides typically work together, they can sometimes disagree[,] which can be a problem as it shares the same body." For us, the Interdisciplinator has come to signify how science can work together with literature toward a shared purpose, sharpening the observations and analytical skills of students and engaging their imagination, whatever their majors and future careers.

Notes

1. In addition to humanities and natural science domain criteria, the course addresses the integrative thinking objective of our institution's general education curriculum. For a description of objectives, see "Learning Objectives."

2. The drawings can be viewed on *Knowledge Commons* at https://doi.org/10.17613/e3x6-1626.

3. The table and image can be viewed on *Knowledge Commons* at https://doi.org/10.17613/b6ys-eh14.

4. An image of the sculptures can be viewed on *Knowledge Commons* at https://doi.org/10.17613/r8rg-4h16.

5. An image of the microscope can be viewed on *Knowledge Commons* at https://doi.org/10.17613/n301-1p40.

6. An image of the dragon can be viewed on *Knowledge Commons* at https://doi.org/10.17613/6zhg-m929.

Works Cited

Aberdeen Bestiary. Aberdeen University Library, MS 24, abdn.ac.uk/bestiary.

Andersen, Ross. "Welcome to Pleistocene Park." *The Atlantic*, Apr. 2017, theatlantic.com/magazine/archive/2017/04/pleistocene-park/517779/.

Aristotle. *The History of Animals*. Translated by D'Arcy Wentworth Thompson. *The Internet Classics Archive*, classics.mit.edu/Aristotle/history_anim.html.

Bacon, Francis. *The New Atlantis*. 1626. *Project Gutenburg*, gutenberg.org/files/2434/2434-h/2434-h.htm.

Barney, Stephen, et al., editors and translators. *The* Etymologies *of Isidore of Seville*. Cambridge UP, 2006.

Beardsley, Monroe C. *Aesthetics: Problems in the Philosophy of Criticism*. Harcourt, Brace and World, 1958.

Blake, William. "The Fly." 1794. *Poets.org*, poets.org/poem/fly.

Brookes, Martin. *Fly: An Experimental Life*. Weidenfeld and Nicolson, 2001.

Brown, Theodore L. *Making Truth: Metaphor in Science*. U of Illinois P, 2003.

Cavendish, Margaret. *Observations upon Experimental Philosophy to Which Is Added the Description of a New Blazing World*. A. Maxwell, 1666. *University of Michigan Library Digital Collections*, 2025, quod.lib.umich.edu/e/eebo/A53049.0001.001.

Cohen, Joel E. "Mathematics Is Biology's Next Microscope, Only Better; Biology Is Mathematics' Next Physics, Only Better." *PLoS Biology*, vol. 2, no. 12, 2004, pp. e439–e440, https://doi.org/10.1371/journal.pbio.0020439.

Cohen, Stanley N., and Herbert W. Boyer. Process for Producing Biologically Functional Molecular Chimeras. US 4,237,224, United States Patent and Trademark Office, 2 Dec. 1980. *US PTO Patent Public Search*, image-ppubs.uspto.gov/dirsearch-public/print/downloadPdf/4237224.

Darwin, Charles. "Does Sea-Water Kill Seeds?" *Gardeners' Chronicle and Agricultural Gazette*, vol. 21, 1855, pp. 356–57. *Darwin Online*, darwin-online.org.uk/content/frameset?itemID=A2299&viewtype=text&pageseq=1.

Darwin, Charles, and Alfred Russel Wallace. "On the Tendency of Species to Form Varieties; and on the Perpetuation of Varieties and Species by Natural Means of Selection." *Zoological Journal of the Linnean Society*, vol. 3, no. 9, Aug. 1858, pp. 45–62, https://doi.org/10.1111/j.1096-3642.1858.tb02500.x.

The Double Helix. Directed by Rob Whittlesey, Howard Hughes Medical Institute, 2013, biointeractive.org/classroom-resources/double-helix.

"*Drosophila melanogaster.*" *Wikipedia*, 16 June 2025, en.wikipedia.org/wiki/Drosophila_melanogaster#.

Falkowski, Paul G. *Life's Engines: How Microbes Made Earth Habitable.* Princeton UP, 2015.

Hooke, Robert. *Micrographia: Some Physiological Descriptions of Minute Bodies Made by Magnifying Glasses with Observations and Inquiries Thereupon.* London, 1665. *Project Gutenburg*, www.gutenberg.org/files/15491/15491-h/15491-h.htm.

"Learning Objectives and Foundation and Domain Criteria." *Penn State Undergraduate Education*, gened.psu.edu/learning-objectives-and-foundation-and-domain-criteria. Accessed 15 Apr. 2025.

Linnaeus, Carl. *Systema Naturae.* Haak, 1735. Translated by M. S. J. Engel-Ledeboer and H. Engel, De Graaf, 1964. *KTH*, kth.se/polopoly_fs/1.199546.1600688273!/Menu/general/column-content/attachment/Linnaeus—extracts.pdf.

———. *Systema Naturae.* 10th ed., Laurentius Salvius, 1758. *Biodiversity Heritage Library*, biodiversitylibrary.org/page/726886.

The Making of a Theory: Darwin, Wallace, and Natural Selection. Directed by John Rubin, Howard Hughes Medical Institute, 2013, biointeractive.org/classroom-resources/origin-species-making-theory.

Mendel, Gregor. "Experiments in Plant Hybridization." 1865. Translated by William Bateson, with modifications by Roger Blumberg, Electronic Scholarly Publishing Project, 1996, old.esp.org/foundations/genetics/classical/gm-65-a.pdf.

Nicholls, Henry. "The Seeds That Sowed a Revolution." *Nautilus*, 6 Feb. 2014, nautil.us/the-seeds-that-sowed-a-revolution-rp-234778/.

Ohl, Michael. *The Art of Naming.* Translated by Elisabeth Lauffer, MIT Press, 2019.

Padel, Ruth. "Salting the Seeds." *Darwin: A Life in Poems*, by Padel, Knopf, 2009, p. 112.

Pliny the Elder. *The Natural History.* Translated and edited by John Bostock, Taylor and Francis, 1855. *Perseus Digital Library*, www.perseus.tufts.edu/hopper/text?doc=Plin.+Nat.+toc.

Swenson, May. "The DNA Molecule." *Poetry*, vol. 113, no. 3, 1968, pp. 175–77. *Poetry Foundation*, poetryfoundation.org/poetrymagazine/browse?contentId=31073.

Watson, James D., and Francis H. C. Crick. "Molecular Structure of Nucleic Acids: A Structure for Deoxyribose Nucleic Acid." *Nature*, vol. 171, 1953, pp. 737–38, https://doi.org/10.1038/171737a0.

Yong, Ed. "The Unique Merger That Made You (and Ewe, and Yew)." *Nautilus*, 3 Feb. 2014, nautil.us/the-unique-merger-that-made-you-and-ewe-and-yew-234769/.

Zimmer, Carl. "Creating Life As We Don't Know It." *Nautilus*, 10 Oct. 2013, nautil.us/creating-life-as-we-dont-know-it-234594/.

Part V

Resources

Professional Associations and Journals

Association for the Study of Literature and Environment (ASLE), asle.org
> Founded in 1992, ASLE is a US-based environmental humanities organization with affiliates in Europe, Asia, and South America. ASLE publishes a quarterly journal, *Interdisciplinary Studies in Literature and Environment* (academic.oup.com/isle). The organization's website contains an extensive pedagogical resources section.

British Society for Literature and Science (BSLS), bsls.ac.uk
> Founded in 2005, BSLS promotes scholarship on literature and science in all historical eras. Especially useful as a teaching resource are the organization's online book reviews (www.bsls.ac.uk/reviews).

H-Sci-Med-Tech, networks.h-net.org/h-sci-med-tech
> Part of *H-Net*, *H-Sci-Med-Tech* is a network for humanities and social sciences scholars who study science, medicine, or technology of any era. Especially useful for pedagogical purposes are the site's "Resources" and "Reviews" sections.

Journal of Literature and Science (*JLS*), literatureandscience.org
> Supported by the ScienceHumanties Initiative at Cardiff University, *JLS* is an open access journal published twice a year.

Modern Language Association Forum TC Science and Literature on *MLA Commons*, mla.hcommons.org/groups/science-and-literature
> The MLA division TC Science and Literature has existed since 1939; divisions have since become forums, with their own online discussion and resource-sharing areas supported by *CORE*, the open access repository for the humanities.

National Association of Science Writers (NASW), www.nasw.org
> NASW is the largest and oldest general science writing organization in the United States. Its website includes a modest but useful pedagogical resources section. Instructors can also point students interested in careers in science writing to this website, which includes resources about the industry.

Science Literacy Foundation Resource Guide, scienceliteracyfoundation.org/resource-guide/index.html
> Assembled by the nonprofit Science Literacy Foundation, this online resource brings together information about science literacy as it relates to journalism, education, and public policy.

Society for Literature, Science, and the Arts (SLSA), litsciarts.org
> Founded in 1985, SLSA remains the premier US-based literature and science professional organization. SLSA publishes a quarterly journal, *Configurations* (www.press.jhu.edu/journals/configurations), and sponsors multiple book series.

Primary Text Anthologies and Databases

The Best American Science and Nature Writing Series
Part of HarperCollins's *The Best American* series, *The Best American Science and Nature Writing* is an annual anthology of popular science articles published in the United States. Books in this series typically feature both well-known and up-and-coming science writers and are suitable for use in a range of humanities courses.

Dawkins, Richard, editor. *The Oxford Book of Modern Science Writing*. Oxford UP, 2009.
Composed largely of short excerpts from longer works, this anthology brings together science writing from the twentieth and twenty-first centuries aimed at a wider audience. Each piece is briefly introduced by the editor.

Harding, Sandra, editor. *The Postcolonial Science and Technology Studies Reader*. Duke UP, 2011.
This collection presents twenty-five previously published essays by international scholars, providing a valuable introduction to postcolonial science and technology studies. Essays consider, variously, the impact and legacy of Eurocentricism and colonialism on science and historiography of science, non-Western and Indigenous ways of knowing, the scientific representation of different cultures, and models for more equitable scientific frameworks and practices.

Otis, Laura, editor. *Literature and Science in the Nineteenth Century*. Oxford UP, 2009.
This anthology offers a broad selection of primary texts, some excerpted, from the nineteenth century. Texts are organized thematically and include literary and scientific texts. The editorial apparatus includes an introduction to each theme and substantial bibliographies of secondary sources.

Philosophical Transactions Archive, royalsocietypublishing.org/loi/rstl
This resource provides open access facsimiles of articles published from 1669 to 1886 by the de facto journal of the Royal Society.

Rogers, Hannah Star, et al., editors. *Routledge Handbook of Art, Science, and Technology Studies*. Routledge, 2021.
This handbook positions itself as an introduction to art, science, and technology studies, an emerging cluster of interdisciplinary approaches to knowledge making and creative endeavor that builds on science and technology studies. Because of its highly conceptual nature, this volume is most suitable for graduate-level courses or for scholars interested in learning about tools for analyzing art-science collaborations.

Science in the Making, makingscience.royalsociety.org
An open access digitization program that aims to make available archival material such as correspondence and drafts related to the publication of the Royal Society's scientific journals.

Series, Companions, and Other Pedagogical Resources

Ahuja, Neel, et al., editors. *The Palgrave Handbook of Twentieth and Twenty-First Century Literature and Science*. Palgrave Macmillan, 2020.

Organized into four sections ("Epistemologies," "Methods and Approaches," "Ethics and Politics," and "Forms and Genres"), this handbook illustrates developments in literature and science from the mid–twentieth century to the present, taking up such topics as biotechnology, energy sciences, and surveillance technologies. It may be especially useful for illustrating how literature and science can be combined with other approaches, such as postcolonial criticism or ecocriticism.

Clarke, Bruce, and Manuela Rossini, editors. *The Routledge Companion to Literature and Science*. Routledge, 2012.

The forty-four essays in this volume address cultures of literature and science from ancient Greece to modern cybernetics. Part 1 presents advanced introductions to disciplinary topics including alchemy, ecology, and mathematics. The essays in part 2 address pre-disciplinary or transdisciplinary approaches such as animal studies and semiotics. The essays in part 3 focus on specific geographic and historical fields.

Gordon, Michael D. *Pseudoscience: A Very Short Introduction*. Oxford UP, 2023.

Suitable for use as a course text, this book offers a historical survey of pseudoscience, including such practices as alchemy, parapsychology, and scientific racism, as well as analysis of contemporary issues such as climate change denial and the anti-vaccine movement.

Gossin, Pamela, editor. *Encyclopedia of Literature and Science*. Bloomsbury Publishing, 2002.

Featuring over 650 signed entries on writers, scientists, theories, themes, and other topics, this encyclopedia bills itself as a resource for undergraduates—or those new to literature and science—as well as more experienced researchers in the field. Entries range in length from fifty to 3,500 words.

Meyer, Steven, editor. *The Cambridge Companion to Literature and Science*. Cambridge UP, 2018.

The essays in this volume are suitable for students and take a range of approaches to the topic of literature and science: a section titled "Snapshots of the Past" includes essays such as Mary Baine Campbell's "Shakespeare and Modern Science" and Devin Griffiths's "Darwin and Literature," whereas the majority of essays are more broadly methodological or theoretical.

Sleigh, Charlotte. *Literature and Science*. Palgrave Macmillan, 2011.

Sleigh's book represents a readable transhistorical study of the field. The introduction is particularly useful for orienting students and instructors alike. Within the book's chronological structure, individual chapters provide case studies that place prose literature and scientific study alongside each other. Examples are drawn from both within and beyond the Anglophone sphere.

Tubbs, Robert, et al., editors. *The Palgrave Handbook of Literature and Mathematics*. Palgrave Macmillan, 2021.
> The thirty-two entries in this handbook, some written by literature scholars and some by mathematicians, examine a range of connections between math and literature, including math in literature (part 1), math and literary forms (part 2), math as it relates to modernism (part 3), the relationship between literature and math in various eras (part 4), and math as literature (part 5).

Willis, Martin. *Literature and Science: A Reader's Guide to Essential Criticism*. Palgrave Macmillan, 2015.
> This introductory volume surveys the field of literature and science and its development. Each of the book's seven chapters focuses on a key area of the discipline—scientific institutions, early criticism, Darwinism, the body, the mind, physical sciences, and the natural world—and provides detailed summaries of significant critical studies up to 2013 together with assessments of their influence.

Wyer, Mary, et al., editors. *Women, Science, and Technology: A Reader in Feminist Science Studies*. 3rd ed., Routledge, 2014.
> Designed for use as a textbook, this reader draws primarily on essays from the journals *Signs* and *Feminist Theory*. Though some of the works are now dated, this volume is nonetheless useful as a source for touchstone essays such as Donna Haraway's essay "Situated Knowledges," referenced in the following section.

Science and Technology Studies: Foundations

Daston, Lorraine, and Peter Galison. *Objectivity*. Zone Books, 2007.
> Daston and Galison explore the evolution of scientific objectivity over time, drawing on scientific atlases to show how such objectivity has been shaped by various factors, including the tools, practices, and cultural norms of different scientific disciplines. This volume is especially useful for introducing students to the shifting relations between subjectivity and objectivity across time.

Haraway, Donna J. "Situated Knowledges: The Science Question in Feminism and the Privilege of Partial Perspective." *Feminist Studies*, vol. 14, no. 3, autumn 1988, pp. 575–99. *JSTOR*, https://doi.org/10.2307/3178066.
> In this landmark work of feminist science and technology studies, Haraway challenges conventional notions of objectivity and truth in scientific inquiry, emphasizing that all knowledge is contingent on one's perspective and context. In a classroom context, the concepts of "situated knowledge" and "partial perspective" can serve as a jumping-off point for discussing the relationships among knowledge, power, and social contexts.

Huxley, Aldous. *Literature and Science*. Harper and Row, 1963.
> In this contribution to the so-called two cultures debate initiated by C. P. Snow, Huxley examines similarities and differences between scientific and

literary language, making the case that each domain influences the other. Although he acknowledges the challenge of interdisciplinary communication, he nevertheless takes his fellow writers to task for ignoring contemporary science.

Kuhn, Thomas S. *The Structure of Scientific Revolutions.* U of Chicago P, 1962.
The publication of this book played a key role in the history of the interdisciplinary field of science studies. Kuhn challenges prevailing positivist conceptions of scientific progress as a linear progression that advances by means of the accumulation of facts and data; instead, he proposes an episodic model of scientific development in which periods of "normal science" are undertaken under a given "paradigm," or a set of concepts and values shared by a scientific community that dictate the possibilities and limits of science. Scientific revolutions occur, Kuhn claims, when anomalies arise, necessitating a "paradigm shift" driven by cultural factors.

Latour, Bruno. *We Have Never Been Modern.* Translated by Catherine Porter, Cambridge UP, 1993.
In this much cited interdisciplinary study, Latour challenges the traditional distinctions between nature and society, arguing that modernity's dualisms have failed to accurately capture the complex interplay between humans and their environment. Ultimately, Latour advocates for a more nuanced, interconnected view of science, technology, and culture.

Latour, Bruno. "Why Has Critique Run Out of Steam? From Matters of Fact to Matters of Concern." *Critical Inquiry*, vol. 30, no. 2, winter 2004, pp. 225–48, https://doi.org/10.1086/421123.
In this provocative essay, Latour critiques traditional modes of criticism in the humanities and social sciences, citing their diminishing relevance in addressing exigent societal issues such a climate change. Notably, this essay corresponds to, and helped initiate, a broader reexamination of critique across academia: for example, it marks the rise of postcritique methods within literary studies.

Latour, Bruno, and Steve Woolgar. *Laboratory Life: The Social Construction of Scientific Facts.* Sage Publications, 1979.
While its technological references and images are now dated, this influential study provides an outside view of a working laboratory that can provide a helpful starting point for class discussion about disciplines and knowledge. Latour and Woolgar explore the processes of scientific study, the steps toward establishing scientific facts, and the stories scientists tell.

Lindberg, David C., and Ronald L. Numbers, general editors. *The Cambridge History of Science.* Cambridge UP, 2002–20. 8 vols.
This indispensable series supplies a bounty of information, interpretation, and analysis on the history of science in texts, practices, and material culture. The volumes on historical periods cover ancient science, medieval science, early modern science, and eighteenth-century science. The remaining

volumes cover topics after 1800: physical and mathematical science, biological and earth sciences, social sciences, and national, transnational, and global contexts.

Pickering, Andrew, editor. *Science as Practice and Culture*. U of Chicago P, 1992. Controversial at the time of its release, this collection of fifteen essays on the sociology of science registers a significant point in scholarship on the cultures and structures of laboratory research.

Snow, C. P. *The Two Cultures*. 1959. Edited by Stefan Collini, Cambridge UP, 2012. A now canonical work from a novelist and former research scientist, Snow's 1959 lecture presents and deplores the polarization of literary intellectuals and scientists, which Snow claims is visible in the former's scientific illiteracy and distance from industry and the latter's lack of engagement with literary culture.

Wilson, Edward O. *Consilience: The Unity of Knowledge*. Random House, 1998. In this influential book, Wilson argues that while the natural sciences have achieved consilience—that is, a concurrence of results, rooted in the Enlightenment ideal of a unified theory of knowledge—the humanities and social sciences have yet to fully embrace disciplinary integration. This book may be most useful in the classroom as a provocation: Wilson's argument is ambitious and, by his own admission, sometimes speculative.

Literature and Science: Conversations

Bono, James J., editor. *Focus: History of Science and Literature and Science: Convergences and Divergences*. Special section of *Isis*. Vol. 101, no. 3, Sept. 2010, pp. 555–98.
    A series of provocative essays aimed at historians, this special section considers the disciplinary boundaries of history of science and literature and science. James J. Bono's introduction provides a helpful reflection on the direction of literature and science studies since 1978 and suggests that the two disciplines can approach their primary material as "forms of making" and can understand science itself as "making" (559). Laura Otis's essay focuses on the role of metaphor and time in teaching contexts (570–77). Laura Dascow Walls considers American nature writing in the context of voice, performance, and authority (590–98). And Henry S. Turner's explanation of how literary scholars employ form as a focus of analysis is a helpful starting point for discussions of methodology (578–89).

Dimock, Wai Chee, and Priscilla Wald, editors. *Literature and Science*. Special issue of *American Literature*. Vol. 74, no. 4, Dec. 2002.
    In the preface to this issue, the editors argue that scientific discourse is inherently literary and that humanists have a public responsibility to address scientific discourse in their scholarship and teaching. The authors respond to

this call with two distinct approaches: first, by exploring fiction as a vehicle for understanding a changing world characterized by rapidly developing scientific ideas and technologies and, second, by employing rhetorical analysis to think through how science itself might be understood as shaped by media, film, literature, and philosophy.

Littlefield, Melissa M., and Martin Willis, editors. *The State of the Unions*. Special issue of *Journal of Literature and Science*. Vol. 10, no. 1, 2017.

The first of a two-part special transatlantic issue coordinated by the UK-based editors of the *Journal of Literature and Science* and the US-based editors of *Configurations* provides an excellent entry point into the key concepts, methodologies, and debates about the possible futures of the study of literature, science, technology, and the arts. Scholars from all career stages engage with questions such as how to define *literature* in the study of literature and science and how the field may evolve as more specialized subfields, such as animal studies, the environmental humanities, and literature and medicine, emerge.

Peterfreund, Stuart, editor. *Literature and Science: Theory and Practice*. Northeastern UP, 1990.

This transhistorical collection includes eight essays by prominent scholars in the field. Each essay addresses the theoretical implications of literature and science with particular attention to methodology.

Rader, Karen. "The Changing Pedagogical Landscapes of History of Science the 'Two Cultures.'" Introduction. *Isis*, vol. 111, no. 3, Sept. 2020, pp. 568–75.

This brief essay introduces a special section of *Isis* focused on pedagogy. Billed as "a series of 'thought pieces' about various ongoing experiments in reconceptualizing the history of science pedagogy" (569), the special cluster takes on such issues as teaching the history of science in general education courses, teaching the history of science with diverse texts and media, and the challenges of interdisciplinary teaching. Two notable themes uniting these essays are their interest in the institutional forces humanists face in today's classrooms and their interest in acknowledging students' diverse lived experiences.

Rousseau, George S. "Literature and Science: The State of the Field." *Isis*, vol. 69, no. 4, Dec. 1978, pp. 583–91, https://doi.org/10.1086/352116.

This essay marks a turning point in literature and science—namely, a shift from "history of ideas" criticism that examined the influence of science on literature to methods that subjected scientific texts to literary analysis. This essay is helpfully contextualized by Michael Whitworth's "Literature and Science," annotated below.

Sudan, Rajani, and Will Tattersdill, editors. *State of the Unions Redux*. Special issue of *Configurations*. Vol. 26, no. 3, summer 2018.

The second of a two-part special issue continues to reflect on the interdisciplinary nature of the field, raising the question of whether the study of literature and science will "continue to generate smaller and smaller derivations" or "remain a 'union,' accruing more territories" (256). This installment is divided into three parts: institutions and narratives, traffic, and pedagogy.

Whitworth, Michael H. "Literature and Science." *Oxford Research Encyclopedia of Literature*, Oxford UP, 28 Sept. 2020, https://doi.org/10.1093/acrefore/9780190201098.013.990.

This essay offers a useful, accessible overview of key developments in literature and science from the early twentieth century, as represented by Marjorie Hope Nicolson's work, to the present. Of note is Whitworth's focus on how theoretical frameworks associated with Bruno Latour predate Latour; thus, this essay may be most useful to readers interested in understanding how historicist investigation of literary-scientific relations relate to parallel developments in science and technology studies.

Zapf, Hubert, editor. *Literature and Science.* Special issue of *Anglia.* Vol. 133, no. 1, 2015.

This special issue includes essays by prominent US and European scholars in literature and science. Topics covered range widely and include such areas as ecocriticism, life writing, biosemiotics, new materialism, cognitive literary studies, and literature and math.

Literature and Science: The Early Modern Period and the Eighteenth Century

Bailes, Melissa. *Questioning Nature: British Women's Scientific Writing and Literary Originality, 1750–1830.* U of Virginia P, 2017.

This monograph reads women's poetry of the second half of the eighteenth century as engaging with the period's fever of botanical classification and collection in the context of shifting debates around the gendered literary canon. Bailes presents a series of case studies on Anna Barbauld, Maria Riddell, Anna Seward, Charlotte Smith, Helen Maria Williams, Mary Shelley, and Felicia Hemans.

Chico, Tita. *The Experimental Imagination.* Stanford UP, 2018.

Chico reads the emergence of natural philosophy as a form of knowledge that needed to define itself against the dominant literary scene. Her book draws on a broad range of literary and natural philosophical sources to argue for the centrality of tropes and figuration to the development and representation, including self-representation, of both science and scientists.

Crane, Mary Thomas. *Losing Touch with Nature: Literature and the New Science in Sixteenth-Century England.* Johns Hopkins UP, 2014.

Crane's monograph presents 1530–1610 as a period of flux between the waning of Galenic, Aristotelian, and Ptolemaic accounts of the universe and the emergence of stable new ideas. Literary texts, including those by Shakespeare, Christopher Marlowe, and Edmund Spenser, are approached here as registering responses to the shifting of a worldview away from what the author terms an intuitive connection with nature.

Knight, Leah. *Reading Green in Early Modern England*. Ashgate, 2014.
Billed as a study of color as a cultural phenomenon, this book explores how scientific and literary writings of the era were shaped by early modern understandings of the color green and its properties, both physical and figurative. Readers interested in the history of medicine will find Knight's discussion of the color's medical applications useful; ecocritics will find her analysis of the period-specific relations between nature and culture useful.

Marchitello, Howard, and Evelyn Tribble, editors. *The Palgrave Handbook of Early Modern Literature and Science*. Palgrave Macmillan, 2017.
The twenty-three essays in this volume reconceive literature and science as inseparable discourses in the early modern period and the eighteenth century. Essays focus on a broad range of texts and contexts, with particular attention to Robert Boyle, Margaret Cavendish, and Francis Bacon, who are representative of the volume's focus on Western scientific culture.

Munroe, Jennifer, et al., editors. *Ecological Approaches to Early Modern English Texts: A Field Guide to Reading and Teaching*. Ashgate, 2015.
Organized into three sections ("Theoretical Approaches," "Reading Ecologically: Texts and Methods," and "Approaches to Teaching Ecologically: Texts and Methodologies"), this book demonstrates how historicized ecocritical approaches can be applied to works by Shakespeare, John Milton, Edmund Spenser, and others. Its focus on pedagogy makes it an ideal starting point for readers interested in how the intersections between science and literature might inform ecological approaches in the classroom.

Nicolson, Marjorie Hope. *Newton Demands the Muse: Newton's* Opticks *and the Eighteenth Century Poets*. Princeton UP, 1946.
Written by a pioneer of literature and science, this book examines how Isaac Newton's *Opticks* shaped the eighteenth-century literary imagination. It is an early example of scholarship that traces mutual lines of influence between literature and science.

Preston, Claire. *The Poetics of Scientific Investigation in Seventeenth-Century England*. Oxford UP, 2015.
This volume analyzes the literary elements of scientific writing in the seventeenth century, including scientists' use of rhetorical figures, neologisms, parody, romance, and verse. Preston examines ways in which scientific practice and expression were intertwined during this period, with natural philosophers employing humanist rhetorical skills and nonscientific writers drawing from scientific ideas and imagery.

Ruston, Sharon. *Creating Romanticism: Case Studies in the Literature, Science and Medicine of the 1790s.* Palgrave Macmillan, 2013.

> Through four case studies, Ruston argues that the category of Romanticism was created as much by science as it was by literature. She shows how writers in the disciplinary culture of the Romantic period participated in a two-way exchange between scientific and literary knowledge, developing and employing a distinctive aesthetic vocabulary of the sublime, nature and the natural, creativity, and imagination.

Literature and Science: The Nineteenth Century

Beer, Gillian. *Darwin's Plots: Evolutionary Narrative in Darwin, George Eliot and Nineteenth-Century Fiction.* Routledge, 1983.

> This landmark work of literature and science demonstrates how Charles Darwin's conceptions of evolution and natural selection not only challenged Victorian religious and philosophical beliefs but also prompted significant shifts in the thematic, formal, and narrative elements of literature.

Griffiths, Devin. *The Age of Analogy: Science and Literature between the Darwins.* Johns Hopkins UP, 2016.

> This book examines how literature influenced Erasmus Darwin and his grandson Charles to develop a technique for describing natural systems that Griffiths refers to as "comparative historicism" (4). Inspired by sources such as the historical fiction of Walter Scott and George Eliot, this mode utilizes the unique properties of analogy, which, Griffiths contends, played a vital role in Victorian scientific and historical thinking.

Holmes, John, and Sharon Ruston, editors. *The Routledge Research Companion to Nineteenth-Century British Literature and Science.* Routledge, 2017.

> This comprehensive volume brings together some twenty-seven essays on broad themes including empire, religion, science for the general reader, and publication contexts. Parts 3 and 4 offer useful topic-based essays on the treatment of particular disciplines—from chemistry to occult sciences and medicine to thermodynamics—in science, literature, and scholarship.

Jenkins, Alice. "Beyond Two Cultures: Science, Literature, and Disciplinary Boundaries." *Oxford Handbook of Victorian Literary Culture*, edited by Juliet John, Oxford UP, 2016, pp. 402–16.

> This essay surveys methodological approaches in historicist literature and science, showing how scholars position themselves in an intellectual lineage of discussion around the two cultures–one culture debate. It offers a helpful summary of the role of analogy in the nineteenth century.

King, Amy M. *Bloom: The Botanical Vernacular in the English Novel.* Oxford UP, 2007.

> Beginning with an investigation of how the Linnaean system of botanical classification made its way into various discourses of the eighteenth and

nineteenth centuries, this book argues that this "botanical vernacular" shaped the representations of sexuality and courtship in poetry and novels. It includes analyses of a wide range of literary texts, from poetry by Charlotte Smith and Erasmus Darwin to novels by Maria Edgeworth, Jane Austen, George Eliot, and Henry James.

Levine, George. *Darwin and the Novelists: Patterns of Science in Victorian Fiction*. Harvard UP, 1988.

In this foundational work of criticism, Levine demonstrates how Victorian science influenced—and was influenced by—novelists such as Charles Dickens and Anthony Trollope. He argues that in contrast to earlier novelists, Victorian writers embraced a Darwinian form of gradualist realism.

Levine, George, editor. *One Culture: Essays in Science and Literature*. U of Wisconsin P, 1987.

The eight essays in this collection mark an important moment in literature and science scholarship in which critics embraced the idea, contra C. P. Snow's famous two cultures argument, that scientists and authors inhabit a shared culture. For these critics, science and literature are different but related expressions of a culture's values, and influence between the two domains runs in both directions.

Menely, Tobias. *Climate and the Making of Worlds: Toward a Geohistorical Poetics*. U of Chicago P, 2021.

This study draws on materialist ecocriticism and the energy humanities to construct a prehistory of the Anthropocene. Menely reads the imprint of Britain's transition from solar to mineral energy in poetry of the long eighteenth century, including in works by John Milton, William Cowper, William Wordsworth, and Charlotte Smith.

Rusert, Britt. *Fugitive Science: Empiricism and Freedom in Early African American Culture*. NYU Press, 2017.

In this volume Rusert explores how nineteenth-century African American writers, artists, and performers pushed back against the scientific racism of their day. Excluded from educational institutions, the figures she examines developed their own "radical empiricisms" (20)—a "fugitive science" that resisted white supremacy.

Literature and Science: The Twentieth and Twenty-First Centuries

Choksey, Lara. *Narrative in the Age of the Genome: Genetic Worlds*. Bloomsbury Publishing, 2021.

Focusing on writers including Doris Lessing, Kazuo Ishiguro, and Jeff VanderMeer, Choksey examines the influence of genomic technologies—specifically, discourses that emerged in the late 1970s surrounding genomic sequencing—on narrative form. Individual chapters consider the relationship of genomics to racism, gender, politics, and the environment.

Crossland, Rachel. *Modernist Physics: Waves, Particles, and Relativities in the Writings of Virginia Woolf and D. H. Lawrence.* Oxford UP, 2018.
Carving out a method between the "direct influence" and "zeitgeist" models of literature and science, Crossland examines how ideas advanced in three papers by Albert Einstein manifest in various forms in the works of Virginia Woolf and D. H. Lawrence. Part 1 examines Woolf in relation to Einstein's work on light quanta. Part 2 explores Lawrence's interest in relativity and its influence on his characterization. Part 3 examines both writers' work as it relates to theories of motion that preoccupied Einstein.

Gill, Josie. *Biofictions: Race, Genetics and the Contemporary Novel.* Bloomsbury Publishing, 2020.
Through a series of case studies that read works of contemporary fiction (Alex Haley's *Roots*, Kazuo Ishiguro's *Never Let Me Go*, Zadie Smith's *White Teeth*, Colson Whitehead's *Apex Hides the Hurt*, Octavia Butler's *Kindred*, and Salman Rushdie's *The Satanic Verses*) alongside the question of race in genetic science, from the African Eve hypothesis to the rise of epigenetics, Gill demonstrates how the social and scientific construction of the concept of race is shaped by both science and fiction.

Goody, Alex, and Ian Whittington, editors. *The Edinburgh Companion to Modernism and Technology.* Edinburgh UP, 2022.
Divided into four sections ("Machines," "Media," "Bodies," and "Systems"), this reference anthology contains twenty-eight essays by leading scholars of modernism on a diverse range of topics such as X-ray technology, birth control, and infrastructure.

Shepherd-Barr, Kirsten E. *Theatre and Evolution from Ibsen to Beckett.* Columbia UP, 2015.
This book explores the influence of evolutionary theory on various forms of performance popular in Europe and the United States in the late nineteenth and early twentieth centuries, including stage plays, circus, pantomime, and vaudeville. Shepherd-Barr argues that, rather than simply incorporating the theories of Charles Darwin, Jean-Baptiste Lamarck, and other evolutionists, playwrights and performers engaged critically with ideas such as biological determinism and gender essentialism. She contends that because of theater's wide reach, it played a key role in disseminating evolutionary concepts to the general public.

Trigoni, Thalia. *The Intelligent Unconscious in Modernist Literature and Science.* Routledge, 2021.
Looking beyond a Freudian model of the unconscious, this book explores modernist writers' embrace of an "intelligent unconscious" capable of

cognition and creativity. Trigoni traces how various versions of an intelligent
unconscious surface in works by D. H. Lawrence, T. S. Eliot, and Virginia
Woolf.

Walter, Christina. *Optical Impersonality: Science, Images, and Literary Modernism*. Johns Hopkins UP, 2014.
This book explores how modern optics and visual culture influenced writers
such as H.D., Mina Loy, and D. H. Lawrence. Drawing on affect theory,
Walter argues that these writers developed models of the human subject
informed by contemporary physiological science. These models were not
merely a rejection of the Romantic self but also a new way of conceptualizing the relationship between aesthetic "impersonality" and the individual's
personality.

Whitworth, Michael H. "Science in the Age of Modernism." *The Oxford Handbook of Modernisms*, edited by Peter Brooker et al., Oxford UP, 2010,
pp. 445–60.
This brief essay provides a helpful summary and assessment of versions of
science in the modernist period, with reference to key cultural texts by
T. S. Eliot, Aldous Huxley, James Joyce, and Virginia Woolf, among others.

Indigenous Science and Indigenous Knowledge: Introductory Resources

Grenz, Jennifer. *Medicine Wheel for the Planet: A Journey toward Personal and
Ecological Healing*. U of Minnesota P, 2024.
Trained in Western scientific methods, Grenz (Nlaka'pamux mixed ancestry)
recounts her gradual disillusionment with the field of restoration ecology
and her subsequent efforts to embrace Indigenous ecology. Grenz argues
that Western ecology must reject that goal of restoring pristine landscapes
and instead embrace the Indigenous vision of purposeful reciprocity with the
environment.

Hernandez, Jessica. *Fresh Banana Leaves: Healing Indigenous Landscapes through
Indigenous Science*. North Atlantic Books, 2022.
Drawing on her activism and other experiences as a Maya Ch'orti' and
Zapotec environmental activist, Hernandez argues that Western environmentalism has long marginalized Indigenous science, leading to ineffective
conservation practices. She urges policymakers and those in the field of
conservation to embrace Indigenous communities and their environmental
stewardship practices.

Kimmerer, Robin Wall. *Braiding Sweetgrass: Indigenous Wisdom, Scientific
Knowledge, and the Teachings of Plants*. Milkweed Editions, 2013.
In *Braiding Sweetgrass*, Kimmerer (Potawatomi) draws on her personal ex-
periences as a botanist and an Indigenous woman to examine the ecological

relationships between and among plant species, animals, and people. Ultimately, she contends that humans must acknowledge and embrace our reciprocal relationships with nonhuman others.

Leonhard, Beth. "Indigenous Knowledges and Methodologies in Higher Education." *Oxford Research Encyclopedia of Education*, Oxford UP, 20 Apr. 2022, https://doi.org/10.1093/acrefore/9780190264093.013.527.
A helpful starting point for those interested in Indigenous knowledge, this article offers descriptions of Indigenous knowledge, methods, and ethics. A case study of Indigenous knowledge in the University of Alaska system illustrates the challenges inherent in integrating Indigenous knowledge and Western higher education. This article also includes a reading list.

Liboiron, Max. *Pollution Is Colonialism*. Duke UP, 2021.
Drawing on their work for the Civic Laboratory for Environmental Action Research, the Métis scholar and activist Liboiron makes the case for anti-colonial scientific research methods founded on Indigenous conceptions of relationality. Using plastic pollution as an example, Liboiron demonstrates that pollution is itself a violent enactment of colonial land relations.

Little Bear, Leroy. "Indigenous Knowledge and Western Science: Contrasts and Similarities." *YouTube*, uploaded by BanffEvents, 14 Jan. 2015, www.you tube.com/watch?v=gJSJ28eEUjI.
In this talk filmed live at the Banff Centre in 2015, Little Bear contrasts Blackfoot ontology with Western quantum physics. As he explains, Native concepts such as "flux" and "relationality" have the potential to reframe dilemmas in Western thought, such as the question of how to parse animacy at the subatomic level.

Medin, Douglas L., and Megan Bang. *Who's Asking? Native Science, Western Science, and Science Education*. MIT Press, 2014.
Medin and Bang analyze relationships within and among science and its practitioners, culture, and science education to argue for increasing cultural diversity among scientists. The first half of the volume lays out their argument about the ways that cultural values influence science; the second half compares Native American and European American science education, with a focus on community-based science education on the Menominee Reservation in Wisconsin and at the American Indian Center in Chicago.

Whyte, Kyle. "Critical Investigations of Resilience: A Brief Introduction to Indigenous Environmental Studies and Sciences." *Daedalus*, vol. 147, no. 2, spring 2018, pp. 136–47, https://doi.org/10.1162/DAED_a_00497.
This article offers an overview of Indigenous environmental studies and sciences, a field that combines historical research with living Indigenous intellectual and research traditions. As Whyte explains, the field centers moral

relationships as the basis of ecological resilience, emphasizing concepts such as responsibility, spirituality, justice, and political advocacy.

Contemporary Readings in Science and Culture

McIntyre, Lee. *Post-Truth*. MIT Press, 2018.
In this volume Lee traces the rise of a "post-truth" reality to a time before social media and the election of Donald Trump, demonstrating that humans' cognitive biases, as well as concerted efforts by conservative groups to leverage postmodern philosophy, play a role in fact denial. This book offers a useful introduction to the phenomenon of science denialism as well as an argument for why "post-truth" should be resisted.

Oreskes, Naomi. *Why Trust Science?* Princeton UP, 2021.
Derived from Oreskes's guest lectures at Princeton, and including essays by several respondents, this book—which is suitable for use as a course text—argues that the social nature of scientific inquiry makes scientific knowledge trustworthy.

Osmundson, Joseph. *Virology: Essays for the Living, the Dead, and the Small Things in Between*. W. W. Norton, 2022.
This book of interdisciplinary essays draws on queer theory from thinkers such as José Esteban Muñoz to examine the mechanics of viruses and their sociopolitical impacts.

Prescod-Weinstein, Chanda. *The Disordered Cosmos: A Journey into Dark Matter, Spacetime, and Dreams Deferred*. Bold Type Books, 2021.
Drawing on her personal experiences as a Black woman physicist, Prescod-Weinstein weaves a critique of racism and other forms of oppression in science into an accessible introduction to concepts in physics such as dark matter.

Schaefer, Donovan O. *Wild Experiment: Feeling Science and Secularism after Darwin*. Duke UP, 2022.
Drawing on affect theory, science and technology studies, and literary criticism, Schaefer, a religious studies scholar, argues that rationality is inseparable from affective processes—as in the excitement and anxiety that attend scientific study or the fascination that attends conspiracy thinking. Drawing on historical and contemporary case studies, Schaefer argues that the embodied aspects of cognition are both a strength and a liability for science.

Zimring, James C. *What Science Is and How It Really Works*. Cambridge UP, 2019.
Aimed at a general audience, this book develops a definition of science designed to help nonscientists assess scientific claims. Zimring—a working scientist—draws on social science and the humanities to explain flaws inherent in human observation and how scientific methods are meant to address these flaws.

Science Communication: Introductory Resources for Writing and General Education Pedagogy

Avraamidou, Lucy, and Jonathan Osborne. "The Role of Narrative in Communicating Science." *International Journal of Science Education*, vol. 31, no. 12, 2009, pp. 1683–707, https://doi.org/10.1080/09500690802380695.
This article argues for the inclusion in science education of fictional texts that communicate concepts. The authors suggest that such texts can mediate between the potentially alienating nature of objective, cumulative science studies and students' own experiences to enable them to engage critically with new ideas.

Bloomfield, Emma Frances. *Science v. Story: Narrative Strategies for Science Communicators.* U of California P, 2024.
In this volume aimed at science communicators, Bloomfield argues that storytelling is at the heart of effective science communication. Borrowing concepts from rhetoric studies and narrative theory, Bloomfield examines as case studies the scientific narratives, and rival counternarratives, surrounding climate change, evolution, vaccines, and COVID-19.

Brauer, David. "Writing between Two Worlds: Science and Discourses of Commitment in the Composition Classroom." *Composition Studies*, vol. 34, no. 1, spring 2006, pp. 71–93.
This article explores the challenges of creating a composition classroom in which differences are respected, a problem Brauer traces to instructors' tendency to focus on disagreements rather than consensus. Using the example of scientific discourse, he suggests that writing instructors must help students enter into dialogue with scientific authority so that they do not merely "submit to scientific authority, or, by extreme contrast, disregard it as meaningless in relation to questions of private belief" (73).

Bucchi, Massimiano, and Brian Trench, editors. *Routledge Handbook of Public Communication of Science and Technology.* 3rd ed., Routledge, 2021.
The third iteration of this evolving collection presents seventeen essays that discuss the state of the field. Contributions from a multidisciplinary group of scholars focus on topics including the practices of public scientists and environmentalists, museums, film, and cross-disciplinary collaboration.

Dahlstrom, Michael F. "Using Narratives and Storytelling to Communicate Science with Nonexpert Audiences." *PNAS*, vol. 111, no. 4, 2014, pp. 13614–20, https://doi.org/10.1073/pnas.1320645111.
Placing current research on narrative communication within a science communication context, this article addresses the role of narrative and personification in mass media and addresses the ethical implications of persuasive science writing.

Guenther, Lars. "Science Journalism." *Oxford Research Encyclopedia of Communication*, Oxford UP, 26 Mar. 2019, https://doi.org/10.1093/acrefore/9780190228613.013.901.
> In addition to a brief history of science journalism, this article outlines several major theoretical approaches to science journalism from a communication studies perspective. It also examines how broader trends in journalism, namely digitization, are influencing science journalists' practices.

Halpern, Orit, and Robert Mitchell. *The Smartness Mandate*. MIT Press, 2023.
> Drawing together the intersecting discourses of computer science, economics, ecology, and evolutionary biology, this book critically examines the promises of smart technologies, ranging from productivity apps and household appliances to artificial intelligence and machine learning.

Hanganu-Bresch, Cristina, et al., editors. *The Routledge Handbook of Scientific Communication*. Routledge, 2021.
> Winner of awards from the Association for Writing Across the Curriculum and the WAC Clearinghouse, this book features thirty-three essays—anchored in a rhetorical perspective—on scientific communication practices in industry, government, and academia. The volume's focus is scientific communication—that is, communication among scientists (including citizen scientists). Notably, contributors engage with matters of race, gender, and ethics. The final section focuses on science communication pedagogy.

Kearns, Faith. *Getting to the Heart of Science Communication: A Guide to Effective Engagement*. Island Press, 2021.
> Kearns, a science communicator, contends that successful science writing requires "relating," "listening," "working with conflict," and "understanding trauma" (concepts that anchor the book's middle chapters). In addition to a history of science communication, this volume discusses topics such as diversity, equity, and inclusion in science communication and self-care for communicators working with difficult subject matter.

Moskovitz, Cary, and David Kellogg. "Primary Science Communication in the First-Year Writing Course." *College Composition and Communication*, vol. 57, no. 2, Dec. 2005, pp. 307–34.
> This article questions the disciplinary norms behind the routine exclusion of intra-expert science writing in composition classes. It assesses the objections to its use before outlining the benefits. It also outlines criteria for text selection and provides suggestions for activities and assignments.

Thaiss, Christopher. *Writing Science in the Twenty-First Century*. Broadview Press, 2019.
> Intended as a textbook for teaching science communication, this book stands out for its focus on rhetoric. Readers of this volume may find it useful as a writing across the curriculum resource or as a resource for interdisciplinary courses.

Zerbe, Michael J. *Composition and the Rhetoric of Science: Engaging the Dominant Discourse*. Southern Illinois UP, 2007.

    In this volume Zerbe urges rhetoric and composition scholars to engage with scientific discourse—including primary scientific texts—in the classroom. He argues that sophisticated scientific literacy is imperative in a society where scientific ideologies pervade public discourse and are sometimes appropriated or misapplied. In addition to a theoretical argument, Zerbe provides specific examples of how to deploy scientific writing in composition courses.

Notes on Contributors

Bridgitte Barclay is professor of English and environmental studies at Aurora University. She writes and teaches about the intersections of gender and the environment in speculative fiction and film as well as public science narratives. Her recent work includes two Lakeshore PBS interviews on environmental and gender issues, an *EcoCast* podcast episode on environmental creature features with Christy Tidwell, an article on feminist ecoscience in Leigh Brackett's archival works, and the edited collection *Gender and Environment in Science Fiction*, among other projects.

James Barilla is the author of several books of narrative nonfiction about the human relationship with the natural world, including *Naturebot: Unconventional Visions of Nature*, *My Backyard Jungle*, and *West with the Rise*. His work has appeared in print or online in *The New York Times*, *National Geographic*, *The Atlantic*, *Conservation*, and *Places*. A recent Fulbright Scholar at the University of Bergen, Barilla is professor of English at the University of South Carolina, where he teaches courses in creative nonfiction and the environmental humanities.

Xan Sarah Chacko is a feminist science studies scholar who writes about the people and practices that are instrumental to science and technology but are rarely credited for their contributions. Chacko is coeditor of *Invisible Labour in Modern Science* (2022). She teaches in and directs the undergraduate program Science, Technology, and Society at Brown University. Her in-progress book manuscript, *The Last Seed: Botanic Futures in Colonial Legacies*, traces a history and dwells on the material and semiotic practices of the seed bank, a technoscientific enterprise that combines the despair and promises of late capitalism.

Julia Dauer is an academic writing coach and editor whose research focuses on early and nineteenth-century American literature, the environmental humanities, and the health humanities. They have held positions as a postdoctoral research associate at the University of Virginia and as an assistant professor of English at Saint Mary's College in Indiana. Their writing has appeared in venues including *Early American Literature*, *Legacy: A Journal* *of American Women Writers*, *Climate and American Literature*, *Edge Effects*, and *Entropy*.

Joshua DiCaglio is associate professor of English at Texas A&M University, College Station, where he studies and teaches rhetoric of science, rhetorical theory, science and technology studies, and environmental rhetoric. His book, *Scale Theory: A Nondisciplinary Inquiry*, examines the theoretical foundations of scale as it manifests in both science and the humanities.

Melissa Dickson is a senior lecturer in literature at the University of Queensland, where her research focuses on the relationships between Victorian literature, science, medicine, and material culture. She is the author of *Cultural Encounters with the Arabian Nights in Nineteenth-Century Britain* (2019) and *Acoustics in Nineteenth-Century Literature and Science* (2025), coauthor of *Anxious Times: Medicine and Modernity in the Nineteenth Century* (2019), and coeditor of *Progress and Pathology: Medicine and Culture in the Nineteenth Century* (2020).

Allison Dushane is professor in the Department of English and Modern Languages at Angelo State University. Her research brings eighteenth- and nineteenth-century literature into conversation with contemporary questions raised by science studies, the environmental humanities, and posthumanism. She is coeditor of the first complete scholarly edition of Erasmus Darwin's *The Botanic Garden* (2017).

Nancy Easterlin is research professor of English and professor of women's and gender studies at the University of New Orleans, where she has taught a broad range of courses in literature and theory for many decades. She is the author of *A Biocultural Approach to Literary Theory and Interpretation* (2012) and *Wordsworth and the Question of "Romantic Religion"* (1996) as well as numerous essays on cognitive-evolutionary approaches to literature and theory. She is editor of three special issues: *Knowledge, Understanding, Well-Being: Cognitive Literary Studies* (*Poetics Today* [2019]), *Cognition in the Classroom* (*Interdisciplinary Literary Studies* [2014]), and *Symposium: Evolution and Literature* (*Philosophy and Literature* [2001]). Her current research integrates the interdisciplinary area of place studies with literary theory and interpretation.

Sandy Feinstein is professor of English at Penn State University, Berks. She has published on alchemy and biology in the works of Geoffrey Chaucer; on chemistry in the works of John Milton, Bram Stoker, Marie Meurdrac, and Margaret Cavendish; and on teaching literature and writing. She and Bryan Shawn Wang, a biologist, have together published creative scholarship in *New Chaucer Studies: Pedagogy and Profession*, *Scientists and Poets #Resist*, *The CEA Critic*, *Angles: New Perspectives on the Anglophone World*, *Pedagogy*, and *Intraspection*, among other venues.

Davy Knittle is assistant professor of English at the University of Delaware, where he teaches queer and trans studies, US literature and literatures of migration, and the urban and environmental humanities. His current book project describes how urban and environmental change shaped the central questions of queer and trans cultural production in the United States from 1950 to 2020. His work has appeared or is forthcoming in *GLQ: A Journal of Lesbian and Gay Studies*, *PMLA*, *ISLE: Interdisciplinary Studies in Literature and Environment*, and *Feminist Formations* and in the collection *In the Daylight of Our Existence: Architectural History and the Promise of Queer Theory*.

Marissa Kopp is a doctoral fellow in ecology at Penn State University, University Park, where she explores how climate, management, and communication can change ecosystem functions. Her work in the humanities centers on environmental communications, British Romantic literature, pastoral poetry, and writing center pedagogy.

Susanna Lee is professor of French and francophone studies at Georgetown University. Her research focuses on nineteenth-century narrative, intellectual history, and comparative literature. Her most recent book, *Detectives in the Shadows: A Hard-Boiled History*, was published in 2020. She is also the author of *Hard-Boiled Crime Fiction and the Decline of Moral Authority* and *A World Abandoned by God* and edited the Norton Critical Editions of Marcel Proust's *Swann's Way* and Stendhal's *The Red and the Black*.

Aylin Malcolm is assistant professor of English at the University of Guelph, where they teach courses on premodern literature and the environmental humanities. Their current research explores medieval accounts of nonhuman animals in relation to reason, experimentation, gender, and grief. Malcolm's work can be found in *New Medieval Literatures*, *The Routledge Companion to Global Chaucer*, and a special issue of *Medieval Ecocriticisms* titled *Trans Natures*. They have also worked on projects, including online editions and podcasts, whose aim is to make premodern literatures accessible to broad audiences.

Aneesha Manocha is pursuing a PhD in energy and resources at the University of California, Berkeley. She conducts research in macro-energy systems modeling and has developed tools to more granularly model technologies in a low-carbon future. Her future research aims to prioritize environmental injustices in modeling frameworks. She was a Kanders Churchill Scholar at the University of Cambridge. She is also a recipient of the National Science Foundation Graduate Research Fellowship, the HMEI Environmental Scholarship, and a Udall Scholarship honorable mention and placed second in the USAEE Case Competition. She has worked at RMI, Prospect14, the Department of Energy, and the Centre for Social and Economic Progress.

Laura McGrath is professor of English and professional writing at Kennesaw State University. Her research examines digital and popular culture as well as rhetorical dimensions of science communication and environmental communication. Her publications include *Collaborative Approaches to the Digital in English Studies*, articles in *Computers and Composition*, *Literacy in Composition Studies*, and *Res Rhetorica*; and contributions to *Avian Aesthetics in Literature and Culture* and *Reading and Writing New Media*.

Nicole M. Merola is professor of environmental humanities and American literatures at the Rhode Island School of Design. She teaches courses on biodiversity and extinction studies, climate change cultures, discourses of the Anthropocene, ecological literary studies, and theories of naturecultures that ask students to consider the role mediating technologies play in apprehending and interrogating structures of classed, gendered, and racialized socioecological experience. Merola's current scholarship focuses on the intersection of affect, form, and socioecologies. Key aims of this work are to historicize environmental emotion and highlight vulnerability at scales from the personal to the planetary.

John MacNeill Miller is the author of *The Ecological Plot: How Stories Gave Rise to a Science* (2024). His essays have appeared in *PMLA*, *Victorian Studies*, and *Environmental Humanities*, among other venues. For ten years he taught courses at the intersection of literature, science, and the environmental humanities at Allegheny College. He currently lives and writes on the outskirts of Pittsburgh.

Matthew Newcomb is professor of English and director of the Faculty Development Center at the State University of New York, New Paltz, where he teaches rhetoric, writing, and literary theory courses with a focus on argument, environmental writing, composition theory, and science writing. He spent a decade as a writing program administrator. He has published work in journals including *College Composition and Communication*, *Interdisciplinary Studies in Literature and the Environment*, *Rhetoric Review*, *JAC*, and *Departures in Critical Qualitative Research*. His monograph, *Religion, Narrative, and the Environmental Humanities: Bridging the Rhetoric Gap*, was published in 2023. He is currently working on projects related to the rhetoric of space exploration.

Nathaniel Otjen is assistant professor of sustainability and environmental studies at Ramapo College. Previously he was a postdoctoral fellow in the High Meadows Environmental Institute at Princeton University. An interdisciplinary environmental humanist, he specializes in multispecies justice theory, critical animal studies, and literary and cultural studies. He is currently writing his first book, "Entangled Lives: Multispecies Selves, Justice, and Narratives," and codirecting an energy humanities project called *Mining for the Climate*. His published and forthcoming research can be read in *Environmental Humanities*, *Animal Studies Journal*, *ISLE: Interdisciplinary Studies in Literature and Environment*, and *A/B: Auto/Biography Studies*, among other venues.

Aaron Ottinger is a tenure-track faculty member in the Department of English at Highline College, where he also teaches in the Department of Diversity and Globalism Studies. His primary research focuses on literature and mathematics of the eighteenth and nineteenth centuries. He has published essays on Lord Byron, Mary Shelley, Laurence Sterne, and William Wordsworth and is currently at work on a manuscript, "Astral Romanticism: Mathematics, Realisms, and Subjectivities."

Lisa Ottum is professor of English at Xavier University, Ohio, where she teaches ecocriticism, literary criticism and theory, composition, and other subjects. She researches diverse texts and artifacts representing a range of time periods, genres, and geographies.

Rosalind Powell is assistant professor of English literature at the University of Amsterdam. She was previously senior lecturer in English at the University of Bristol and moved to the Netherlands after over a decade of teaching in British universities. Her research focuses on literature and science of the long eighteenth century. She is the author of *Christopher Smart's English Lyrics* (2014) and *Perception and Analogy: Poetry, Science, and Religion in the Eighteenth Century* (2021).

Arielle Rivera is an associate planning engineer for the Generation Integration team in interconnection projects at the New York Independent System Operator. In this role she coordinates, performs, and reviews technical studies related to the interconnection of proposed new generation, transmission, and load facilities. Previously she worked for the Federal Energy Regulatory Commission's Office of Electric Reliability, the Environmental Defense Fund, and La Cooperativa Hidroeléctrica de la Montaña.

Luke Rodewald is assistant professor of writing studies at Florida International University, where he teaches courses about environmental rhetoric and writing. His research and teaching interests concern the intersections of critical plant studies, climate change, and rhetoric and composition. His writing can be found or is forthcoming in venues such as *ISLE: Interdisciplinary Studies in Literature and Environment*, *Resistance: A Journal of Radical Environmental Humanities*, *The Journal for the Study of Religion, Nature and Culture*, and *The Journal of Environmental Education*.

Scott C. Thompson is assistant instructional professor in the University Writing Program at the University of Florida. He specializes in teaching writing in the disciplines, with a particular interest in health and science writing. His research interests include Victorian literature, health humanities, the history of science and psychology, sensation fiction, and the novel and narrative theory. His work has appeared in outlets such as *Studies in the Novel*, *Victorian Review*, *George Eliot–George Henry Lewes Studies*, and *Victorian Popular Fictions*.

Bryan Shawn Wang is teaching professor of biology at Penn State University, Berks. In addition to reports of his scientific research, he has published fiction in literary magazines and, with Sandy Feinstein and others, articles on interdisciplinary thinking and teaching in the college classroom and beyond in *Comparative Media Arts Journal*, *Scholarship and Practice of Undergraduate Research*, and *Journal of Sustainability Education*.